From Bomba to Hip-Hop

Popular Cultures, Everyday Lives

Robin D. G. Kelley and Janice Radway, Editors

Popular Cultures, Everyday Lives
Robin D. G. Kelley and Janice Radway, Editors

From Bomba to Hip-Hop

Puerto Rican Culture and Latino Identity

JUAN FLORES

Columbia University Press

NEW YORK

Columbia University Press

Publishers Since 1893

New York   Chichester, West Sussex

Copyright © 2000 Columbia University Press

All rights reserved

Library of Congress Cataloging-in-Publication Data

Flores, Juan.

From bomba to hip-hop : Puerto Rican culture and Latino identity / Juan Flores.

p.   cm.

Includes index.

ISBN 978-0-231-11076-1 (cloth : alk. paper) — ISBN 978-0-231-11077-8 (paper : alk. paper)

1. Puerto Ricans—United States—Social life and customs. 2. Puerto Ricans—United
States—Ethnic identity. 3. Arts, Puerto Rican—United States. 4. Popular culture—United
States. 5. United States—Social life and customs—1971– I. Title.

E184.P85 F58 2000

305.868'7295073—dc21   99-049285

Casebound editions of Columbia University Press books are
printed on permanent and durable acid-free paper.

Printed in the United States of America

c 10 9 8 7 6 5 4 3 2 1
p 10 9 8

Some of the material in this book is reprinted by permission
of holders of copyright and publication rights. See page 253
for acknowledgments.

Contents

The concept of *popularity* itself is
not particularly popular.
—BERTOLT BRECHT

From Bomba to Hip-Hop

Break Battle in playground, Upper West Side (1983)

(Photo by Máximo R. Colón)

Prelude

FROM BOMBA TO HIP-HOP

The excitement level was high, and the young people—mostly Puerto Ricans, Dominicans, and other Latinos—kept filing into the large student lounge at Hunter College wondering what would *really* be happening. The word *hip-hop* must surely have caught their attention (for the event itself was titled "From Bomba to Hip-Hop"), though the main draw was probably Latin Empire, the best-known rap group. It was late November 1994, just a few nights after the historic "Muévete" conference at Columbia University, where thousands of Puerto Rican and Latino youth had gathered to talk about a range of social issues and to take up, through discussion and performance, the complex question of their own cultural identity.

So the spirit was in the air, the time was visibly ripe for talking, negotiating, affirming, questioning—who are we? where do we come from? who do we relate to? how do we relate to each other, and to "others"? Questions that stir young people's hearts and minds every day, on topics that trouble, confuse, agitate, but that matter, and that one way or the other strongly move Latino youth in these changing times—that was the agenda. Tonight these items would be on the table, for open debate, and everyone was encouraged to speak out.

Hip-hop, OK—but *bomba?* What's that? Reference to the folkloric ancestor of Puerto Rican popular dance and music probably escaped most of the youthful audience, as did the descriptive subheading of the event: "A Celebration of the Continuity of Puerto Rican Culture." They came to hear some Spanglish rap and be with their cultural peers, to talk about what was on their minds as Latino teenagers trying to make sense out of life in the "Big Manzana" of the gruesome 1990s. Their idea of culture and identity

I

was for the most part practical and spontaneous, based on the blows of racism, elitism, sexism, cultural chauvinism, and all the other forms of prejudice and exclusion they encounter in daily life, and the wellspring of pride and defiant affirmation with which they commonly respond. What historical dimension there was to this process of identification came, certainly not from the public schools, which tend to distort all things Puerto Rican, Dominican, or Mexican, when they even mention them, but in lively, real, but anecdotal form from their parents, aunts and uncles, cousins, and—the lucky ones at least—from their dear grandmothers, *sus abuelitas*.

What an eye-opener it was for many of them, then, to find out about *la bomba* and *la plena*, and to learn that these expressive cultural practices from their own backgrounds as Puerto Ricans weren't so different after all, in their day, from the latest hip-hop styles many in the crowd considered uniquely their own. It was José Rivera, the *panderetero* and vocalist-composer for Los Pleneros de la 21, the foremost *bomba y plena* group in New York City, who brought this message home most dramatically. Here was a New York Puerto Rican not much older than they (José's around forty) who was raised on bomba and plena music—his father was the legendary Ramón "Chín" Rivera—and who could illustrate the musical kinship between bomba and rap by marking beats on the tabletop. Talking about the casita "Rincón Criollo" in the South Bronx which he himself had helped build and where he hangs out, José brought the social setting of bomba and of plena to life for the young Latino audience, and showed that the function of those performative experiences and the sector of the population to partake of them corresponded in many ways with the origins and originators of hip-hop in the South Bronx and Harlem some fifteen years before.

These historical links and continuities were made even stronger by another presenter, Charlie Chase, a well-spoken Nuyorican of about thirty, who had been the deejay for the Cold Crush Brothers, one of the most popular rap groups in the early days, the late seventies, before hip-hop music had been recorded or gained any commercial success. Charlie (whose real name is Carlos Mandes) began as a bass player in Latin bands, playing the salsa and merengue circuit with musicians older than himself. But then one day, attentive to the musical preferences of so many of his teenage Puerto Rican peers, he decided to break into rap as a deejay, scratching, mixing, sampling, and in general providing the rhythmic ground for the hugely popular, all African American group, Cold Crush. He told of the suspicions he sometimes evoked "because he wasn't Black" and of his determined rivalry with the greatest deejay of those years, Grandmaster Flash; as he explained, his street and stage name indicated, at least to himself, that he was "chasin' the Flash." But he also made clear something that the commercial media and dominant story of hip-hop tend to leave out: that Puerto Ricans were involved in this contemporary youth style from the beginning, and that Puerto Rican and other Caribbean practices and traditions are woven into the very fabric of this supposedly "American" or strictly "African American" genre in all its subsequent manifestations.

Another speaker, Raquel Rivera, added a further link to the chain of associations by explaining to the New York audience that rap had arrived in Puerto Rico and was already the most widespread form of cultural identification among young people on the Island, especially the poor urban youth. Raquel, now a doctoral student in sociology and cultural studies at the CUNY Graduate School, had recently moved from Puerto Rico, where she completed her master's degree at the Centro de Estudios Avanzados del Caribe with a thesis on rap in Puerto Rico. She described her struggle to establish rap as an integral part of contemporary Puerto Rican culture, and not as just another example of imposed and imported fads from the States ("de allá," as the saying goes). She spoke of several articles on this theme which she had published in newspapers on the Island, and how strongly some of the conservative cultural elite (of all political stripes) had objected to her efforts to open up the cultural debate and break it away from the kind of static, monolithic categories that tend to keep it removed from the everyday experiences and tastes of the majority of the population. Referring to Vico C, Rubén DJ, Lisa M, and many of the lesser-known rappers of the day, she demonstrated how, rather than just a slavish import or imitation of North American expressive modes, rap on the Island had taken on a life of its own, adopting as themes—in Spanish—the realities of everyday life in Puerto Rican society, and influenced musically more by Caribbean styles like merengue and reggae than by any recent innovations in the United States.

The presentations were inspiring, and the discussion provoked by each of them was lively, dynamic, and straight from the heart. The audience spoke out energetically, asking José if he had done any "bomba-raps," Charlie Chase if the Cold Crush Brothers had also referred to women as "bitches and 'hos," and Raquel if she saw any parallels between so-called "gangsta rap" and "underground" on the Island. Several slightly older members of the audience, maybe pushing fifty, raised the issue of salsa, which most people identify as "our music" much more than rap, or even the "old-fashioned" folksy styles of the trios, "la música jíbara," or bomba and plena. One person even mentioned loving boogaloo music in the sixties and suggested that, with its bold connection between Puerto Rican and Black American styles, it seemed like an important link in the bomba–hip-hop chain.

But the highlight of the event was clearly Latin Empire. These two cousins from the South Bronx, Rick Rodríguez ("Puerto Rock") and Anthony Boston (aka MC KT—"Krazy Taino"), were familiar to most of those present, even though they were still then, more than ten years after they had started performing, awaiting their first major recording. Free of all pomp and circumstance, Latin Empire captivated the already spirited gathering, mixing their well-known standards like "Puerto Rican and Proud, Boy-ee," "En mi viejo South Bronx," and "Así es la cosa" with new rhymes touching on the street themes of our own days. They also blended performance with conversation, fielding questions and challenges from many sides, relating instructive anecdotes, and venturing bold philosophical reflections. The atmosphere during the most heated exchanges was simply electric, charged with what seemed a collective need to address issues like sex, violence, drugs, school, the commercialization of rap, and, of course, the "continuity of Puerto Rican culture."

This memorable youth gathering was billed a *tertulia*, the traditional Spanish word for an open, free-wheeling forum, a kind of modest, topical town hall meeting. Whatever the theme at hand, the aim is an open, stimulating, and free environment where all in attendance can feel comfortable setting out their ideas and asking questions. As people lingered talking and gradually filing out of the lounge, we all had a sense that it is this kind of environment where we can best talk about things like culture and identity. When the subject is popular culture, and participation and performance the vehicles of exchange, suddenly it seems possible to begin reconstructing Latino history and repair that "broken memory" so that it can serve as an active force in the challenging social struggles ahead.

Sunday afternoon jam at Bethesda Fountain, Central Park (1975)

(Photo by Carlos Ortíz)

Introduction

As the populations of Latin American and Caribbean background in the United States increase rapidly in size and diversity, it becomes all the more important to understand the particular histories and cultures of each of the nationalities and regional groups. For over a decade now, the categories "Hispanic" and "Latino" have been taking hold in the public vocabulary, with the obvious effect of blurring such distinctions and treating peoples with roots in Mexico, Puerto Rico, Cuba, the Dominican Republic, El Salvador, Colombia, and many other countries as though they were all of common stock and circumstance. Many people now considered "Latino" or "Hispanic" find objection to this composite label, taking offense at the confusion of their special personal and historical heritage with those of others. Not that they have anything against any other group with whom they may be equated, and in fact may often feel close bonds with other Latinos along cultural and political lines. I once asked a class of mostly Dominican students what had drawn them to a course on Puerto Rican history; several of them answered that when they see the words "Puerto Rican" in the U.S. setting, they figure it must pertain to them as well. But even in such cases of cross-group identification, there always seems to be an important stake in upholding the specifics of one's own nationality, and a strong sense that "if I'm Latino or Hispanic, then I am Dominican, or Puerto Rican, or Mexican American first."

In my writings I take the position that while there is a certain inevitability in the formation of pan-ethnic concepts like "Latino," or "Asian American," and may well be some significant strategic advantages to their deployment in political movements for change, their validity as sociological constructs depends overridingly on the attention paid to the specifics of each of the constituent groups and their historical placement within U.S. society. That is, there is "Latino" only from the point of view and as lived by the Mexican, the Puerto Rican, the Cuban, and so forth; without denying the congruencies and threads of interconnection among them that the term implies, "Latino" or "Hispanic" only holds up when qualified by the national-group angle or optic from which it is uttered: there is a "Chicano/Latino" or "Cuban/Latino" perspective, but no meaningful one that is simply "Latino." For the generic, unqualified usage, aside from generating and perpetuating stereotypes of a derogatory or otherwise distorting kind, also is employed to mislead the public into thinking that all members and constituents of the composite are in basically the same position in the society and are all progressing toward acceptance and self-advancement from the same starting line, and at the same pace. Evading a rigorously comparative structural analysis (i.e., how each group is positioned within the existing relations of power and privilege of U.S. society), the public image typically gravitates toward the upper or most successful examples of "Latino" life—what I call the highest common denominator— with the suggestion that those who fail to match up to this pattern of accommodation have primarily themselves to blame. Thus, what presents itself as a category of inclusion and compatibility functions as a tool of exclusion and internal "othering."

It is for this reason that in seeking to approach the thorny issue of Latino identity I arrive there only by first elaborating some dimensions of the national discourses and diasporic experiences of one of them; whatever in my notion of "Latino" pertains to other or all of the groups included in the term does so because of the complexity of the "Puerto Rican/Latino" identity formations which I present in the varied essays included in the present collection. That the focus is on the Puerto Rican is of central importance, for of all the groups it is the one most characteristically cast as the bottom rung, the "exception" to the Hispanic rule. For though they have long been the second largest of the groups, enjoy a history here second in duration only to the Mexicans, and are as fully part of the American cultural landscape as any, it is the Puerto Rican population that is most commonly pointed to as the most nagging "problem" presented by the need for a cultural fit between the Anglo-American north and the Hispanic south of the hemisphere. Since at least the 1950s, the "Hispanic" conundrum has been epitomized by the racialized, stigmatized, inner-city Puerto

Rican, the "spic," whose only cultural cousin has been the similarly placed "pachuco" and "greaser" from the cities of the Southwest. In our times, with the many middle-class Cuban Americans and South American exiles to serve as foils, the relegation of the Puerto Rican has taken an even more virulent form than ever, with age-old social pathologies and theories of cultural deficiency now buttressed by the loudly touted success stories of so many of their presumed "Hispanic" cohorts.

I attribute this special, and especially unfavorable, position and representation of Puerto Ricans to the colonial relation between the United States and their country of origin. Unlike the other Latino groups, the Puerto Rican diaspora hails from a nation that has languished in a dependent and tightly controlled political status for its entire history, a condition that has persisted throughout the twentieth century. To this day, more than one hundred years since U.S. troops landed on the Island in 1898 and the growing world power set up a government of military occupation, Puerto Rico remains strapped with an unresolved and vigilantly manipulated place in the world of modern nations. Thus, long after the wave of decolonization swept the so-called Third World in the post–World War II period, and at a time when the most fashionable theory of diplomatic affairs goes under the name of the "postcolonial," this island nation is still a colony by all indicators of international relations, its economic and political life fully orchestrated by its mighty neighbor to the north, the putative leader of world democracy and sovereignty. Of course the euphemisms abound, such as "commonwealth" status or "free associated statehood," as do the denials and convoluted circumlocutions, but the reality—and supposed anomaly—of direct bondage and lack of national autonomy stares the world in the face, and goes to condition every aspect of Puerto Rican life, including the migration process itself as well as the social experience of the emigrant community.

Latino immigration, in general, has transpired under the sway of U.S. power. Directly or indirectly, for positive or negative reasons, this inequality and dependency have catalyzed the immense gravitational pull across the hemispheric divide which has been swelling exponentially over the past half century. In this sense, the Puerto Rican experience has been paradigmatic rather than exceptional of the general Latino process of propelled movement and the challenge of resettlement. But for reasons of historical reconfiguration and new forms of ideological suasion, the lever of colonialism and international domination has all but vanished from social analytical parlance, its place taken by the sundry guises of globalism, transnational movements and networks and, at a domestic level, multiculturalism and identity politics. As a result, the worldwide experience of diasporic displacement and realignment often appears dislodged from any causal connection to relations of disproportionate political and economic power among nations, as have the redefined cultural "differences" among the newly interacting populations. Such differences, as for example those between "Latinos" and "Americans," or among the varied Latino groups, are typically relativized, and reduced largely to their symbolic dimensions, with histories and structures of power thereby losing in analytical relevance.

With the nagging "unfinished business" of Puerto Rico, the concept and pertinence of colonialism cannot be extricated from the new cultural politics of difference, nor from the meaning and range of "Latino" culture and identities. The direct colonial tie as in the case of Puerto Rico is the exception, of course, the extreme limit in the range of "postcolonial," and "Latino," grid lines. But the idea of the "colonial" becomes more widely applicable if not paradigmatic for most Latinos when it is taken more generally to refer to structures of inequality and domination, and histories of conquest and enslavement. In such terms, the seeming anomaly of the "postcolonial colony" of Puerto Rico and its unassimilable diaspora takes its place alongside its closest historical kins on the American ethnic landscape: the Mexican Americans, the American Indians, and the African Americans. Variously referred to as "colonial minorities," "conquered peoples," or "racialized subjects," these structured forms of affiliation belie any too facile and culturally determined version of "Latino difference." This common "internally colonial" condition serves to weave the "Latino" discourse into the fabric of U.S. cultural and racial politics, thus defying any overly "Latin Americanized" sense of the pan-national mix. Puerto Ricans in the United States indeed belong among other Latinos, because of obvious cultural affinities starting with language background and important historical parallels; but in other ways, perhaps including their colonial situation, they also belong among other groups. In terms of long-standing association of a social and cultural nature, as well as common socioeconomic indicators, they have shared as much with African Americans as with any Latino counterpart.

But in addition to this "internal" pressure, the salience of the colonial status issue in the Puerto Rican case also drives home the need for an active transnational and political frame of reference in understanding "Latino matters" in an integral way. More graphically perhaps than in other instances but in no way unique, for Puerto Ricans what happens "over there," what happens in and to the homeland or the diaspora, conditions what happens "here." The entire process of migration and resettlement, spanning a full century, has been forged and shaped by that relationship, including its sheer demographic magnitude, which for several decades has been hovering, astoundingly, at around half of the total Puerto Rican population. With increasing intensity over the decades, there has been an interpenetration of life and culture of the two "sides" of Puerto Rican social experience, its quality always defined and orchestrated as a result of political and economic decision-making at a transnational level. The fallacy of conjuring the Latino "difference" in the confines of domestic politics of ethnicities surfaces most visibly in considering the situation of Puerto Ricans, an ironic twist given that other Latin Americans and Caribbeans have so often viewed them as the most Americanized and integrated into U.S. affairs. But despite the huge gap between the public political life on the Island and in U.S. communities, and the apparent indifference and widespread cynicism in both directions, there is a structured codependency in the Puerto Rican "trans-colony" that invalidates any hasty separation between the situation of "Latinos" on the domestic scene from the happenings in and to their countries of origin.

From the perspective of "Puerto Rican/Latinos," then, the category "Latino" into which they are grouped in the 1990s has utility only if it can account for the colonial dimension of "difference" in the U.S. setting and as an international background. Because of their shared coloniality with other, "non-Latino" groups, the "Latino" concept needs to be seen as conjoined and partially overlapping with, rather than categorically distinct from, that of other "different" groups, such as African Americans, Asian Americans, non-Hispanic Caribbeans, or American Indians. As is indicated by the general Puerto Rican refusal of the hyphen, however, this immersion in U.S. culture and politics is not to be confused with "assimilation in American life" in the sense of incorporation, and of feeling definitively, and comfortably, at home. On the contrary, this positioning and self-positioning inside points outward, toward the continued bearing of "foreign" policy questions and "national cultures," however remote they are made to seem, on their everyday life in the diaspora. The Puerto Rican optic thus tugs the purportedly expansive "Latino" category in both directions—inward into the "entrails" of the "non-Latino" North American culture, and outward toward national and regional histories of Latin America and the Caribbean.

The essays that make up *From Bomba to Hip-Hop* were assembled with these perspectives in mind. After an opening reflection on the contemporary meanings of "popular culture," the term and social practice which are of central interest throughout (and to which I will return for further comments), the subsequent two chapters take up aspects of the recent cultural discourse on the Island, on the eve of the centenary of U.S. presence in 1998. In "The Lite Colonial" and "Broken English Memories," attention goes to the radical challenges to traditional concepts of nation and nationalism which have gained currency among theorists and in public opinion in Puerto Rico, and the attempts to redefine the colonial relation in the light of the social and intellectual changes of our times. In each case the diasporic experience is drawn into the analytical equation, as its virtual omission from even the most innovative revisions of the national history signals an unwitting continuity with the very inadequacies which they aim to address. An underestimation of the importance of the diasporic break, or misunderstanding of the dynamic relation between diaspora and "national" life, make an integral, translocal mode of analysis elusive at best. By introducing the epithet "lite" into the contemporary discussion of colonialism, I do not mean to blunt the edge, or "heavy," contestatory nature of colonial contradictions in the Puerto Rican or any other case. As a playful alternative to more familiar, yet evidently unsatisfactory, prefixes like "post-," "late," or "neo-," the idea is that colonialism has been taking on a new face as its economic and political legitimations become so thoroughly veiled by cultural and commercial ones, and the colonial subject is mostly visibly so as a consumer. As it imposed modernity on the colony, so colonialism is imposing postmodernity as well, and even, perhaps, some of the aura of the "postcolonial."

The remainder of the book, from chapter 4 on, has to do specifically with the diaspora, with the varied and changing experiences and expressions of "Nuyorican" life. Architecture and urban space, musical styles and cultural movements, and literary traditions provide some of the sites and moments of a cultural world defined by the interplay of continuity and transformation, heritage and innovation, roots and fusions. The creative reinvention of national traditions exemplified by casita and plena culture contrasts with the bold adoption and reworking of African American and other U.S. expressive currents in Latin boogaloo, a striking 1960s forebear to the role of Puerto Ricans in hip-hop in more recent generations. The common thread running through all of them, as well as the story of "Nuyorican" literature in its present-day status, is the phenomenon of oblivion and exclusion they face in prevailing cultural discourses, both in the U.S. and in Latin America. Not only the past but the present of Puerto Rican cultural practices encounters a kind of social amnesia by which they are buried or subsumed under more prominent, or more familiar, or more accommodating, rubrics of group identification. Once again, I would attribute these processes of exclusion and invisibility to the mechanisms of colonial control.

Which brings us back, after these powerful instances of cultural particularity, to the pan-ethnic "Latino" label and the uneasy Puerto Rican fit within it. Beginning with chapter 7, "Pan-Latino/Trans-Latino," the problematic of the particular and the general is subject to close scrutiny, first at a demographic and discursive level, then as exemplified in the contrast between the emergent concept of "Latino literature" and the historical contours of "Nuyorican" writing through the decades. The "life off the hyphen" of Puerto Ricans in a "Latinized" New York, the literary expression and circumstances of the "lowercase people," point up the exclusions and hierarchies of privilege at work in the public use and conceptualization of "Latinismo" in current parlance. Finally, in "The Latino Imaginary" and "Latino Studies," I suggest ways of taking account of such exclusions and divisions while also seeking to probe beyond them for strategies of cultural and educational change. The closing call for a "new kind of university" which would include Latino Studies in critical and inclusive terms also serves as a return to the spirit of the youth *tertulia* evoked in the prelude, where a free and politically savvy exchange over the pressing issues of community and identity is possible—that is, where cultural history is, at it should be, a matter of survival. (I have added a "postscript" datelined 1998 so as to bring the discussions contained in the book current with the situation in that symbolically important year in Puerto Rican, and Latino, history.)

As mentioned, the conceptual concern that here crosscuts the discussion of national and ethnic identity has to do with another beleaguered and polemical term, *popular culture*. I foreground its importance not only because of my own personal tastes and predilections, but because it retains the dimensions of class and cultural capital which are so easily lost sight of in considerations of group identities and interactions along ethnic cultural lines. The socioeconomic and power-defined tension implicit in the idea of the popular, even when limited to the differential decoding of mediated commercial culture, helps to ground the discourse of Puerto Rican or "Latino" culture, or the relation between them, in the impinging realities of social position. The argument advanced here, though, is that this limitation in the conceptual reference of popular culture is especially untenable in the case of the cultural practices of colonial and diasporic peoples, where the "old" and supposedly outmoded forms of vernacular, community, and "folk" culture—the earlier denotation of popular culture—are still very much alive. Needless to say, much of my analysis and speculation about Puerto Rican and "Latino" popular culture should rightfully be complemented by a deeper account of issues of the culture industries and of media and other public representations of and by Latinos. But economic and political disenfranchisement also involves a relatively greater remove from all available means of cultural reproduction, such that any sense of cultural agency on the part of Puerto Rican/Latinos tends to be more visibly located in the field of direct, community-based expressive practices usually dismissed as residual enclaves or subcultures of anachronistic "folklore." For as one contemporary theorist of popular culture reminds us, "Keeping up with the rate of change in our discipline can lead us to ignore the way that a rhetoric or a problematic deemed 'dead' or 'dated' in one context can be alive and kicking in another."[1]

Finally, giving full play to the role of popular cultural practices poses the underlying question of contemporaneity, and thus of history. All of the essays included here are from the 1990s, and with the exception of the study of the boogaloo era, all are about cultural and intellectual phenomena of the last decade of the twentieth century. They are also delimited geographically, for the most part set in and drawing their ethnographic and textual evidence from New York City. Here again, there is a deliberate methodological stress on the local and the particular as a means of approaching the global and the general. But as Johannes Fabian maintains, creative and critical attention to the popular also shows that the focus on contemporary, and of course temporary, manifestations of cultural expression and discourse may reinforce rather than diminish our historical sense, as it also, more obviously, may serve to counteract dangers of a historicist and positivist kind. By privileging temporality and movement and establishing what I term "popular culture in time," it is possible to bring into association telling cultural "moments" which remain disconnected in official and "larger" historical narratives. The "coexistence of tradition and modernity" that Fabian identifies as the sine qua non for the recognition of popular culture "as contemporary practice," involves the indissoluble, but nonlinear and noncausal, relationship between past and present, memory and desire.[2]

It is in the practice of popular music and dance, that quintessential "art of timing," that this concept of historical and performative temporality is of course most richly exemplified; an expressive practice constituted by the interplay of tempos, cadences, rhythms, and syncopations bears an obvious and special relationship to the social experience of time. Indeed, my usage "in time" intends to resonate with the title of the book *Del canto y el tiempo* by Cuban musicologist Argeliers León, and with its adaptation by the Puerto Rican cultural historian Angel G. Quintero Rivera in the opening chapter, "Del canto, el baile . . . y el tiempo," of his book *¡Salsa, sabor y control!: Sociología de la música tropical.*[3]

The title *From Bomba to Hip-Hop* is intended in this sense as incorporating the constituents of a genealogy of Puerto Rican popular culture, or what Fabian in somewhat more fanciful terms refers to as "historiology" as distinct from historiography in any accepted understanding of that intellectual endeavor. The path *from* some primordial Puerto Rican cultural practice (bomba) *to* an advertently parallel one in the here and now (hip-hop) is anything but direct and unidirectional, much less is it causal in the sense of an influence or continuity of influences, whether conscious or as mediated through intervening styles, movements, or periods. Though "temporal" calls attention to "moments," conjunctures, and contexts, the nexus between "from" and "to" actually marks off historically associated "spaces" of cultural practice—performative locations from which Puerto Ricans, notably poor and black Puerto Ricans and Latinos, find it possible to exercise the "freedom" of cultural expression and identification. The youth gathering whose title, "From Bomba to Hip-Hop," was adopted for the present collection, was just such an instance of popular culture genealogy, an energetic placing "in time" of their own complex social and cultural presence.

Los Pleneros de la 21 at Caribbean street festival, New York City (1984)

(Photo by Máximo R. Colón)

I

"pueblo pueblo"
POPULAR CULTURE IN TIME

1

Popular culture is energized in "moments of freedom," specific, local plays of power and flashes of collective imagination. It is "popular" because it is the culture of "the people," the common folk, the poor and the powerless who make up the majority of society. The creative subject of popular culture is the "popular classes," and its content the traditions and everyday life of communities and their resistance to social domination. It is typically referred to as "low" culture, or "subculture," and marked off from the "high" culture of the elite. In another familiar image, it is "marginal" culture or the culture of marginality, thus sidelined from the core "mainstream" cultural life and values of society. It is this topography of top and bottom, center and periphery, that is upset and radically unsettled in the "moments of freedom," those pregnant conjunctures and contexts when it becomes clear, however fleetingly, that the top is "frequently dependent on the low-Other . . . [and even] *includes* that low symbolically." This dependence and this secret desire for what is excluded and disdained go to account for the deepest irony of popular culture, that "what is socially peripheral is so frequently *symbolically* central."[1]

Midway through its two-hundred-year life since the late eighteenth century, the idea of popular culture began a gradual shift of focus from this traditional, collective creativity, commonly called "folklore," to the domain of the mass media, the "mass culture" of technical reproduction and industrial commercialization.[2] This shift has intensified over the course of the twentieth century, as new means of reproduction and diffusion came into place in the cultural sphere, such that by the 1940s and 1950s, especially with the advent of television, the mediated culture *for* the people came to eclipse and replace, in most theoretical assessments, the expressive culture *of* the people which had been the object of knowledge of popular culture and folklore studies in earlier generations. While the critical theorists Theodor Adorno and Walter Benjamin in their writings of the 1930s were the first to describe and analyze this change, in the United States it can be traced with some precision to the "mass culture debate" of the 1950s as exemplified in the thinking of critics and commentators like Dwight Mac-Donald, Oscar Handlin, and Clement Greenberg. MacDonald, for example, went so far as to revise the title of his most influential essay, from "Theory of Popular Culture" in its original 1944 version to "Theory of Mass Culture" for the publication of 1953. Even more explicitly, Handlin in the same years so much as pronounced a requiem for traditional popular culture with the advent of the mass media; the dean of American immigration historians bemoaned the demise of regionally and ethnically differentiated popular cultures as a result of the leveling effects of mediated mass culture. In subsequent decades this narrative of the effective replacement of popular cultures by mass culture became common sense, such that by our times any discussion of traditional, community-based cultural experience has come to be regarded as a sign of romantic nostalgia which flies in the face of contemporary realities. In most recent work, including much of that conducted in the name of "cultural studies," the concept of popular culture is directly equated with the offerings of the "culture industry" and their consumption; any productive agency or oppositionality on the part of "the people" is effectively reduced to its ability to consume in a differential and critical way.[3]

Another basis for the generalized skepticism as to the persistence and theoretical utility of popular culture in its traditional sense has been the ideological manipulation of the concept of "the people" in the hands of populism in its various twentieth-century guises. The recurrent appeal to "the people" in opportunistic political mobilizations of left, right, and center, whether in the name of democracy, national liberation, the free world, or the cause of labor, has so perverted that slogan as to empty it of all meaning, contestatory or otherwise. The work of Ernesto Laclau is often cited as the most rigorous critical exposé of the vagaries of populism as rhetoric and ideology; it has served recent cultural theorists like Stuart Hall and John Frow to rethink notions of "the people" and "the popular" in radically skeptical terms as constructs deployed for the purpose of deflecting political and cultural movements from more solidly verifiable realities of class as well as racial and sexual contestation, particularly in view of the conservative hegemonies of the 1980s.[4] Latin American social theorists like Nestor García Canclini have also propounded a trenchant critique of populism, in this case even more squarely associated with the remnants of retrogressive folklorism in the social sciences.[5] Reeling from the horrors of the dictatorship period, García Canclini and other contemporary scholars of "popular cultures" are concluding that it has become necessary to dispense with that category altogether, in favor of what are considered less misleading concepts like citizenship and civil society.[6] Along similar lines, the idea of "public culture" has been advanced, and has gained favor, as an alternative to "popular culture" in its diverse significations.[7]

Thus discredited by the compelling forces of global and regional modernity, the ideas of vernacular popular culture and "the people" have been reduced to a tenuous status at best, with the interventions of some postmodernist thinking only adding to the general skepticism by casting it as still another of the spurious master narratives that go to obscure the multiplicity and heterogeneity of cultural subjects and perspectives in present-day social experience. In a characteristic move, both of the component terms—*the people* and *culture*—are taken to be salvageable only when pluralized—*peoples* and *cultures*—and beyond that, only when employed in their adjectival form, as in the opting for "the cultural" rather than "culture" or "cultures" in the suggestive work of Arjun Appadurai.[8] The shift away from a sense of popular culture as products and traditions to a complex idea of signifying "practice," performance, and institutional process, as in the writings of Michel de Certeau and Pierre Bourdieu, has given the field new life and sophistication, but has by no means gone to counteract the near consensual reluctance to sustain the tenability of the concept in contemporary social analysis. The word *folklore*, the only terminological recourse to differentiate popular cultural expression from the engulfing phenomenon of popular culture qua mass cultural consumption, is so patently outmoded and laden with ideological baggage that its use only sets up the intellectual endeavor for further ridicule. Even the notion of "traditional" as distinguished from "modern" popular culture explicitly projects the community-based, expressive variant into a past tense, and cedes to the mass-mediated experience the crucial space of contemporaneity.

Is there any life left in "the people" as a social concept after the deadening impact of industrial mediation and ideological manipulation? Does the household term *popular culture* still bear any substantive content, or has it been become so replete with referents to every aspect and detail of social experience as to have been depleted of any and all specificity? Even if it is acknowledged that such cultural agency does exist, is there any way of talking about it without falling into some kind or other of essentialism or reductive simplification, and without minimizing the omnipresent role of the media and the active reelaboration of cultural meanings on the part of the public? Put another way, is it possible to engage this direct, expressive cultural practice of everyday life—those "moments of freedom" which Johannes Fabian sees at the core of popular culture—without positing some space outside of and unaffected by the industrial, ideological, and mobile demographic conditions that so obviously prevail in contemporary society on a world scale?

2

"It takes moments of freedom to catch moments of freedom," Fabian writes in a phrase whose insistently temporal imagery suggests an alternative way of conceptualizing popular culture.[9] He invites us to think of popular culture not so much as an entity comprised of products and processes, or as a bounded social space such as low or marginal, but as a relation or system of relations. Rather than marking off boundaries and defining separate spheres of cultural practice, perhaps popular culture is about the traversing and transgressing of them, and characterized by a dialogic among classes and social sectors, such as the popular and nonpopular, high and low, restricted and mass. As for thinking popular culture and developing a concept of the popular, the main correlation has to do with the "catching," the interplay between practice and theory, the "people" as subject and as object of knowledge, between lived social reality and the observer.

The familiar old ethnographic dilemma is at the heart of popular culture as an idea, but it is important to see—with Fabian—the relation between the people and the writer in terms of time, temporally, and as a historical relationship. For only in this way can the concept of popular culture address the need for contemporaneity and be rescued from its relegation to archaic and residual roles in today's global modernity and mass culture. Fabian concludes: "Observations on the privileging, in received culture theory, of shape over movement and of space over time made me consider the problem of contemporaneity as it poses itself specifically in the study of popular culture: as the coexistence of tradition and modernity. Such coexistence must be assumed and understood if our ambition is to recognize popular culture as contemporary practice, that is, as neither derivative epiphenomenon nor something that, in some evolutionary perspective on history, inevitably follows tradition when the latter disappears under the onslaught of modernity."[10]

There needs to be a correspondence, or a congruence of some kind, between the energized "moments of freedom" of popular cultural practice and the disposition of the writer at the moment and in the act of "catching." That symbiosis is temporal, an accordance in time and history, and conditioned by the "coexistence of tradition and modernity." If popular cultural practices are "arts of timing," in de Certeau's phrase, then the ethnographic intervention is a corresponding "art of timing," and the relative accuracy of our interpretation of those practices will depend on the quality of that correspondence. By historicizing the ethnographic relation, the reflexive presence of the writer may help contextualize cultural practice and dramatize the coexistence and interpenetration of historical periods, stages, and generations. While crossing multiple social spaces, the writer ignites associations across time not immediately visible at the site of cultural activity, yet latent as meanings and indispensable to its conceptualization.

"It should already be becoming clear," says the writer at the beginning of Edgardo Rodríguez Juliá's memoir *El entierro de Cortijo* (1983), "that this chronicle will be the encounter of many historical crossings."[11] Like many works of recent Puerto Rican writing, *El entierro de Cortijo* is a "chronicle" of contemporary popular culture and aims to "catch" the styles and language of everyday life in the colony in the wake of its aborted—or at least contorted—modernization process under the refurbished imperial arrangement of commonwealth status. And Rodríguez Juliá's chronicler goes straight to "the people": moved by the occasion of the funeral for his favorite popular musician Rafael Cortijo, the conspicuously middle-class intellectual ventures into the notoriously "underclass" housing projects called Lloréns Torres, after the laureled national poet Luis Lloréns Torres, in the heart of Cortijo's home neighborhood and where the deceased musician's body lay in wake. Amidst the family, friends, and local folk who have come to pay their respects, mostly poor and uneducated black women, men, and children, the bespectacled writer of visibly Mallorcan stock is nervously self-conscious of being himself "othered" by the "Other," and sets to thinking about the meaning of it all. He notices that, with all the solemnity of the occasion, there is a sense of playfulness and even festivity in the air, and he himself seems to let his guard down so as to make the most of this "moment of freedom," this fortunate "art of timing."

Surveying the scene, he sees people, regular Puerto Rican people, paying tribute to an emblem of their culture, Cortijo, whose music stands as a supreme example of popular culture and of the "coexistence of tradition and modernity." Yet the event itself, marking the popular artist's passing, is also an act of popular culture, and it includes the writer himself and his complex, paradoxical relation to it. The sparks of historical associations fly, and he waxes philosophical about the meaning of death, the question of immortality, and how "the people," *those* people yet at the same time *his* people, might be defined. "How to define this people?" he asks, and responds with an explanation which points to a novel way to get beneath the representational and ideological constructions of popular culture that prevail in the public mind. "To define it is easy," he says, "but how difficult it is to describe it! It is people people [pueblo pueblo], my Puerto Rican people in all its contradictory diversity: . . ."[12] The distinction drawn between "definition" and "description" is an important one, as it signals the need to go beyond a facile naming or labeling based on political rhetoric or sociological categorizing ("definir"), and to somehow account for the variety, richness, and the complexity of the phenomenon ("describir"), that is, to retain a sense of concreteness and specificity while generalizing. The doubling of the noun "pueblo" has to do, first of all, with emphasis; perhaps the English equivalent would be "real people," or "down-home people." But from the context it is clear that the reiterated "pueblo pueblo" is the term appropriate to "description" rather than "definition," that in order to make it clear that he is talking about living human beings and not the abstract slogan and category "the people" used to objectify them, it is necessary to say it twice, "people people."

Yet the writer is also wary of the pitfall of essentialism implicit in the claim to unmediated experience and authenticity. His version of "the people" is itself mediated through his own perceptions and explicitly stated social position. Nevertheless, Rodríguez Juliá—and Johannes Fabian— would insist that, without positing some "popular" experience outside the dominant ideological field or mass media culture, there is a difference between mediation as a creative and intellectual activity and that of the media with their commercial and political overdeterminations. The Colombian cultural theorist Jesús Martín Barbero titled his important book "From the media to mediations" (*De los medios a las mediaciones*),[13] and argues for the value of keeping the historical sense of popular culture as "folklore" alive even while recognizing the encompassing role of the media in twentieth-century culture.

The medium of the literary ethnographer or chronicler of popular culture, which allows for the closest possible approximation to the perspective of that culture, is the imagination, a faculty referred to emphatically by Rodríguez Juliá along with other contemporary theorists like Fabian and Appadurai.[14] The work of the imagination in this sense is historical memory, that is, the association of social experiences through and in time by means of interpretive recognition and recollection. Immediately after his programmatic reference to "pueblo pueblo," the phrase "in all its contradictory diversity" is followed by a colon, and the chronicler offers an example: "the sickly-looking woman with her hair in a bun and wearing sneakers because of her bunions, you know, like the bunions in the plena song 'Los juanetes de Juana' " ("la *jipata* señora de moño calza tenis para los *juanetes* de Juana"). The ethnographic mediation continues when this succinct but culturally rich description is brought into association with similar class and cultural experiences as awakened in the author's own recollection; the "little beads of greasy sweat" he notices on the woman's brow "remind me of those self-sacrificing ironing-women and domestic cooks who used to pass by on Saturdays along the streets of my childhood and head off to their proletarian places of evangelical worship [al proletario culto evangélico]."[15] The black working-class woman he sees there at the wake for Cortijo takes on emblematic significance as an embodiment of "pueblo pueblo" not for some hidden essence or archetypicality, but by force of the historical parallels and richly contradictory mnemonic associations her presence evokes. It is important to understand that along with the obvious continuities between the woman before him and those of his memories, there is also a sharp contrast because of the historical lapse resulting from the colonial modernization process and its so-called "lumpenizing" or de-proletarianizing consequences. Both are "pueblo pueblo," their visage and beads of sweat may be identifiable, but intervening historical change has brought alterations in their everyday social practices and beliefs. In both cases, though, their concreteness and specificity are maintained, and imaginative memory allows for the study of popular culture in time.

3

More than merely emphasis, the effect of the doubling in the term "pueblo pueblo" is to provide a necessary marker of specification or qualification. It is a sign of internal difference and contradiction, and of the abiding need to address the questions, "*Which* people?" and "*Which* popular culture?" With the hegemonic meaning of the term *popular culture* so identified with global media culture and communication, some specification of the time or site of the popular becomes indispensable. It is this need for specification that Stuart Hall stresses when he takes up, in cautiously nonessentialist terms, the thorny question, "What Is This 'Black' in Black Popular Culture?"[16] He recognizes bluntly that popular culture has become "the scene, par excellence, of commodification," "the space of homogenization where stereotyping and the formulaic mercilessly process the material and experiences it draws into its web, where control over narratives and representations passes into the hands of the established cultural bureaucracies, sometimes without a murmur."[17] Though openly "available for expropriation," however, popular culture may signal alternative spaces, temporalities, and practices when the marker "Black" is added—that is, when there is a qualifying reference to the experiences of a historically specified people. Accounting for these two distinct levels of meaning, Hall demonstrates how this doubling of the term through social markers helps in establishing a more dynamic understanding of contemporary popular culture: "However deformed, incorporated, and inauthentic are the forms in which black people and black communities and traditions appear and are represented in popular culture," he writes, "we continue to see, in the figures and repertoires on which popular culture draws, the experiences that stand behind them. In its expressivity, its musicality, its orality, in its rich, deep, and varied attention to speech, in its inflections toward the vernacular and the local, in its rich production of counternarratives, and above all, in its metaphorical use of the musical vocabulary, black popular culture has enabled the surfacing, inside the mixed and contradictory modes even of some mainstream popular culture, of elements of a discourse that is different—other forms of life, other traditions of representation."[18]

"It is this mark of difference *inside* forms of popular culture," Hall concludes, "that is carried by the signifier 'black'," and he sees what is called "American popular culture" as a prime example of this internal differentiation: "the fact of American popular culture itself, which has always contained within it, whether silenced or not, black American popular vernacular traditions."[19] To further underscore his strictly historical intentions, Hall is emphatic in stating that the "difference" marked off has to do not only with race but with other forms of marginality and difference as well, and that "blackness" has preeminently to do with unifying experiences of colonization, enslavement, and diasporic displacement. The point of the signifier, and the value of such seeming tautologies as "popular vernacular" and "pueblo pueblo," is specification in historical time and social position, which is why Hall speaks so affirmatively of Gramsci's concept of "the national-popular." Though some contemporary theorists, like the Brazilian Renato Ortiz, claim that the "national-popular" is by now fully eclipsed by what he calls "uma cultura internacional popular,"[20] Hall argues that this national qualification remains cogent and continues to alter the meaning of the "popular" in our times: "The role of the 'popular' in popular culture is to fix the authenticity of popular forms, rooting them in the experiences of popular communities from which they draw their strength, allowing us to see them as expressive of a particular subordinate social life that resists its being constantly made over as low and outside."[21] Inside and behind the surface of commonality and the homogenizing pressure of "popular culture" in its hegemonic appearance, there is the popular culture defined by historical experiences of exclusion and subordination, of "difference" along the axes of social power.

It is important to recall that this dimension of national and colonial particularity has intersected the sense of popular culture as a "common," class-unified culture since the earliest conceptualization of the term. Long before Gramsci, Herder and the Grimm brothers along with other "discoverers" of the popular had in mind this differentiation along lines of national and center-periphery contrast in their quest for some alternative to the cultural hegemony of France and England.[22] The history of the term, in fact, has witnessed this tension between the popular as "low" or "common" within a given society and that of some variant of what Gramsci then came to call the "national-popular," the national marker always indicating a colonial or peripheralizing relation of power. As engulfing as the "international-popular" may have become, the vector of national and regional hierarchies has by no evidence been effaced, and thus continues to point up contexts of popular cultural expression of a local and community-based kind.[23]

Rather than among advertently isolated and disconnected groups, in our time these "national-popular" contexts are particularly alive in diasporic settings, and under conditions, not of purity or boundedness, but of what García Canclini refers to, in his influential book, as "hybrid cultures."[24] The preservation and reenergizing of national traditions is most active at the seams of contemporary transnational formations, at the point of rupture and refashioning characteristic of diasporic conditions and migratory peoples, where an appeal to those traditions helps to provide a sense of grounding in place and time. The particularity characteristic of popular culture practice is now present not so much in some presumed untampered lineage of native heritage as in the very hybridization itself, in the blending and juxtaposition of seemingly disparate elements of divergent traditions and practices.

4

But cultural hybridity in García Canclini's sense refers to more than the fusion of cultural traditions resulting from the mutual influence among intersecting groups, a phenomenon which he studies closely in his work on Tijuana and the Mexican-U.S. border culture.[25] He is also referring to the mixing and interpenetration of the cultural domains themselves, the blurring of the age-old distinctions between high and low, and between elite, folkloric, and mass cultures. His guiding conceptual term is "reconversion," by which he means the constant use of supposedly "high" culture features by the "low" (whether folk or mass), and vice versa, such that as a result of multidirectional "reconversions" the cultural field becomes in our time—in "postmodernity," he would say—a field of influences and interactions unified by transnational demographic movements and consumption practices. Such an interpretation of cultural relations has its obvious appeal among contemporary readers in Latin America and elsewhere (which accounts for the book's huge influence), for it helps free the conceptualization of popular culture from the usual binarisms of high and low, inside or outside. It also allows for a more careful reading of Bakhtin's idea of cultural inversion and the topsy-turvy creativity of the carnivalesque. As Hall points out, "The carnivalesque is not simply an upturning of two things which remain locked within their oppositional frameworks; it is also crosscut by what Bakhtin calls the dialogic."[26]

An especially rich example of cultural reconversion and the dialogic interplay of high and low may be seen in the current strategies of the Walt Disney Company.[27] The entertainment colossus, long the world's supreme purveyor of mass culture, is resolutely going upscale, dedicating a surprisingly large share of its $22.5 billion in revenues (for 1998) to the patronage of high culture. Disney chairman and CEO Michael Eisner, described as "a man who can shape culture on a global basis like perhaps no other person in history," is now "the Medici behind Disney's high art." Currently, he is commissioning two choral symphonies to mark the millennium, an idea that came to him while attending a performance of Mahler's Eighth Symphony, the "Symphony of a Thousand," at Carnegie Hall in 1996. Similar ventures in sophistication are afoot in the areas of theater and architecture, and the pretensions of elite cultural status are most evident and serious, as might be expected, in France and in the vast endeavors of EuroDisney. In 1989 Eisner hired Jean-Luc Choplin, of indubitable high-culture pedigree as the former managing director of the Paris Opera Ballet, to program the entertainment at Disneyland Paris. In a move that would leave Theodor Adorno and the Frankfurt School theorists aghast, the quintessential "culture industry" is on a mission to "help new culture flower," as one of the commissioned composers has it, "when what we're seeing is this overwhelming junk culture."

And, of course, neither patron Eisner nor ambassador Choplin sees any contradiction between their "serious culture" endeavors and what Disney has done all along. As always, it is about the marriage, or symbiosis, between culture and business; as Eisner responds to the many attacks on his entertainment corporation, "To be broadly commercial, you have to be broadly talented, so nothing we do now is inconsistent with what Walt did with his early pioneering work in animation, or with 'Fantasia' or with working with Westinghouse to adapt the technology of his day to his theme parks." Choplin in turn, more at ease with his imbued cultural capital than with marketing projections, is expansive in his justification of Disney's quest for cultural sophistication; in his view, it is the long history of "reconversion," the age-old interdependence of the high and the low, that lies at the heart of the Disney mission and points to the vision for the future. With references ranging widely to Boticelli, Mahler, Sibelius, and Charles Ives, he states that "they were all inspired by popular traditions, by roots. I think we have explored a lot of one-way streets at the end of the twentieth century, and I think art needs to go back to more popular roots. And roots are not in the ether; they're in popular culture." The process of reconversion is thus multidirectional, and in this case may be seen to come full circle: what starts as commercial mass culture turning to elite culture be-

comes the recognition by the newfound purveyors of high culture of the
need for "roots" in popular culture traditions.

5

The playing field of contemporary culture may be new but it is still not
level; lines have been redrawn but not erased. García Canclini is careful to
distinguish between "reconversión hegemónica" and "reconversión popular," and thereby to lodge his theory of cultural hybridizations in structures
of corporate and state power. Homogenizing tendencies engendered by
global consumer culture are met by countervailing moves of reappropria-
tion and reindigenization. Diasporic experiences demonstrate that the global encounters opposition not only at the local but at the translocal level as
well, and thus belie the logic of a narrowly territorial geopolitics of cultural
relations. The persistence of structures of social domination in general involves their persistence in the cultural field as well, though the relational
lines between them, between social and cultural power, are shifting and
oblique. That is, the socially dominant is also the culturally dominant, but
the Bakhtinian paradox has it that the exercise of cultural domination inherently entails a "dependency on the low-Other," and further that "the top
includes that low symbolically, as a primary eroticized constituent of its own
fantasy life."[28]

No matter how the field of cultural practices is reconfigured in line with
political and economic changes, popular culture of the vernacular, community-based kind will continue to be present as a mode of social relations,
not to be wished away or analyzed out of existence in response to the per-
vasiveness of media consumption. The need for "roots" is unrelenting, if
not intensifying, in our times, and because of the carnivalesque inversion—that "what is socially peripheral is so frequently *symbolically* central"—the roots of popular culture traditions are strongest among colonized nationalities and racialized communities and peoples. Here is where
those "moments of freedom" are most visible, the "arts of timing" characteristic of popular culture in refusing incorporation and retaining what
Hall calls "the cutting edge of difference and transgression."[29] But to "cap-
ture" such moments, as Fabian continues his temporal imagery, requires
an acute and perhaps redefined sense of time and temporal relations: it in
turns calls for "moments of freedom" and "arts of timing" as well. This
means, most obviously, historical awareness in order to counteract the ex-

cessively spatial conception of cultural relations that prevails in popular culture theory; the primacy of context in history over the usual privileging of an ahistorically constructed "location" in social space. The imperative is temporality not just historicity, though, because too often history, and historical contexts, are confused with a teleology of progress and "development," and the puzzling over "modernity" with the sense that modernity (and postmodernity) are somehow the goal or end-result of cultural experience on an individual and collective level.

Popular culture "in time" calls for historical rather than preponderantly spatial contexts, but above all it refers to the enactment and the "capturing" of popular culture as the establishing of temporal relations, associations fashioned by acts of memory and imagination. Relations in space and time, of course, interactions and intersections among social classes, racialized groups, diasporic locations, periods in history, generations—all are at work, and revealed, through popular cultural practice and interpretation. But what is particular about popular culture is its particularity, and as "moments of freedom" the particularity of time in popular culture is that it is momentary, that with all its embeddedness in tradition and the historical past, it is present, it is contemporary, it is always *now*.

> The concept of *popularity* itself is not particularly popular. It is not realistic to believe that it is. There is a whole series of abstract nouns in "ity" which must be viewed with caution. Think of *utility, sovereignty, sanctity*; and we know that the concept of *nationality* has a quite particular, sacramental, pompous and suspicious connotation, which we dare not overlook. We must not ignore this connotation, just because we so urgently need the concept *popular*.   —BERTOLT BRECHT

Puerto Rican Day parade, along Fifth Avenue (1997)

(Photo by José Rosario, courtesy of *El Diario–La Prensa*)

2

The Lite Colonial

DIVERSIONS OF PUERTO RICAN DISCOURSE

EL GIRLIE SHOW

The leader of the Independence Party called it an "infamy without parallel in the history of our country." Public figures of all stripes and persuasions chimed in—politicians, journalists, church leaders, media personalities— all indignant at this ultimate act of desecration. At a concert in Bayamón in October 1993 none other than pop icon Madonna, the "Material Girl," had suggestively passed the Puerto Rican flag between her legs, bringing that most sacred of national symbols into sacrilegious contact with "those dishonorable zones" ("esas zonas deshonradas"), as antiabortion, antigay crusader Father Mateo Mateo put it. Patriotic and moral sensitivities converged, finding in the defiled flag a common, consensual object of honor and adoration.[1]

Yet it didn't take the infamous "Madonna incident" to get Puerto Ricans to rally around the flag. In recent years, increasingly as we approach the centenary of the planting of the Stars and Stripes on Puerto Rican soil in 1898, the "one-star flag" ("la monoestrellada") has assumed its role as the most venerated singular emblem of the Puerto Rican nationality. "¡SOLA!" was the single-word headline that took up the entire front page of the daily newspapers in December 1995, the one-hundredth birthday of the national banner, which to this day according to colonial jurisdiction can legally be displayed only in the company of Old Glory. But on that December morning the Puerto Rican flag waved proud and all on its own above the hallowed halls of the Ateneo Puertorriqueño, long considered the official seat of the national culture. Again, the ideological and other rifts that mark Puerto Rican public life seemed to have been suspended, as statehooders, independentistas, and autonomists shared in this ironic and mildly defiant outburst of patriotic celebration.

The irony is that as recently as the 1970s that same object of collective veneration was considered a mark of nationalist insolence if not transgression, and many today still recall being apprehended and harassed for brandishing a flag on their bumper stickers or T-shirts. What is new, of course, is not the intense national sentiment but its outing, not the meaning of the flag but its legitimation in the public sphere, official and other. In fact, as the "Madonna incident" shows, it is its commercial visibility more than any moral umbrage that helps propel the national flag into the open and out of its restricted political and ideological field of signification. In view of this proliferation and commercial use of the flag, there were even those who took less offense at Madonna's spectacle; one diehard Madonna fan (referred to dismissively as a "cocolo") is quoted as responding, "I don't know why there's all the noise, because our flag ["la monoestrellada"] has never waved so pretty. Better between Madonna's legs than on Macho Camacho's ass."[2] This irreverent remark suggests that it is not actually the eroticization of the flag that desecrates it but its crass and ubiquitous commodification—don't blame Madonna but rather the sway of the global marketplace and mass consumption for stripping the paramount national symbol of its traditional spiritual aura. As one commentator put it, that unflustered "cocolo" is only reminding the outraged public that long before the Material Girl came along to fondle the flag, that cherished symbol had been used on boxers' shorts, baseball hats, ass-patches, T-shirts, scarves, beer cans, and in cigarette and rum ads as well as ads by American Airlines, Pizza Hut, and MacDonald's—and yet somehow nobody's patriotic honor seemed to be offended.[3]

Madonna of course is not just any old commodity, and her self-advertisement serves to market not any product or brand name in particular, but is part and parcel of transnational consumer culture as such. The bleach-blonde gringa flaunting the largesse of imperial morality sets off special signals in the colonial public sphere at many levels. Indeed, when in the following year R. J. Reynolds ran a multimillion-dollar ad campaign for Winston, featuring the flag draped around a young man's body and the slogan "100% Puertorriqueño," objections resonated from many quarters, culminating in its denunciation by the newly appointed president of the Puerto Rican Senate, Charlie Rodríguez, in his inaugural address. The clamor was such that R. J. Reynolds was impelled to retract its use of the flag, though it held onto its long-standing image identifying Winston with "pure" Puerto Rican-ness. Interestingly, the loudest outcry came not so much from offended nationalists but from proponents of statehood like Charlie Rodríguez and journalist Luis Dávila Colón, who claimed that with its use of the flag the Winston ad was pushing the cause of Puerto Rican nationalism! Madison Avenue, it seems, is now accused of picking up where Pedro Albizu Campos left off, waging "the latest offensive in the ideological warfare that consumes us and has contaminated our civil society."[4]

But it is the "Madonna incident," with its range of moral, racial, sexual, and political implications, that sparked the most heated ideological reactions and points up most clearly the range of contemporary intellectual debate in Puerto Rico. One extended reflection, by cultural critic and university professor Carlos Pabón, was titled "De Albizu a Madonna: para armar y desarmar la nacionalidad" ("From Albizu to Madonna: Arming and disarming the nationality") and accompanied by a photomontage featuring the head of the famed nationalist leader atop Madonna's scantily clad torso. Pabón takes the occasion to point up "the theoretical and political limitations of the neo-nationalist and Puerto Ricanist discourse that dominates the debate about identity in Puerto Rico." In tune with much current theorizing on the Island, he speaks of the nation as constructed, commodified, and antiessentialist, and of the conversion of political nationalism of earlier years into a watered-down, consensual, and noncontestatory "cultural nationalism": "The discourse of Puerto Rican-ness has been constituted as a paradigm of social consensus. Nationalism has been converted into a state ideology and market culture, and in the process a problematic discourse was domesticated."[5] Interrogating the widespread indignation over Madonna's desecration of the flag, critics like Pabón and Madeline Román in her essay "El Girlie Show: Madonna, las polémicas nacionales y los pánicos morales" ("El Girlie Show: Madonna, national polemics, and moral panic") place in question the very concept of the nation itself, pointing up its historical contingency, moral arbitrariness, and ultimately conservative role as a sustaining ideological metanarrative. Román in particular emphasizes its complementarity with other, more obviously conservative metanarratives of moral puritanism, elitism, patriarchy, and heterosexism.

Over against the "essentialism of the neo-nationalist discourse," this line of recent criticism poses the "cultural hybridity (heterogeneity and plurality) of our contemporary cultural formation," the profound contradictions inherent in the national construct, and its unboundedness and relational interaction with other "national" cultures. In the theoretical language of the 1990s, published in journals with names like *Postdata, Bordes,* and *Nómadas,* Puerto Rican identity is described as multiple, nomadic, diasporic, and disengaged from the categorical moorings of the nation in its traditional conception. The undermining of the hegemony of the national concept has gone so far as to lead some to abandon the independence project altogether in favor of the polemically charged idea of "radical statehood," thus driving a wedge in the long-held equation of independentism and the political struggle for democracy.[6] In a highly resonant phrase, there is a call to abandon the "heavy," totalizing, propagandistic nationalism of earlier years in favor of what is termed "la independencia lite."[7]

Needless to say, there has been a response, sometimes vehement, to these heretical notions, most extensively in the book-length essay by journalist and editor Luis Fernando Coss entitled *La nación en la orilla: repuesta a los posmodernos pesimistas* (The nation on the shore: Response to the postmodern pesimists) (1996). Taking issue with the positions assumed by Carlos Pabón and others, Coss argues on behalf of the independence movement not as an ideological ploy but as an eclectic, nonsectarian progressive tradition in Puerto Rican history, a democratic, anticolonial public sphere. Like other stalwarts of the independence movement, Coss retains with faint disclaimers the "heavy," totalizing nationalist stance, including its traces of Hispanophilia, patriarchy, and cultural elitism. If not flag-waving and triumphalist, Coss is driven by his disgust over offenses like the "Madonna incident" and those who are not equally outraged to a heated defense of the national culture and national dignity. The nation in this view is not just a "discourse," "text," or "imagined community," but a historical category and verifiable site of lived social experience.[8]

THINKING LITE

After a century of U.S. control over Puerto Rico, then, the debate over the status and future options for the society rages as widely and intensely as ever, with many of the present-day positions echoing closely the lines drawn over the decades. What is perhaps new about today's polemic, aside from the postmodernist vocabulary, is the current of skepticism as to the viability and validity of the national concept itself, and the appeal to other forms of solidarity and contestation often obscured by the univocal call for unity and self-determination along patriotic lines. Never before have the articles of faith of Puerto Rican political and cultural self-understanding been subjected to such radical rethinking, nor has there been such an intricate gradation of intermediate and qualifying perspectives. Ranging among the three formal political alternatives—autonomy, statehood, and independence—liberals and neoliberals, conservatives and U.S.-style Republicans, feminists and postfeminists, Marxists, neo-Marxists, and post-Marxists, postmodern pessimists and optimists, radical statehooders and old-line nationalists, and countless other positions have been staked out during the present generation, converting the battleground of earlier periods into a veritable free-for-all of divergences and modifications. Ambiguity and vacillation reign supreme, with fin-de-siécle Puerto Rico being described as "a paramount instance of the present-day 'heterotopia,' a marked-off geographical space housing a heterogeneity of social desires."9

Yet as the carefully monitored plebiscites and referenda of recent years make evident, the present collective ambiguity is more than ever an orchestrated one, a reflex of the vagaries and complexities of U.S. and transnational priorities and rearrangements. Indeed, if there is consensus on any issue, it is that Puerto Rico is a "colony." Whether the preferred option is annexation, increased autonomy, or national sovereignty, and whether the theoretical perspective is primarily guided by ideas of democracy, socialism, feminism, anti-imperialism, or antiracism, all programs are propounded with the purported aim of decolonization—that is, the recognition of an ongoing condition of subordination and external tutelage and the need to put an end to it. Though it carries a seemingly endless array of meanings, and the formulas for challenging it span the full range of political options, the word *colony*, or its connotations, resonates virtually unchallenged in Puerto Rican public life.

It is this bottom-line, largely unarticulated consensus as to the persistence of coloniality that may account for the reluctance to engage the concepts of postcolonial theory in the eclectic intellectual landscape of the current debates. With all the receptivity toward the many shadings and inroads of recent social theory in its poststructuralist, postmodernist, deconstructionist, even postnationalist variants, the idea of the postcolonial has singularly fallen on deaf ears. If it is true that postcolonial theorizing evidences a spirit of "premature celebration" (as is claimed by critics like Anne McClintock and Ella Shohat),10 then Puerto Rico is surely an obvious case in point. Like Palestine—the example cited by Homi Bhabha and others—Puerto Rico stands as "exceptional" and unusual in "still" being a colony in the context of postcolonial globality. Puerto Rico today stands as a test of the universalist claims of postcolonial theory, bringing to the foreground the relation between a purported global "condition" ("post-" as an "aftermath") and the reality of national and regional conditions. That is, both the globalizing claims of postcolonial theory and the geopolitical specification of the Caribbean as a paradigmatic postcolonial region, rest for their validity on the inclusion of the still-colonial Puerto Rico.

Yet it is also clear that Puerto Rico is a colony in a different way, jibing only partially and uncomfortably with the inherited notion or stereotype of the classical colony with its earmarks of rampant socioeconomic misery, direct and total political and military control, and peripheralized public life contrasting graphically with that of the metropolis. The postcolonial, it would seem, involves not so much the elimination or supercession of colonialism but its pluralization; it signals the existence of multiple colonialisms—gradations and varieties, faces and masks of colonial experience, as a legacy, as an ongoing and modulating state, as an emergent anticipation, or even as a return to a prior condition. If anything, the case of Puerto Rico demonstrates the need for a new and more differentiated vocabulary for postcolonial discourse: if neither the familiar old "colonial nation" nor a newfangled "postcolonial postnation" are appropriate, what about the variously propounded ideas of neo-, late, or "modern" colony, or—in order to account for diasporic fragmentations—the de-territorialized concepts of "ethnonation" or "transnation"?[11] Or, if colonization is perceived more as a process or historical dynamic than as a finite state or condition, what about "re-colonial," or when thinking of parts of the world like eastern Europe, Central America, or the Pacific Rim, may we not even speak of "precolonial"?

Or, to return to the specific case of Puerto Rico, the apparently anomalous postcolonial colony, what about the "lite colonial"? It has the advantage of resonating with "late colonial," which helps locate it historically in the period coinciding with and following the global decolonization process. Rather than as a formula or program, the term "lite" may help signal the "structure of feeling" of contemporary intellectual and cultural sensibilities in the period since the 1970s, and especially in the decade of the 1990s. Aside from its ubiquity in the media-speak that saturates much public discourse on the Island, cultural critics like Juan Duchesne Winter, Carlos Gil, and Carlos Pabón have given it a lively currency in the theoretical debates of the 1990s, and topical author Juan Antonio Ramos subtitles a recent

(1993) book of stories and sketches "ocurrencias 'lite.' " While Duchesne introduced it by way of a call for a more moderate, toned-down independentista "temperament," Pabón speaks of "the rise of a 'lite capitalism'," meaning "a capitalism that has become Puerto Ricanist by exploiting for its own benefit the national symbols, which like the flag, represent 'our' customs, traditions, and way of life. This is a post-Fordist capitalism which as a result of the processes of economic and cultural globalization and internationalization seeks to incorporate 'the other.' "[12] "Lite" in this sense is intended to contrast to the heavy, hard, rough, "dark" colonial reality and discourse, including the anticolonial struggle and stance, of the modernist and modernizing period. It involves the analytical disengagement of the age-old paired concepts of nation and nation-state, politics and culture, patriotism and nationalism, consensus and contestation, which are so much at issue in the current debate.

Yet as idiosyncratic as the qualifier "lite" may be to present-day Puerto Rican discourse, its currency may also apply in a more far-reaching way to the quality of colonial relations in late or postcolonial times. Might we now speak of a process of "flexible" colonization to match the often-discussed "flexibility" of contemporary capitalist accumulation? Much of the recent literature on transnational political economy, from a range of political agendas, suggests such a realignment of power relations, as is evident, for example, in the writings of Paul Krugman (*Peddling Prosperity* and *Pop Internationalism*), William Greider (*One World, Ready or Not*), or Robert Kuttner (*Everything for Sale*), or more recently (1993) in the book *The Commanding Heights: The Battle Between Government and the Marketplace That Is Remaking the Modern World* by Daniel Yergin and Joseph Stanislaw. A critical perspective might well dismiss some of this literature as a lot of "globaloney," or "global babble," but the interesting policy article, "The Rise of 'Lite' Powers: A Strategy for the Postmodern State," illustrates the potential attractiveness of the "lite" category in current social theory on a world scale.[13] In a similar vein, in *Michael Jordan and the New Global Capitalism* Walter LaFeber makes valuable use of the term "soft power" to refer to the "influence of U.S. culture and commerce, rather than its military and political muscle."[14]

Without recourse to the term "lite" itself, Stuart Hall characterizes the economic underpinnings of this new market-driven form of hegemony in more substantive terms in his essay "The Local and the Global": "Not everywhere, by any means, but in some of the most advanced parts of the globalization process what one finds are new regimes of accumulation, much more flexible regimes founded not simply on the logics of mass production and of mass consumption but on new flexible accumulation strategies, on segmented markets, on post-Fordist styles of organization, on lifestyle and identity-specific forms of marketing, driven by the market, driven by just-in-time production, driven by the ability to address not just the mass audience, or the mass consumer, but by penetrating to the very specific smaller groups, to individuals, in its appeal." In another phrase, Hall speaks of "this concentrated, corporate, over-corporate, over-integrated, over-concentrated, and condensed form of economic power which lives culturally through difference and which is constantly teasing itself with the pleasures of the transgressive other."[15]

Getting beyond the obvious trendiness of the term, then, the catchphrase "lite" indicates that as colonial subordination becomes transnationalized it also tends to shift from a primarily political, state-, and institution-driven force to a commercial one impelled by markets and oriented toward consumers. In contrast to a colonialism based on production, the "lite colonial" is grounded on consumption. "Lite," after all, especially in its cute phonetic spelling, is primordially the language of advertising, of commercial culture, and of an empire of signs maintained for the purpose of social pacification and need-creation, including the stimulation and satisfaction of ideological needs.[16] The "lite colonial" is eminently discursive colonialism, a thickly symbolic form of transnational domination which emphasizes both a consensual identity ("we are all Puerto Ricans, across all lines") and at the same time multiple identities of a nonmonolithic, fragmented kind, including the diasporic. In accord with such "lite colonial" conditions, the move for decolonization needs also to be flexible, dynamic, and democratic in the sense of skepticism toward the postulation of a singular vanguard force or an obligatory teleology of state power.

Under conditions of the "lite colonial" intended in this way, it is understandable why events like the "Madonna incident" take on such explosive public significance in Puerto Rican discourse, and why the analysis of their meaning for everyday life is so intricately linked with critical interventions of a more directly economic and political kind. Colonial legitimation thus resting strongly on the logic of commercial persuasion and its incursion into the cultural discourse, the struggle for interpretive power moves to the foreground of anticolonial projects, with the deconstruction of corporate-sponsored salsa concerts, media coverage of the "chupacabras" ("goat sucker") episode, or the differential reaction to the Puerto Rican Barbie Doll, arousing active political reaction and debate.

Yet it should be borne in mind that the consumer catchphrase "lite" also carries the implication of light-weight, watered-down, without the edge or the kick. In order to build consumer markets with a view toward modern-day health and environmental consciousness (or hype), products must be deprived of some of their "fat," or substance, or at least be promoted as such. Correspondingly, an exclusive focus on the "lite" quality of contemporary colonial relations without moorings in a critique of political and economic conditions may also signal a superficial and thin analysis, an interpretation that takes at face value the camouflages and ploys of commercial colonialism. It is, in a word appropriately laden with ambiguity, a "diversion," or in the usage expounded by Edouard Glissant, a "détour."[17]

POINTS OF ENTANGLEMENT

The Martinican writer and theorist Edouard Glissant builds his monumental treatise *Caribbean Discourse* (*Discours antillais*, 1981) on the concept of "diversion" or "détour." Given the notorious gulfs separating the varied political cultures of the Caribbean, it may appear far-fetched to look to a Francophone thinker like Glissant for insights into the complex and distinctive experience of "lite colonial" Puerto Rico. But as "modern colonies," which retain nonindependent status and relations under conditions of postcolonial globality, Puerto Rico and Martinique today bear stronger similarities than in earlier periods.[18] In fact, since the departmentalization of Martinique and the establishment of commonwealth status in Puerto Rico, both adjustments dating from the late 1940s, the two countries have encountered similar assimilationist and consensualist tendencies in their colonial accommodation, along with the growing prospect of a soft or gradualist decolonization process. There is thus in present-day Puerto Rico an intriguing resonance in Glissant's words about his fellow Martinicans, as when he describes them as "a people wedged in an impossible situation," or even in his definition of the term *diversion*: "The community has tried to exorcise the impossibility of return by what I call the practice of diversion."[19]

Rather than an essentializing metaphor, as guides the writings of other Caribbean cultural theorists like Fernando Ortíz or Antonio Benítez-Rojo, Glissant's concept of diversion would seek the unifying thread of a pan-Caribbean discourse in a "practice," that is, a gesture or performative tactic. Glissant's term is also useful because it retains the ambiguity of the word in its everyday usage: diversion means both fun or "divertissement," including the sense of making fun of or ironically (re)signifying (what Achille Mbembe refers to as "how the people trick, play, toy with power"),[20] and at the same time a distraction or deflection, a "detour" in the literal sense. Unpacking this central concept in his poetic/politics on Caribbean "discourse," Glissant explains that "diversion is not a systematic refusal to see. No, it is not a kind of self-inflicted blindness nor a conscious strategy of flight in the face of reality. Rather, we would say that it is formed, like a habit, from an interweaving of negative forces that go unchallenged."[21]

In another passage which would seem equally pertinent to contemporary Puerto Rican cultural experience, Glissant speaks of diversion as "the ultimate resource of a population whose domination by an Other is concealed: it must search *elsewhere* for the principle of domination (which is not only exploitation, which is not only misery, which is not only underdevelopment, but actually the complete eradication of an economic entity) and is not directly tangible."[22]

In its existential presentness and situational, unsystematic inversion or displacement of an imposed reality, Glissant's "diversion" bears obvious traces of the carnivalesque, but it is important that the practice of "détour" occurs in dialectical interplay with that of "reversion" or "rétour." Here again two meanings are harbored in the same term, one being "reversion" in the primordialist, nostalgic sense, or in Glissant's explanation, "the obsession with a single origin: one must not alter the absolute state of being. To revert is to consecrate permanence, to negate contact. Reversion will be recommended by those who favor single origins." But Glissant has another, more historical and contextual notion of what reversion can be, where it serves to counterbalance the strategy of diversion: "Diversion is not a useful ploy unless it is nourished by reversion: not a return to the longing for origins, to some immutable state of Being, but a return to the point of entanglement, from which we were forcefully turned away; that is where we must effectively put to work the forces of creolization, or perish."[23]

With this coupled tactic of diversion and reversion, situational deflection and collective genealogy, Glissant's dynamic model offers an account of colonial/anticolonial cultural practice which pertains to much of the Caribbean in its postcolonial condition (though Glissant, writing *Caribbean Discourse* in the 1970s, is really a pre- or perhaps proto-postcolonial thinker), and which applies with particular resonance in "lite colonial" Puerto Rico or his native Martinique. How this practical and theoretical dynamic plays it-self out, and what the historical "entanglements" and "creolization" com-prise, will of course vary from country to country, and need to be approached from, and inclusive of, particular national contexts and constructs. But as an analytical paradigm or method, the dialectic of diversion and reversion pro-vides a valuable supplement to the tenets of postcolonial theory in critiquing contemporary colonial culture. It also allows for an analysis of the "excep-tional" case of contemporary Puerto Rico in a Caribbean regional context.

UNSETTLING FRAGMENTS

It has often been noted that it is the diasporic situation, rather than the re-alities of the formerly colonial nations themselves, which most directly en-genders postcolonial theorizing.[24] The postcolony implies and necessarily includes its diaspora(s), and the rethinking of national identities and boundaries faces a key challenge in the translocal, translocational, and transcontextual character of diasporic history. Though usually ignored or relegated in "Puerto Rican discourse" (and in much "Caribbean discourse" as well), the diaspora is integral and relational to the national and region-al; it constitutes the most obvious and profound instance of fragmentation of the national and the most vibrant site of contemporary "creolization."[25]

Though modern-day Martinique and the Martinican diaspora communi-ties are certainly an obvious case in point, Glissant is less specific in this re-gard. "There is a difference," he writes in the opening sentence of the *Dis-cours*, "between the transplanting (by exile or dispersion) of a people who continue to survive elsewhere and the transfer (by the slave trade) of a pop-ulation to another place where they change into something different, into a new set of possiblities."[26] Though it contains the important reminder that the Caribbean nations are themselves diasporic in their historical constitu-tion, and that their histories attest above all to an African diaspora, his dis-tinction is less helpful when assessing the contemporary context. For in today's Caribbean diasporas (notably the Puerto Rican and the Martinican), there is some of both, survival and change, and certainly no fundamental "difference." Nevertheless, whether he is speaking of transplants or trans-fers, Glissant's general point about the relational force of diasporic experi-ence still holds: "The history of a transplanted population, but one which elsewhere becomes another people, allows us to resist generalization and the limitations it imposes. Relationship [*relationalité*] (at the same time link and linked, act and speech) is emphasized over what in appearance would be conceived as a governing principle, the so-called universal 'controlling force.' "[27] Diasporic experiences—African in the Caribbean, and Caribbean in the imperial metropoles—have the effect of relativizing and de-essential-izing, and of course de-territorializing, the traditional national construct and its hegemonies.

For conceptualizing Caribbean diasporic identity, though, I find another set of conceptual/processual terms more useful. Though it articulates well with Glissant's diversion/reversion dialectic (which he refers to as a "dialog-ic relationship'), the paradigm outlined by Stuart Hall in his important essay, "Cultural Identity and Diaspora" (1990), moves closer to the situation of the (post)colonial diaspora in the contemporary world. For Hall, this situation is "'framed' by two axes or vectors, simultaneously operative: the vector of sim-ilarity and continuity; and the vector of difference and rupture. . . . The one gives us grounding in, some continuity with the past. The second reminds us that what we share is precisely the experience of a profound discontinu-ity."[28] Hall says that this second axis of understanding—that is, cultural identity in terms of ruptures and discontinuities—is "much less familiar, and more unsettling," and even claims that it "constitutes, precisely, the Caribbean's 'uniqueness.'" "It is only from this second position," he contin-ues, "that we can properly understand the traumatic character of 'the colo-nial experience.' "[29]

Both dimensions of (post)colonial identity are intensified by the physi-cal and geocultural remove and resonance of the diasporic location: a more intense urge for continuity and a more dramatic sense of rupture. In an important theoretical turn, the aspect of break or disjuncture, which would seem the most debilitating, and colonizing, of experiences, actually har-bors a sense of process, freedom, agency, and an alternative historical po-sition. "Cultural identity," Hall continues, "is a matter of 'becoming' as well as of 'being.' It belongs to the future as much as to the past. It is not something which already exists, transcending place, time, history and cul-ture. Cultural identities come from somewhere, undergo constant trans-formation. Far from being eternally fixed in some essentialised past, they are subject to the continuous 'play' of history, culture and power. Far from being grounded in mere 'recovery' of the past, which is waiting to be found, and which when found, will secure our sense of ourselves into eter-nity, identities are the names we give to the different ways we are posi-tioned by, and position ourselves within, the narratives of the past."[30]

What is so "unsettling" about this disjunctural aspect of diasporic experience is clearly the newfound and unknown flexibility, fluidity, and muta-
bility of identity moorings and reference points, the loss of sanctity of national symbols, the relativity of cultural needs and imperatives. To carry
Hall's point even further in view of the Puerto Rican diaspora, a "Caribbean
location" as a site of the postcolonial must include and account for the apparent drift-away, the colonial diaspora entrenched in a history of internal
(re)colonialism, a history which would seem in many ways to contradict, or
consider an impediment, or even to dispense with, the past as narrated.

SPIDERTOWN

An especially poignant, dramatic example of this radical diasporic discontinuity, in fact its dramatization as an existential process, may be found in
the writings and personal stance of the young Nuyorican (or perhaps "post-
Nuyorican") author Abraham Rodriguez. A reading of the title story of his
book *The Boy Without a Flag* (1992) presents in sharp, jarring terms that
particular mixed sense of being definitively broken off from, yet demanding inclusion in, the new national reality and trajectory. It also offers occasion to return to the constant repositioning and resemanticizing of the national symbol—the Puerto Rican flag.

In "The Boy Without a Flag" Rodriguez examines the education of a
young diasporic, South Bronx Puerto Rican in what it means to be Puerto
Rican. Whichever way he turns in his crack-ridden, hip-hop–crazed environment, this Generation X Young Lord-without-a-cause finds himself betrayed by his fellow Puerto Ricans. To drive the point home, though it is set
deep in the U.S. inner city, all of the characters in the story are Puerto
Rican. And whether it is his teachers, classmates, the principal, or most
significantly his father, he finds no allies in his defiant refusal to salute "that
flag." "Were those people really Puerto Ricans?" he asks. "Why should a
Puerto Rican salute an American flag?"[31] While the school environment impresses him with how Americanized his compatriots can get, his father in-
culcates him with a "heavy" nationalist, anti-imperialist rhetoric and education, and the young rebel senses a common fate with the hero Albizu
Campos he has been reading about: "They were bound to break me the way
Albizu was broken, not by young smiling American troops bearing choco-
late bars, but by conniving, double-dealing, self-serving Puerto Rican land-
owners and their ilk, who dared say they were the future. They spoke of dig-

nity and democracy while teaching Puerto Ricans how to cling to the great coat of that powerful northern neighbor. Puerto Rico, the shining star, the great lap-dog of the Caribbean" (23). Yet even his father, who had railed against the "Yankee flag-wavers," will betray him by going along with the disciplinary posture of the school authorities. "Are you crazy?" he mutters to his son. "Don't you know anything about dignity, about respect?" (28).

Not that the Puerto Rican flag represents any real alternative for him either, as is clear from his experience in the school auditorium, which he recounts in starkly suggestive imagery: "All I could make out was that great star-spangled unfurling, twitching thing that looked like it would fall as it approached all those bored young heads. The Puerto Rican flag walked beside it, looking smaller and less confident. It clung to its pole" (14). At the end, he is indeed "without a flag," estranged from the national symbols of both of the cultures that would define him.

Yet, interestingly, he is left with some kind of insight beyond the flags, beyond the disillusionment over his "father's betrayal." It is not so much conciliation (at no point does he disavow his anticolonial stance), as it is a deeper understanding of his own social position. Perhaps this restrospective wisdom is an expression of (postcolonial) diasporic identity, the dialogic between diversion and reversion, continuity and rupture. For, once the ordeal is over, and his teacher Miss Colon tells him to "go home and listen to the Beatles," the story ends with these sanguine musings: "I stepped out into the sunshine, came down the white stone steps, and stood on the sidewalk. I stared at the towering school building, white and perfect in the sun, indomitable. Across the street, the dingy row of tattered uneven tenements where I lived. I thought of my father. Her [the teacher's] words made me feel sorry for him, but I felt sorrier for myself. I couldn't understand back then about a father's love and what a father might give to insure his son safe transit. He had already navigated treacherous waters and now couldn't have me rock the boat. I still had to learn that he had made peace with The Enemy, that The Enemy was already in us. Like the flag I must salute, we were inseparable, yet his compromise made me feel ashamed and defeated. Then I knew I had to find my own peace, away from the bondage of obedience. I had to accept that flag, and my father, someone I would love forever, even if at times to my young, feeble mind he seemed a little imperfect" (29–30).

Like the boy in his story, Abraham Rodriguez is merciless in his relation to Puerto Rico and being Puerto Rican, and feels "stranded" and betrayed by the Island, which he says is no more than a "myth" to him. In an interview, the author tells of the time when he tore up a T-shirt bearing the Puerto Rican flag that he had received as a gift. When his girlfriend asked him why he was doing that, his answer was, "It's because I always thought that the flag was a dishrag, so here's a dishrag, it's for the dishes."[32] Yet this iconoclasm should not be mistaken for indifference, nor his sense of individual transcendence for a lack of interest in politics. By his own account he follows events on the Island closely, explaining that his disdain for the flag has to do with his feeling that it has been robbed of its deeper contestatory meaning. "There was no Nationalist kind of feeling," he contends. "That's why I don't like that flag." Then, referring to the controversial "Madonna incident," he makes clear that from the vantage point of the diaspora and its problems, such spectacles of the "lite colonial" amount to "diversions" in the sense of distractions or deflections from the underlying political realities: "You know what mystifies me?" he goes on. "Madonna goes to Puerto Rico, and she takes the Puerto Rican flag and she puts it between her legs for a little hanky panky. The situation that Puerto Ricans find themselves in here, in the inner city, or in any inner city in this nation, or even in Puerto Rico, where you get drug traffickers attacking police, is a problem directly imported from the United States, and this is a result of a political decision that was made on the island. It's ironic to me that Puerto Ricans have these amazing problems, and the one thing that makes them get into an uproar is when some white woman takes the Puerto Rican flag and puts it between her legs. Let's face it: Congress has been doing that to the island now for how many years? . . . We have bigger problems to confront than our depiction in a movie or that Madonna plays with the Puerto Rican flag."[33]

Under conditions of global postcoloniality, then, Puerto Rican culture necessarily includes "Spidertown," the eerily mythic South Bronx setting of Rodriguez's work and the title of his first novel, just as contemporary "Puerto Rican discourse" must also in important ways be constituted right there, in "mi viejo South Bronx," the postnational fragment gone adrift. This thought is most troubling, of course, to those who would cling to ideas of colonial nationality appropriate, if ever, to earlier political economic arrangements, and who insistently disavow the hybridity and multiplicity of identity formations under the transnational conditions of our times.[34] But even commentators intent on challenging those outworn positions, including some of the theorists of a "lite colonialism" cited here, are still groping for a concept of national identity elastic and malleable enough to account for social experiences at such blatant odds with what remains a territorially circumscribed universe of cultural discourse. After all, Abraham Rodriguez's "Spidertown" is not Central Park during the Puerto Rican Day Parade, with Puerto Rican flags of all shapes and sizes waving everywhere in view, and bedecking everything from sidewalks to clothing and bead necklaces to tattooed fingernails and eyelids.

The diaspora not as a monolith or inert social mass, but as a complex and dynamic reality woven inextricably into the social fiber of the metropolis, is also an integral part of the "lite colony" and its discourse. It is the most visible sign of the de-territorialization and de-centering of colonial boundaries, and of the constitutive role played by translocal consumption practices in the forging of contemporary cultural identities. What Abraham Rodriguez's irreverent and idiosyncratic outbursts signal is that it is not only the offspring of Operation Bootstrap and the great migration who demand inclusion in the national self-reflection, but their children and grandchildren, as well the many orphans and outcasts gathered along the historical sidelines.

"WHERE THE SUN DON'T SHINE . . ."

The infamous "Madonna incident" was there in the news and quickly gone, an article in "yesterday's newspaper" ("el periódico de ayer"), swept along in the seemingly endless maelstrom of similar diversions, spectacles and cultural ephemera which make for headline news in the "lite colony." Maybe the punchy, statehood-oriented reporter Luis Dávila Colón has a point with his tongue-in-cheek comment that "the 'Material Girl' invented a brand-new dimension of patriotism." "Wow!" he chuckles. "I'd heard of having the flag glued to your heart, or having the flag in one's mind, or of boxers sporting the flag on their backside to catch low blows, or Olympic fans donning it as a hat. But never of flying it at half-mast, down where the sun don't shine."[35]

With all its scandalous novelty, though, this episode of "erotic patriotism" is of fleeting interest in Puerto Rican political culture, eminently an event of October immediately to be overshadowed by Halloween, and then the imminent cataclysms of November. An "infamy without parallel in the history of our country," as the Independence Party leader proclaimed? Hardly, and it is striking what a stunted historical memory is displayed by the country's present political leadership, and how ready they are to suc-cumb to the everyday hype of the ubiquitous mass culture. Dávila Colón ends his comments by predicting the victory of more-of-the-same in the upcoming (1993) plebiscite, all to the gyrations of Michael Jackson and the moonwalk: "Gulp. Did you see what happened in October? You didn't like it? Take it easy, don't get worked up. 'You ain't seen nothing yet' [in English]. Didn't I tell you what November would bring? Madonna has left. But on November 14, on the night of the plebiscite, the Island awaits the arrival of the 'Dangerous Tour' of the King of Pop, Michael Jackson. Once Halloween is over, lock your kids in the house. And get ready to dance the moonwalk when victory goes once again to ELA [Estado Libre Asociado (Free Associ-ated State, the formal term for commonwealth status)]."[36]

As pervasive as the "lite" sensibility may appear, and as symptomatic of the current political culture, it nevertheless remains a "diversion" in the varied senses of the word. While indicative of a real restructuring of colo-nial relations, it is also a mirage, a simulation of non- or postcolonial cir-cumstances aimed at diverting attention from the continuities of colonial history. While suggesting new ways of thinking about colonialism and de-colonization processes, when taken at face value it is also a "making light," a euphemistic "detour" from the ongoing anticolonial project. As in the commercial culture from which it derives, the "lite" may serve to conceal the "hard" and "heavy" ingredients of the product being promot-ed. In view of the bankruptcy of traditional forms of colonial legitimation, the diversions of empire rest increasingly on such discursive camouflage, and on the obscuring of the deep social inequities and the repressive con-trol which continue to mark off colonial oppression from other modes of transnational interaction.

Taller Puertorriqueño, a community-based art center in Philadelphia
(Courtesy of the Taller Collection)

3

Broken English Memories

LANGUAGES IN THE TRANS-COLONY

1

Historical memory is an active, creative force, not just a receptacle for storing the dead weight of times gone by. *Memory* has been associated, since its earliest usages, with the act of inscribing, engraving, or, in a sense that carries over into our own electronic times, "recording" (*grabar*). It is not so much the record itself as the putting-on-record, the gathering and sorting of materials from the past in accordance with the needs and interests of the present. Remembering thus always involves selecting and shaping, constituting out of what was something new that never was, yet now assuredly is, in the imaginary of the present, and in the memory of the future. And the process of memory is open, without closure or conclusion: the struggle to (re)establish continuities and to tell the "whole" story only uncovers new breaks and new exclusions.

It is in the terms of such weighty verities that the well-known critic and Princeton professor Arcadio Díaz-Quiñones ponders the condition of contemporary Puerto Rican culture. In *La memoria rota* (1993), his much-discussed collection of essays from the 1980s and early 1990s, Díaz-Quiñones identifies the most glaring lapses in Puerto Rican historical memory, the ruptures and repressions that have left present-day public discourse devoid of any recognizable field of critical reference.[1] The "broken memory" that he attributes to the current generation is rooted in centuries of imperial mutilation of social consciousness, culminating in his own lived memory in the triumphalist rhetoric of progress and modernization of the midcentury years. His point about the present, end-of-the-century condition is that even though the persuasiveness of that populist, accomodationist narrative seems to have waned definitively, the historical gaps grounding those earlier hegemonies remain largely unfilled. Despite Díaz-Quiñones' emphatic disclaimer of all "totalizing" presumptions and of any intention to set forth a "rigorous theory," La memoria rota, loosely unified around the suggestive metaphor of the broken memory, may well turn out to be the book of the decade in Puerto Rican cultural theory, the 1990s counterpart to José Luis González's El país de cuatro pisos of the 1980s, or René Marqués's El puertorriqueño dócil of the 1960s, or Antonio S. Pedreira's Insularismo of the 1930s.

Díaz-Quiñones' critical eye ranges widely over Puerto Rican political and literary history; his familiarity with the particular national landscape is enriched by continual references to congruent and kindred concerns of other cultural theorists, from Theodor Adorno to Frantz Fanon, from Edward Said to Angel Rama. Rhetorically, the disjunctures he signals in the official story of the national culture take the form of euphemisms having the effect of minimizing the abruptness and violence of imposed historical change, most notably European colonization, centuries of slavery, U.S. occupation, the ideological decimation of the independence and socialist movements, and mass emigration to the United States. He shows how the dominant memory needs to sweeten the pill of colonial power and constantly to construct and refurbish the illusion of internal harmony, compliance, consensus. Emotionally charged catchwords like family, symphony of progress, and cultural affirmation hide the seams and muffle the discord that make up the real fabric of society, which without these comforting mythologies appears as an intricate patchwork of contending claims and social meanings. In La memoria rota, the very concept of "the national"—what it means to be Puerto Rican—has become a battlefield in the ongoing struggle for interpretive power.

One exclusion to which Díaz-Quiñones draws repeated attention—perhaps the most pronounced break in collective memory—is the emigrant Puerto Rican community in the United States. The exodus of Puerto Ricans between the late 1940s and the early 1960s, an integral and orchestrated part of the country's passage into "modernity," is still occluded from the national history; in another new essay, "Puerto Rico: Cultura, memoria y diáspora" (1994), the author even cites two recent history textbooks, Historia general de Puerto Rico (1986) by Fernando Picó and La historia de Puerto Rico (1987) by Blanca Silvestrini and María Dolores Luque de Sánchez, neither of which devotes more than a few pages to the emigrant Puerto Rican community.[2] With all its revisionist correctives to the colonial, class, gender, and racial biases of the traditional narrative of the nation, the "new historiography" which has gained such prestigious intellectual ground since the 1970s continues to present that "other half" of the Puerto Rican population as just that, an "other" lurking in the wings of the main national drama. Puerto Ricans *en el destierro*, or simply *de allá*, persist as a footnote, sympathetic at best but ultimately dismissive and uncomprehending.

To its immense credit, *La memoria rota* places the life of Puerto Ricans in the United States squarely on the agenda of contemporary historical analysis. Díaz-Quiñones' insistence no doubt is fueled by his many years of living and working in New Jersey. He points up the long reach of collective experience back to the late nineteenth century and acknowledges the many other writers and thinkers who have recognized its importance, such as Bernardo Vega, César Andreu Iglesias, and José Luis González. More than merely filling in historical blanks that they have left, though, Díaz-Quiñones asserts the central, constitutive role of Puerto Ricans in the United States in the making and breaking of the Puerto Rican nation in the twentieth century. His allusions to other contemporary theorists of diasporic, transnational identity, such as Said, Partha Chatterjee, and Renato Rosaldo, serve him well in contextualizing that dramatic divide in modern-day Puerto Rican history. Far from being unique or exceptional, the cultural disjunctures, ambiguities, and reconnections undergone by Puerto Ricans in both localities are paradigmatic of experiences familiar to more and more people, and nations, of the world.

Yet for all his stitching and patching, Díaz-Quiñones still leaves the Puerto Rican broken memory in need of serious repair. It is not enough to point to the break and glue the pieces together by mentioning forgotten names and events. The seams and borders of national experience need to be understood not as absences or vacuums but as sites of new meanings and relations. Here again, as in the exclusionary vision Díaz-Quiñones would transcend, the Puerto Rican community in the United States still appears as an extension of discourses based on the Island, its history an appendage of *the* national history, with no evident contours or dynamic in its own right. To attend to the "break" that migration has meant in Puerto Rican history, it is necessary to remember the whole national "project" from the perspectives of the breaking-point itself, from aboard the *guagua aérea*, the proverbial "air bus."[3]

Remembering in Puerto Rican today inherently involves a dual vision, a communication where languages bifurcate and recombine. Puerto Rican memories are mixed-code memories, lodged at the points where English breaks Spanish and Spanish breaks English. The act of memory defies uniformity; it undermines the privilege typically accorded either of the sundered fragments—Spanish or English, *acá* or *allá*—over the living relation between them, as evidenced in the rupture itself. On this point the metaphor of Puerto Rico's broken memory, and the elegant arguments that sustain it, backs away from its deeper theoretical implications.

2

A people's memory and sense of collective continuity is broken not only by the abrupt, imposed course of historical events themselves but by the exclusionary discourses that accompany and legitimate them. Thus, while the massive emigration of the Puerto Rican population to the United States has involved a geographical and cultural divide unprecedented in the national history, it is the dismissive rhetoric of "assimilation" and "cultural genocide" that has effected the glaring omission of Puerto Rican life in the United States from the historical record. In *La memoria rota* Díaz-Quiñones repeatedly takes this ideological agenda to task and reinstates creative agency and continuity in the cultural experience of the emigrant community.

In one of the most moving passages in the lead essay, "La vida inclemente," Díaz-Quiñones argues that "the emigrant reinforced—in a manner unforeseen by the exclusionary discourse of some sectors of the Puerto Rican elite—the need to maintain identities, and even the need to form new descriptions of identity." Rather than leave the Island behind and forget about their homeland, "in those Puerto Rican communities there existed the possibility of a new future that required the preservation of certain real and symbolic places and that lent a new value to the geography of the Island, its rivers and hills, and its barrios."[4]

Geographic separation and distance, rather than deadening all sense of community and cultural origins, may have the contrary effect of heightening the collective awareness of belonging and affirmation. Referring to Edward Said's accounts of life in present-day Palestinian communities, Díaz-Quiñones contends that "the sense of belonging, a feeling for 'home' and community, is affirmed with the strongest emphasis from a distance, when there is an uncertainty as to place. Perhaps this goes to explain the paradoxical situation that people, say in Guaynabo, can take their culture for granted, while others in Philadelphia defend it passionately."[5]

The accuracy of the "paradoxical" inversion of geographical location and cultural belonging resounds in the countless tales of emigrants feeling more Puerto Rican than ever when in the New York setting; in the flourishing of *bomba y plena* and *música jíbara* groups in all the emigrant neighborhoods, from Hartford, Connecticut, to Lorraine, Ohio, from Hawaii to Perth Amboy, in the fashioning of Island-style casitas in the abandoned lots of the South Bronx and Williamsburg, Brooklyn. The contrasting attitudes toward cultural continuity find dramatic expression in much of the literary and artistic work by Puerto Ricans in the United States, most forcefully perhaps in Tato Laviera's memorable poem "nuyorican." The title identifies, in English, the speaker of the poem, a monologue addressed by an irate New York Puerto Rican, in Spanish, to his lost island homeland. "Nuyorican" is an impassioned plea by a son of the migration to his beloved "puerto rico" not to forget why he was born "native of foreign lands" ["nativo en otras tierras"] and to be aware of the real play of cultural loyalties:

> yo peleo por tí puerto rico, ¿sabes?
> Yo me defiendo por tu nombre, ¿sabes?
> Entro en tu isla, me siento extraño, ¿sabes?
> Entro a buscar más y más, ¿sabes?
> Pero tú con tus calumnias,
> me niegas tu sonrisa
> me siento mal, agallao
> yo soy tu hijo,
> de una migración
> pecado forzado,
> me mandaste a nacer nativo en otras tierras
> por qué, porque éramos pobres, ¿verdad?
> Porque tú querías vaciarte de tu gente pobre,
> ahora regreso, con un corazón boricua, y tú,
> me desprecias, me miras mal, me atacas mi hablar,
> mientras comes mcdonalds en discotecas americanas,
> y no pude bailarla salsa en san juan, la que yo
> bailo en mis barrios llenos de todas tus costumbres,
> así que, si tú no me quieres, pues yo tengo
> un puerto rico sabrosísimo en que buscar refugio
> en nueva york, y en muchos otros callejones

que honran tu presencia, preservando todos
tus valores, así que, no me
hagas sufrir, ¿sabes?[6]

[I fight for you, puerto rico, you know?
I defend myself for your name, you know?
I enter your island, i feel foreign, you know?
I enter searching for more and more, you know?
but you, with your insults,
you deny me your smile,
i feel bad, indignant.
I am your son,
of a migration,
a sin forced on me,
you sent me to be born a native of other lands.
why? because we were poor, right?
because you wanted to empty yourself of poor people.
Now i return, with a *boricua* heart, and you,
you scorn me, you look askance, you attack the way i speak,
while you're out there eating mcdonalds in american discotheques,
and i couldn't even dance salsa in san juan, which i
can dance in my neighborhoods full of your customs.
So that, if you don't want me, well, i have
a delicious puerto rico where i can seek refuge
in new york, and in lots of other alleyways
that honor your presence, preserving all
of your values, so that, please, don't make
me suffer, you know?]

Such texts, structured for their emotional force around the clash between an imaginary and a "real" Puerto Rico, and between jarring identity claims of "here" and "there," abound in "Nuyorican" literature.
Works by Sandra María Esteves and Victor Hernández Cruz, Edward
Rivera and Esmeralda Santiago, show that "la memoria rota" is the site
not merely of exclusion and fragmentation but also of new meanings and
identity. They attest to the act of memory at the break itself and thereby
move from the pieces of broken memory to the creative practice of
"breaking memory." Discontinuity, rather than a threat to cultural sur-

vival and inclusion, helps us critically examine prevailing continuities and imagine and create new ones. Homi Bhabha, for whom Díaz-Quiñones expresses great admiration in *La memoria rota*, provides an excellent description of ironically privileged positionality "at the break." Inspired by Said's move from Foucault to the scene of the Palestinian struggle, "from the Left Bank to the West Bank," Bhabha speaks in an interview in the early 1990s of

> the possibilities of being, somehow, *in between*, of occupying an interstitial space that was not fully governed by the recognizable traditions from which you came. For the interaction or overdetermination often produces another third space. It does not necessarily produce some higher, more inclusive, or representative reality. Instead, it opens up a space that is skeptical of cultural totalization, of notions of identity which depend for their authority on being "originary," or concepts of culture which depend for their value on being pure, or of tradition, which depends for its effectivity on being continuous. A space where, to put it very simply, I saw great political and poetic and conceptual value in forms of cultural identification which subverted authority, not by claiming their total difference from it, but were able to actually use authorized images, and turn them against themselves to reveal a different history. And I saw this little figure of subversion intervening in the interstices, as being different from the big critical batallions that always wanted to have a dominating authority, opposed by an equally subordinated agency: victim and oppressor, sparsely and starkly blocked out.[7]

The experience of being "in between," so deeply familiar to Puerto Ricans in the United States, thus harbors the possibility of an intricate politics of freedom and resistance. Understood in this way as a kind of phenomenology or philosophy of experiential space, the "break" appears as both a limit and a breaking of the limit. The "third space" and "little figure of subversion" identified by Bhabha summon the notion of transgression and its constant crossing of lines and demarcated limits. In *Language, Counter-Memory, Practice*, Foucault describes this relation between transgression and limit: "Transgression is an action which involves the limit, that narrow zone of a line where it displays the flash of its passage, but perhaps also its entire trajectory, even its origin; it is likely that transgression has its entire space in the line it crosses."[8]

Rather than negate the limit by crossing it, transgression foregrounds and mediates contrasts by illuminating the spaces on either side of the limit. In a striking metaphor, Foucault suggests that the relationship between the limit and its transgression "is like a flash of lightning in the night which . . . gives a dense and black intensity to the night it denies, which lights up the night from the inside, from top to bottom, and yet owes to the dark the stark clarity of its manifestation" (34).

Such insights from contemporary cultural theory point up the need to appreciate the complexity of Puerto Rico's "broken memory" from the vantage point of those living "in between," in the space of the "break" itself. Sandra María Esteves gives voice to this complexity in the opening lines of her poem "Not Neither," where she identifies as both "Puertorriqueña" and "Americana," yet feels that she is neither a "jíbara" nor a "gringa":

> Pero ni portorra, pero sí portorra too
> Pero ni que what am I?[9]

Occupying and transgressing the limit can be baffling, bewildering to the point of existential anguish, yet facing up to the confounding reality can allow for a newfound sense of confidence and identity. Esmeralda Santiago, for one, after years of jostling and juggling between the Puerto Rican and U.S. parts of her life, has finally "learned to insist on my peculiar brand of Puerto Rican identity. One not bound by geographical, linguistic or behavioral boundaries, but rather, by a deep identification with a place, a people and a culture which, in spite of appearances, define my behavior and determine the rhythms of my days. An identity in which I've forgiven myself for having to look up a recipe for 'arroz con pollo' in a Puerto Rican cookbook meant for people who don't know a 'sombrero' from a 'sofrito.'"[10]

3

In what language do we remember? Is it the language we use when we speak with friends and family in our everyday lives? Or does our choice of a language of memory involve a transposition, a translation in the literal sense of moving across: *trasladar*, "de un lado a otro" [from one side to the other]? For Puerto Ricans, half of whom may be on either "side" at any given time, a symbiosis between language and place, and between identity and memory, is especially salient today. Spanish, English, Spanglish, all in the plural and in lowercase, make for an abundant reservoir of expressive codes with which to relate (to) the past. For language is not only the supreme mnemonic medium, the vehicle for the transmission of memory; fifty years of Puerto Rican history have shown that language can also be the site and theme of historical action, the locus of contention over issues of identity and community that reach far beyond our preference for, or reliance on, this or that word or grammar. "La memoria rota," the fragmenting of Puerto Rican historical memory as a result of selective privileges and suppressions, makes its most palpable appearance as "la lengua rota," or, as Antonio Martorell puts it in his inspired performance piece, "la lengua mechada" [stuffed tongue].[11]

In his essay "La política del olvido" (1991), Arcadio Díaz-Quiñones shows that it is not necessary to accept the inaccurate, colonially charged claim that Puerto Rico is a "bilingual nation" in order to stand in equally critical opposition to the officialization of Spanish as the national language. For while the annexationist impulse behind the bilingual-nation idea is evident, Díaz-Quiñones recognizes the "Spanish-only" campaign as no more than chronic recourse of the autonomist leaders (in this case then-governor Rafael Hernández Colón) in their most desperate moments of opportunism. "What can be gained," he asks, "from defining an *only* language in the face of the hybridity and mixing of Spanish, English, and Spanglish that one hears spoken in Bayamón, Puerto Nuevo, or Union City? The Puerto Rican elites have good reason to defend their bilingualism: it allows them to read Toni Morrison or Faulkner and partake of the high culture of the Metropolitan Museum or the New York City Ballet, and of course Wall Street. The diaspora of Puerto Rican emigrants has been mixing their languages over and over, in their continual trip back and forth."[12]

New York, Díaz-Quiñones reminds us, has been a Caribbean and Puerto Rican city for over a century now, witness to and deeply influenced by the lives and writings, the songs and struggles, of many illustrious Puerto Ricans, along with Cubans of the prominence of José Martí and Celia Cruz. "I prefer the hybridity of nationalities" ["Yo prefiero la hibridez de las nacionalizaciones"], he continues, and concludes his reflections on the politics of language with the challenging question, addressed toward Puerto Ricans on both sides of the linguistic divide: "Will we have the capacity to decolonize our imaginary, to take leave of the colonial fog that Hostos spoke of without relinquishing that special 'mess' that identifies us?"[13]

When it comes to language, "este revolú que nos identifica" amounts to a veritable stew, if such a tired and overloaded expression may be pardoned in the interest of differentiating the dynamic of blending and multiple intersection from notions of transition, transfer, interference, or even back-and-forth movement. It's a *sancocho* whose ingredients include, as Esmeralda Santiago has learned, *sofrito* and not sombreros, because it is not random, much less a sign of confusion and incoherence, as the "English or Español Only-ists" would have it. On closer look, bilingualism as practiced by Puerto Ricans on both sides of *el charco*, but especially by the half "over here," constitutes an intricate tactic and strategy of response and assertion, with deep poetic and political implications. "Broken" English, "broken" Spanish, English and Spanish "breaking" (into) each other—who with any contact at all with Puerto Ricans can fail to hear the semantic micropolitics at play in usages like "Cógelo con take it easy!" or "No problema," or in the bent meanings in the use of words like *anyway*, *OK*, or *brother* (pronounced "brō-ther") in a Spanish context, or *pero*, *verdad*, *este*, or *mira* when speaking English? Whether the primary code is Spanish or English, colloquial Puerto Rican is characterized by its porousness, its undermining and breaking, of the authority of monolingual discourse. Collective memory and identity find their appropriate articulation in this lively, "macaronic" sensibility, where the mixed-code vernacular voice responds in both directions to the imposition of official, standard constructs of "the" national language. Puerto Rican dreams are "broken English dreams," as Pedro Pietri announced in one of his signature poems from the early 1970s.[14] The cultural idiom of many Puerto Ricans and other Latinos in the United States, their language of expression and fantasy, is captured well in the title of the book by the Cuban American cultural critic Coco Fusco, who calls her essays on "cultural fusion in the Americas" *English Is Broken Here*.[15]

Yet as fluid as this interlingual practice may be, there is still a here and a there. Its being "translocal" does not erase the efficacy of "locus"; boundaries of difference and distance remain, most obviously in relation to place and location. Geography is the richest metaphorical field for the politics of linguistic and cultural breaking; the contrast between here and there permeates the idiom, from everyday speech to the lingo of popular songs to the twists and turns of bilingual poetry. The "there" is not only imaginary; it is acknowledged and even thematized as imaginary. The imaginary "there and then" serves as an accessible foil to the intensity of lived presence, and often,

as in the poetry of Sandra María Esteves and Victor Hernández Cruz, becomes a resource for self-discovery and political insight.

Tato Laviera takes this locational counterpoint as the structuring principle of his dramatic poem "migración," where the lyrics of the proverbially
nostalgiac ballad "En mi viejo San Juan" share the same lines and stanzas
with the words, also in Spanish, of a Puerto Rican on the frozen winter
streets of the Lower East Side as he reflects on the death of the song's composer, Noel Estrada. Eventually, the emotionally laden chords of "En mi
viejo San Juan," often considered the anthem of the Puerto Rican and Latin
American emigrant, bring out the sun and, as they resound in barbershops
and nightspots in El Barrio, play their consoling yet challenging role in the
familiar here and now. This sharp dramatic interplay between two cultural
places, the quoted "there" and the unmediated physical "here," allows for
a new mode of identity-formation freed from the categorical fixity of place.
In his essay "Migratorias," the critic Julio Ramos concludes his comments
on Laviera's "migración" by speaking of a practical, "portable" identity: "It
is a way of conceiving identity that defies the usual topographical connec-
tions, along with rigid categories of territoriality and their telluric meta-
phorization. In Laviera, 'roots' may amount to that foundation as a citation,
reinscribed as the syllable of a song. Roots that are portable, disposed to
use in a 'mainstream ethic,' based on practices of identity, on identity as
practice of judgment in the course of traveling."[16]

The themes of spatial, historical, and linguistic counterpoint are joined
by Laviera in his remarkable poem "melao," which enacts paradigmatical-
ly what I have been calling broken English and Spanish memories:

> melao was nineteen years old
> when he arrrived from santurce
> spanish speaking streets
>
> melao is thirty-nine years old
> in new york still speaking
> santurce spanish streets
>
> melaíto his son now answered
> in black american soul english talk
> with native plena sounds
> and primitive urban salsa beats

somehow melao was not concerned
at the neighborly criticism
of his son's disparate sounding
talk

melao remembered he was criticized
back in puerto rico for speaking
arrabal black spanish
in the required english class

melao knew that if anybody
called his son american
they would shout puertorro
in english and spanish
meaning i am puerto rican
coming from yo soy boricua
i am a jíbaro
dual mixtures
of melao and melaíto's
spanglish speaking son
así es la cosa papá[17]

Though the narrative voice is in English, Spanish words, sounds, and meanings burst through the monolingual seams; every shift in geographic and biographical reference undermines the "official" status of either language standard. Close and repeated reading reveals a vernacular Spanish subtext that explodes at the end but collides and colludes with English semantics in the dead center of the poem. The centrally placed word *disparate*, spelled the same in both languages, also "means" in both languages, but the simultaneous meanings are not the same. The concealed (Spanish) phonetics harbors a repressed signification, and the poetics of convergence and divergence underlies an everyday politics of the break in cultural and historical memory.

"La memoria rota," evocative image of the fragmentation of Puerto Rican historical consciousness, is thus most appropriate, especially as it refers to the migratory experience, when reimagined as an active process of breaking and re-membering. Arcadio Díaz-Quiñones has succeeded in placing those lapses and exclusions indelibly on the contemporary intellectual agenda and has signaled the attendant political implications of a needed historical revision. But for Puerto Rican memory to be "repaired," for it to assume greater coherence and continuity, its incoherences and discontinuities must be probed as they manifest themselves in lived experience and expression. "Ese revolú que nos identifica," the elusive mortar of Puerto Rican cultural identity, appears as a magnetic field of unity and diversity, relations and translations. Puerto Rican memory gets "unbroken" by melao, and by melaito, his "disparate sounding" son, as well as by "melaito's spanglish speaking son" when he affirms his "dual mixture" by proclaiming, "así es la cosa papá."

Casita in El Barrio, East Harlem (early 1990s)

(Photo by Martha Cooper; © Martha Cooper)

4

☐:

"Salvación Casita"

SPACE, PERFORMANCE, AND COMMUNITY

The casita people had the Smithsonian jumping that night. It was February 2, 1991, and the occasion was the opening celebration of the new Experimental Gallery, a space within the Smithsonian Institution's Arts and Industries Building intended to "showcase innovative artists, scientists, educators and designers from local, national and international communities." As stated in the invitation, "The Experimental Gallery pushes the edges of our museum knowledge by encouraging risk-taking in exhibition technique and style." Care is taken to assure us that the experimentation is to be that of the exhibit makers, and that "Content and Subject are not the Experiment!"[1]

Yet, with all these cautionary distinctions, the central space of the new gallery was dedicated to what was clearly the featured inaugural exhibit, "Las Casitas: An Urban Cultural Alternative." What an experiment in content and subject for the "national museum" of the United States! For on display was the world of those little houses, modeled after the humble dwellings in rural Puerto Rico of years gone by, which have sprung up in the vacant lots of New York's impoverished Puerto Rican neighborhoods since the late 1980s. Wherever you go in the South Bronx and East Harlem (El Barrio) these days you're liable to catch sight of a casita, in its design and atmosphere magically evocative of the rural Caribbean and now serving as a social club and cultural center for inhabitants of the surrounding tenements.[2]

I'll never forget the feeling I had as I made my way through the crowd of art-world professionals and museum officials hobnobbing in the huge domed rotunda and first set my eyes on that spanking, bright turquoise ca-

63

sita, "Rincón Criollo" (roughly, "Hometown Corner"), so familiar to me from my forays to Brook Avenue in the South Bronx, transplanted to such an unlikely site! The program called it a "built environment," a "living installation, a living space of rescued images that reinforce Puerto Rican cultural identity." Clearly the innovation was not just that of the gallery staff but of the people who built the casita "environment" in the first place. To me, the sight of a casita in the Smithsonian was an uncanny example of the title of the book I happened to have with me that night, Sally Price's *Primitive Art in Civilized Places* (1989).

The little building assumed an imposing but somehow uncomfortable presence there in the center of that gaping, uncluttered space, and seemed intruded upon by the oohs and ahs of its sophisticated visitors as they filed up the "cute" porch and into the "quaint" interior. Lining the walls, the life-scale photos of "real" casitas in their "real" home settings helped bridge the gap somewhat, as did the explanatory captions, the decorative and functional "objects" of casita culture, and the video showings set off in the far corner.

But what made the difference, and brought this "experimental" representation in the nation's capital back in touch with the South Bronx, was the presence of the casita people themselves. There was José Rivera, one of the original builders of Rincón Criollo and for some years its president. There was his brother Ramón ("Papo Chín"), who helped José build the replica and install it in the Experimental Gallery. There was Cepeda (hardly anyone knows him by his first name), another long-time Rincón Criollo mainstay, who aside from his regular role as cook and emcee at casita events has taken on the joyful task of documenting everything on video. So there, too, was Cepeda, with his contagious toothy smile, tilted Panama hat, starched guayabera shirt, and camcorder tucked under his chin. Norma Cruz and Benny Ayala, the casita's resident teachers of music, instrument-making, and dance, were also present, as was José Manuel Soto, or "Chema" as everybody knows him, the founding and guiding spirit behind the casita since even before the lot was cleared. In fact, people from the neighborhood even call Rincón Criollo "la casa de Chema." And sharing the excitement were other familiar faces, those of the friends of casita culture like Betti-Sue Hertz, the director and curator of the project, Bill Aguado, director of the Bronx Council on the Arts, project photographer Martha Cooper, consulting urban anthropologists Joe Sciorra and Susan Slyomovics, and participating architect Luis Aponte-Pares.

The initial awkwardness and incongruity of the scene then began to give way to congeniality and, as we drifted into the rotunda to partake of the abundant food and drinks, to an air of festivity. And when the superb salsa band, Manny Oquendo's Libre, took the stage and started blasting its hot *guarachas* and plenas, that venerable rotunda of the Smithsonian Institution seemed like a casita party, transposed and out of its habitat, but still exuding that boisterous human energy which only comes of living vernacular performance. Tweed suit jackets and lush evening gowns swirling to those irresistible salsa sounds, museum administrators trying vigorously to keep up with the confident steps of South Bronx street people, Libre's congas and trombones filling every cranny of the institution's vast halls with tropical sounds straight from New York City—beyond anyone's expectations, the casita had indeed proved itself to be "a living installation, a living space of rescued images that reinforce Puerto Rican cultural identity."

A month or so later, on a day in early spring, José Rivera called to invite me to a special event at the casita. They were calling it "Salvación Casita," and there was a sense of urgency in his voice. It seems that the developers and housing authorities were hounding them once again, not with any explicit threats but by floating the idea that they were considering use of the "vacant" land for some kind of construction and development. The purpose of "Salvación Casita" was to show, by force of sheer human presence and activity, that the space is not at all vacant and is already being put to valid use. As at eviction parties of years gone by, casita members recognize that the best way to keep the authorities at bay is to celebrate the blatant fact of collective occupancy.

I arrived early, in the late afternoon, to the smell of barbecued chicken wafting from the backyard and the bustle of people, men and women, old and young, setting up for the event. Inside the casita was like a dressing room, with Norma Cruz seeing to the makeup and costumes of her young dance students as they got ready to perform. On the porch, José, Benny Ayala, and some of the other musicians were testing microphones and tuning instruments, while Cepeda was already at the mike welcoming arriving friends and neighbors and announcing future casita events and "salvation" plans. In this homegrown performance space, the front porch is the stage, or rather the bandshell, as the formal and spontaneous dance presentations take place among the public in the yard directly in front of the porch. José even told me once that they built the porch a little wider than casita custom would have it precisely with this stage function in mind, extending it so as to accommodate all the musicians, instruments, and sound equipment needed for full participation in bomba and plena performance.

The front yard, or *batey*, gradually started filling with people—casita regulars and associates, guests invited and uninvited, neighbors from the surrounding tenements, and friends and family from El Barrio, Brooklyn, and other parts of the Bronx. Though nearly everyone was Puerto Rican, it would be difficult and even pointless to generalize in any other sense about the assortment of people gathered for the casita event. There were as many women as men, there were blacks and whites, toddlers and elders, and everything in between. Though dress tended to be very casual, the range of styles was strikingly varied as well: baseball hats and panamas, linen blouses and tank-tops, full dresses and cutoffs, tattered jeans and baggy slacks, Nikes, dance flats and even a few spike heels.

The human atmosphere, despite the forbidding location and the expressed urgency of the occasion, was consistently relaxed, congenial, and respectful. Not a trace of fear, anger, or aggressiveness was evident, nobody seemed inclined to get "out of hand," and even the unknowing interloper could not help but feel welcome and comfortable. Lively gestures and hearty laughter accompanied casual conversation, young children danced on their parents' laps, teeny-boppers flipped motley-colored skateboards, a young couple strolled over to the improvised bar to buy a beer, bystanders stood idly along the chainlink fence, passersby congregated on the street and sidewalk to look on and wave, now and then drifting in when they recognized a familiar face.

The hub of these many disparate styles and activities, drawing them together into a single shared event, was the presence of the casita itself. Architectural shape and detail, extemporaneous and crafted decor, spatial arrangement and location conspire to lend the casita and its environs a unifying emblematic weight, and to convert the easy ambience of the scene into an occasion of community history. Leisurely playfulness and everyday sociability, when in close range of the casita, become performance.

Cepeda finishes his welcome and announcements by promising "un poquito de salsa." Carefully he places the mike in front of a Sanyo tape player, puts on his favorite cassette, and takes to circulating with his trusty camcorder. Technology is clearly no stranger to the casitas, which are often equipped with refrigerators, television sets and VCRs, stereos, and even jukeboxes. The gathering crowd delights in the first sounds as they wait, with growing anticipation, for the musicians and dancers to assemble. As the sun sets behind the buildings on Third Avenue, the scattered groups begin to take shape as an audience, and the glow of a single lightbulb sets off the porch as a theatrical stage.

Four hours of live music are interrupted only by further announcements, calls for donations to support the casita, and the introduction of new groups. Of the variety of songs played—there were merengues, boleros, *seises, sones, guarachas*—by far the most common and favorite were bombas and plenas. It was these African-based forms of Puerto Rican popular music that got everyone moving, clapping and shouting in chorus. Increasingly as the night progressed, the line between audience and performers faded, so that by the last hour the porch was overflowing with men and women of all ages singing and keeping the beat with *panderetas, güiros,* or whatever else was at hand. What had first seemed like a picnic or block party, and then a concert, took on the air of a carnival.

Who were these *pleneros* that served as the catalysts of such an outburst of collective participation? The answer is close at hand: José, Papo, Benny, Chema, the same people who founded and built Rincón Criollo. As one plena chorus puts it, "Le cambiaron el nombre / a la casita de Chema / ahora la están llamando / la institución de la plena" ["They changed the name / of the casita of Chema / now they're calling it / the institute of the plena"]. The plena is the musical expression of the casita and its cultural habitat; its tones and themes seem to mesh perfectly with the collective needs and moods of the people. It is no accident that the most celebrated plena group in New York for some years now, Los Pleneros de la 21, was formed and based at Rincón Criollo.

Though it originated and gained its initial popularity in the coastal towns of Puerto Rico early in the century, the plena has a long history in New York, as do all the forms of Puerto Rican popular song.[3] The first commercial recordings of plena, by Canario (Manuel Jiménez) y Su Grupo, were made in RCA's New York studios in the late 1920s, and over the subsequent decades all the most famous *pleneros*—notably Canario, César Concepción, Rafael Cortijo, and Mon Rivera—performed, recorded, and lived for some time in New York. Some important but lesser known plena groups, like those of Victor Montañez and Matías Pérez, enjoyed their entire careers here in New York and were hardly familiar to audiences on the Island. Since the beginnings of the emigrant Puerto Rican community, and still today, plenas have been a favored genre of musical entertainment at social clubs, house parties, and political and social gatherings for all occasions.

A key person to influence the grounding of the plena in New York's Puerto Rican neighborhoods, especially the down-home, street variety, is the legendary Marcial Reyes. For some thirty years Marcial was known throughout El Barrio and the South Bronx for his unique style of *pandereta* playing and his hundreds of plena compositions. A native of Santurce, he tirelessly taught the arts of playing, singing, and instrument-making, and was centrally responsible for organizing plena groups, such as Victor Montañez y Sus Pleneros de la 110, which enjoyed popularity over many years in New York's Puerto Rican neighborhoods. Today's *pleneros* also mention other important names, like Henny Alvarez, Johnny Flores, and Pepe Castillo; and of course the towering figures of Rafael Cortijo and Ismael Rivera, with whom most of them seem to have played at one time or another, looms large in all of plena history since the 1950s.[4] But it is Marcial Reyes, in recent years back in Puerto Rico and still as active as ever, who is most widely acknowledged for his role in promoting the *bomba y plena* traditions in the New York Puerto Rican communities.

Marcial was also one of the founders of Rincón Criollo. He was there, always raising hell, throughout the clearing and building process and even before, when Chema's hangout was still a storefront social club across the street. He was a fixture in all the jams on the porch in the first years, and around 1983 he helped draw together some of the most accomplished practitioners, many of them regulars of Rincón Criollo, to form Los Pleneros de la 21. Identifying the members of the group was made easier because, like other forms of traditional popular music, plena performance has often been shared from generation to generation along family lines. Even among the Rincón Criollo mainstays, several are from families of *pleneros* and *bomberos*; most notably, José and Papo Chín are the sons of Ramón "Chín" Rivera, the renowned *panderetero*, vocalist, and composer who played with the likes of Rafael Cepeda, Mon Rivera *padre*, Vicente Pichón, and even "Bumbún" Oppenheimer.

The worlds of the casita and the plena are thus symbiotically related as forms of performative expression of working-class Puerto Ricans, especially those of Afro-Caribbean origins from the coastal areas of the Island. Both are rooted in the everyday life of the participants, and their improvisational quality make both optimally inclusive as to the terms of involvement. Just as anyone of good will is welcome at casita events, so taking part in plena jams is open to any newcomer who can to keep a beat. One of Chema's compositions says it clearly: "Oye todo el que llega / sin instrumento desea tocar / coge hasta una botella, un cuchillo de mesa / y pega a marcar" ["Anyone who shows up wanting to play / even without an instrument / pick up a bottle and knife from the table / and keep the beat"].

It seems that this affinity between architectural and musical expression goes back a long way, to the origins of both practices at the beginning of the century. Old photos of Barrio San Antón in the southern coastal city of Ponce, considered the birthplace of the plena, show unpaved streets lined with casitas. The structural concept is the same as that evident in New York today, most notably with the front porch facing out onto an open public space. It takes no great stretch of the imagination to place a group of *pleneros* behind the porch railing and people socializing and dancing in the front yard.

Despite their conscious adherence to early traditions, both casita and plena practice evidence inevitable adjustments in their contemporary New York setting. With the casitas this change is obvious, because of such impinging factors as land-use codes and the winter climate. In one of his compositions, a takeoff on the well-known song "Los Carboneros," José Rivera remembers being in the casita before it had heat, and playfully complains to the negligent "super" to provide some coal: "Super, hace frío, carbón / me levanto por la mañana / pa' irme a trabajar / el super no se levanta / y a mí me pasmá" ["Super, it's cold, burn some coal / I get up in the morning / to go to work / the super doesn't get up / and I'm freezing to death"]. The irony in this song refrain is of course double, since unlike their antecedents in Puerto Rico the casitas here are not intended, or allowed, to be lived in. And as that icy winter scene suggests, the immediate reference-points for New York casitas, everything from construction materials to furnishings and décor, all pertain to the surrounding urban setting.

The changes in the plena involve not only the role of amplification, recording, and thematic references to life in New York. Here there is also a mingling of vocal and instrumental styles which in traditional, Island-based plena remained differentiated according to region or individual artist. In speaking of the members of Los Pleneros de la 21, for example, José readily identifies styles from Mayagüez or Santurce, or the trademarks of Mon Rivera *padre* or Emilio Escobar.

Another interesting and important difference is the role of women. While in the tradition, plena musical presentation has been an overwhelmingly

male experience, with women only present as dancers or an occasional vocalist, at Rincón Criollo the women came forward as instrumentalists. At
"Salvación Casita" the women were slamming away at the *pandereta*, a sight
which I'm told is virtually unimaginable in the Puerto Rico of recent memory. Maybe this is still another throwback, like casita architecture, to very early
times, since history has it that two of the first masters at the *pandereta* were
women: Catherine George, known as Doña Catín, and her daughter Carolina
Mora Clark, who went by the name of Carola among friends and neighbors
in her native Ponce.[5]

Though live bomba and plena music is the central activity at the casita
event, the musical porch / stage is situated spatially between two other performance areas, the dance floor / yard directly in front and the casita interior backstage, each of which stands in a different relation to the musical
presentation. The space for dancing allows for immediate, kinetic interaction with the rhythms and flows emanating from the porch; in the *batey*,
physical communication with the musicians and instruments is all but inevitable. Inside the casita, on the other hand, even when the carnival atmosphere reaches its highest pitch, there always seem to be people just sitting around talking, or children playing on the floor or watching television,
apparently heedless of the whole boisterous affair.

The front yard of Rincón Criollo is paved with bricks, unlike other casitas where the *batey* is either bare earth or covered with cement. This special effect came about accidentally, it seems, when one of the associates, a
bricklayer by trade, started placing down bricks he had gathered from a de-
molished building nearby just to see what it would look like. Everyone liked
it right away, José recalls, because of what they called the "Old San Juan effect," and before you knew it, after they all pitched in to help, the *batey* of
Rincón Criollo was fashioned with colonial-style pavement.

Dancing at the "Salvación Casita" party, as in other casita activities, took
on the full range of forms, from individual and couple steps to open group
participation, from inconspicuous head-bobbing and foot-tapping to the
formal presentation, in folkloric costume, of the young women in Norma
Cruz's *bomba y plena* class. At several points in the evening, most notably
during this rehearsed display of coordinated shimmying and traditional
movements, the crowd in attendance was an audience. They also moved
aside to admire and cheer when a particularly adept couple, like Norma
Cruz and her partner Consorte, took to the center of the *batey* to demon-

strate the perfect synchronization that comes of years of dancing plena together. Another memorable and more unusual display, which brought hilarious delight to the party, was when a man in his sixties, clearly one of the neighborhood personalities, got out there and danced a whole number by himself. Sporting a weathered, hip-length leather jacket and a black baseball cap turned slightly to one side, he shimmied, twisted, and jerked his way through the entire ten-minute piece with remarkable timing, all the while oblivious to the friendly snickers and guffaws of the onlookers.

Aside from these moments of choreographic exhibition, most of the crowd was out there on the brick floor. There was none of the self-consciousness that sometimes prevails at dance clubs and even house parties, as people moved about in every which way, young with old, tall with short, gliders with hoppers, women with women, even, at some points, men with men. As the energy level rose, those seated on the sidelines joined in as well, clapping and swaying in their seats, and groups of onlookers outside the fence took to dancing on the sidewalk. The energy of collective performance radiated outward from the incandescent wooden porch filled with waving *panderetas, güiros,* congas, and accordions.

Inside the casita was like another world, though only a thin wooden wall and a few yards separated it from the porch trembling with percussive sound. Two women and an elderly man sat at a kitchen table talking. Four or five children were watching *Saturday Night Live.* A toddler was playing with a cat on the floor. A teenage couple was whispering and giggling in the back doorway. Another woman was busy rearranging some of the wall hangings: a calendar with the Puerto Rican flag, a picture of nationalist leader Pedro Albizu Campos, a leaflet with the face of the woman poet Julia de Burgos. Out through the back door you could see a few people lined up waiting to use the outhouse. There was a tranquility and everydayness that offered a welcome respite from the eventful intensity outside. And yet, despite the contrast, this peaceful scene was also, in some remarkable way, an integral part of the performance. The completeness of the event required somehow this space for the nonevent, as though it were a reminder that when the party is over the casita itself, the community's home away from home, will still be there.

In Puerto Rico the casitas were often clustered at the mouths of rivers. Peasants and rural workers displaced by the abrupt economic changes under American rule, and again at midcentury by the beginnings of industrialization, found along the riverbanks and marshy deltas the only land available for them to settle. There, removed from the facilities of the nearby towns and cities, they would patch together their makeshift shanties and eke out their subsistence by fishing, truck gardening, and seasonal stints on the huge sugar plantations. As they built their humble dwellings these squatter families always knew that their days there were probably numbered, and that at any moment agents of the government or the corporations could lay claim to the land and send them packing.

Papo Chín and José Rivera remember such moments from their childhood in "El Fanguito," the crowded slum in the mangroves of Santurce where they grew up in the 1950s. When the eviction notices came, they and their neighbors would disassemble the casitas, transport the wood planks and panels to the other side of the lagoon, and set them up again. And life, they recall with a wry smile, would return to normal, as though nothing had happened. "What did we care which side of the water we lived on?"

Since its earliest use, casita architecture has been eminently portable; casita settlements were built more with the dream than with the real prospect of settling in mind. With displacement the most pressing fact of life, the illusion of permanence becomes paramount. The same is true of the cultural world of the casita people: while the music, dancing, pig roasts, and everyday activities give the impression that they are rooted there and always have been, they are lived with the knowledge that it had all occurred somewhere else yesterday, and could well be happening somewhere else tomorrow.

This duality between apparent fixity and imminent relocation may account for the special appeal of casita design among the impoverished and disenfranchised residents of the South Bronx. Under the present conditions of inner-city life, they too, like their nomadic ancestors in Puerto Rico or at some earlier time in their own lives, face the constant threat of removal, of having to pick up and do it somewhere else. Potential displacement is especially the condition of their gathering sites for cultural and recreational activity. For while they may enjoy a semblance of stability, however tenuous, in their tenement apartments or housing projects, over the years economic circumstances have forced them to move their public get-togethers from the dance halls to the storefront social clubs to the vacant lots. And from the vacant lot where to but another vacant lot?

The scramble for public space converged with the need to clean up the rubble and treacherous abandon left by the demolition ball and the arsonists, and then to plant and harvest. In some cases the first little structures were intended as tool sheds for the neighborhood gardeners, who were then spurred on by a reluctant nod from the city agencies in the form of Operation Greenthumb. The transition to the present casita as cultural center with adjoining mini-farm was only a matter of time and lively cultural memory, but at the price of stricter official vigilance, more elaborate security measures, and, of course, a far heightened sense of impermanence.

Such social conditions, in addition to their dense historical symbolism, make the casita settings themselves into acts of performative expression. Whatever may be going on at any given moment, the whole scene—casita, garden, *batey*, farm animals, outhouse, people milling and playing—is like a moveable stage, an array of theatrical props that can readily be packed up and reassembled in some other place and time. The chainlink fence around the yard, aside from its obvious security function, goes to accent the sense of enclosure, of boundedness and fixity within certain marked-off confines. Here we are, it seems to say, nestled between these particular buildings on this particular block, and we're comfortable and having a good time here. But this insistence on demarcation and spatial specificity is actually a performative response to the very fluidity of cultural and social borders characteristic of their historical experience.

The aesthetic of casita performance thus needs to be viewed from two perspectives: performance at the casita and the casita itself as performance. Spatially, there is an angle on the multiple levels and zones of performative expression inside the fence, and an angle from outside the fence, where the casita and its enclosure appear as though from aerial range in their larger architectural context. It is from this second optical approach, where the surrounding buildings, sidewalks and streets, and the whole urban design come into play, that performance refers to an act of imaginative transposition, or construction as anticipated provisionality and recontextualization. For the community, building and being at the casita kindles a performative sense of vividly imagined place and time: it is "as if" we were in Puerto Rico or Puerto Rico were here, or "as if" Puerto Rico were still as it was back in the days when people like us lived in casitas. But from the wider angle the constructed illusion means that casitas exist "as if" there really were a set place proper to the community. Either place engenders metaphor, or place itself is metaphor.

Beyond its practical and symbolic functions for the community in which it is located, the casita stands as a highly suggestive emblem of contemporary Puerto Rican culture, and of diasporic vernacular culture in general. For peoples caught up in circulatory, back-and-forth migratory motion and thereby subject to the constant renewal of personal and historical ties, culture is experienced as dramatic movement and change, adaptability and resilience. Uniqueness, stasis, and even the inexorability of territory and sequence give way to a logic of negotiation and interchangeability. The performance act, object, and site are all eminently transferable, replaceable, mutable; borders, however vigilantly patrolled, are traversable and ultimately collapsible. If economic and political conditions forbid such transactional mobility, performative memory makes it possible, or even necessary. We did this back then, over there, so let's do it again now, over here. In fact, we'd better if we're going to survive.

As emblem, the casita is intended to mean many different things to different people. It is no wonder, then, that artisans in Puerto Rico are making plaster-cast miniature casitas for home adornments, that there are casita T-shirts and casitas in ads for all kinds of products, that a town festival in Cabo Rojo featured a "real" casita and casita kiosks in the plaza, or that additions atop some flat-roof *urbanizaciones* (suburban housing developments) are designed after casitas. Nor is it an incongruity that when it could no longer afford a regular site the former Black and White in Color Gallery decided to become mobile as the Casita Gallery, or that Puerto Rican artist Humberto Figueroa's exhibit at the Museo del Barrio a few years ago included two prefab casitas in the center of the gallery floor.

Nevertheless, despite the casitas' seemingly boundless, protean adaptability, there are still grounds for some serious misgivings about the sight of a replica of Rincón Criollo in the halls of the Smithsonian Institution in Washington. The tourists from middle America and the D.C. cultural elite will surely never make it up to Brook Avenue and 159th Street, and it is unlikely that they will come to appreciate the pressing human conditions that made this "quaint" little structure possible, or necessary. On the other hand, if they are willing, for even an hour, to give themselves over to the intense performance energy of Manny Oquendo's Libre and Los Pleneros de la 21, then maybe they will be able to listen in on casita language in a way that will dramatize their own relationship to the people of the South Bronx. But when I saw those fancy coattails and evening gowns flying to the rhythms of salsa and plena, and José and Cepeda grinning, I was able to sense more deeply than ever the irony in the phrase "primitive art in civilized places."

Even as a happy recollection, that euphoria of conviviality and taste of carnival could only be momentary and, in view of the historical meanings of casitas, ultimately illusory. For however benevolent and "innovative" the intentions guiding the inauguration of the Experimental Gallery, the very format and location of "Las Casitas: An Urban Cultural Alternative" only serve to illustrate with particular poignancy the ideological weight surrounding the concepts "primitive" and "civilized" and any account of their supposed conciliation. The very idea of limiting "risk-taking" to exhibition style and technique, and the emphatic disclaimer that "Content and Subject are not the Experiment!," fits perfectly into critical analyses of hegemonic cultural theory and practice like that of Sally Price.

As tenaciously as those die-hard dichotomies of the "civilized" and the "primitive" and "technique" and "content" tend to hold sway in cultural discourse, it is the other paired terms of the title, "art" and "places," which suggest more fruitful lines of thinking about casitas and their contextual transformations. On what grounds and to what end are casitas to be considered "art," and what role do shifting and contrasting "places," understood spatially and temporally, play in deepening our critical involvement? Both in the Smithsonian and in the South Bronx, and even in their "original" appearance in Puerto Rico, casitas mark off "alternative spaces," scenes, and practices which diverge from and as such challenge prescribed arrangements and uses of social space. But clearly they are "alternative" in different ways, and it is close historical attention to the changing relations between "art" and "place," expressive practice and sociocultural geography, that allows for some insights into these critical distinctions.

In their passage from Puerto Rico in the first half of the century to the South Bronx in the 1980s to the Smithsonian in 1991, casitas have occupied three different "places," and their construction and use constitute, or relate to, "art" in three different ways. Between its primarily functional, habitational presence in the Puerto Rico of not-too-distant memory and its recreational, nostalgic reincarnation in the Bronx and El Barrio in more recent years, and between these homegrown community centers and "Las Casitas" in a museum gallery, two major transformations occur in the meaning of casitas as sites and forms of cultural practice. Though both attest to the seemingly limitless adaptability and negotiability inherent in what I have termed a casita "aesthetic," these changes are obviously of a very different order. In broad terms, but with the idea of "place" in view, the first move is one of de-alienation, the second of alienation. Casitas like Rincón Criollo have the effect—and surely this is their intention—of bridging distances of space and time, and of providing a respite from the inhospitable and atomizing conditions of their tenement apartments. With its heightened symbolic reference, the "home" for poor families in Puerto Rico of yesteryear becomes a "home away from home" for poor Puerto Rican communities in the U.S. inner city today.

The Smithsonian's "Rincón Criollo," on the other hand, is the casita as sheer display, disengaged from any community-based needs and desires. Though in relation to their "originals" in Puerto Rico the new casitas also have a museum-like sense of preservation and exhibition, the "public" served by its construction and use is in sociological terms the same population, only at a later chapter in its history, and the casita's functionality for everyday collective life, while rearticulated, is still present. What was, at least in part, the casita as community museum is now the casita "installed" in a museum; if not exactly a commodity, it has become an artifact, an object, and in any case no longer a process and ongoing expressive and representational practice. And again, though the intention may be to bridge the disparate worlds of the museumgoers and the casita people, whatever proximity is achieved is itself a simulation. The net effect, after the inaugural ball is over, is an accentuation of distance, difference, and ultimate incompatibility based on hierarchies of cultural power. The museum casita, with all its rhetoric of welcoming respect, amounts to cultural tourism of a special kind: instead of intruding on turf by going to it and interloping, the museum exhibit of vernacular culture does so by "installing" the cultural turf on display in one's own turf. Even the casita people themselves, whose presence did so much to enliven and authenticate the encounter, were there as part of the display, as "performers" in a masked, scripted sense rather than as participants in a process of cultural creativity and reenactment.

For it is clear, when the historical trajectory of casita life is brought to bear, that the other face of the validation and celebration of community culture by the dominant society is its repudiation and eventual suppression. By analytically juxtaposing "casita as community museum" and "casita within institutional museum," we can recognize how powerless folkloristic fancy is in detaining the advances of the bulldozer. The "preservation" of the community's own cultural reality, the act of "salvación casita," finally falls to the casita community itself.

So far at least, the "Salvación Casita" campaign has been a success: Rincón Criollo is still there, literally holding ground against the constant incursion of the developers and housing authorities. The surrounding lots, vacant over the years and allowing for a sense of open space and wide horizons, are now, after the mid-1990s, filled with new housing units, of the two- and three-story "post-projects" variety, harbingers of bigger, better, and—for the casita people—more threatening developments ahead. Yet not a Mother's Day or New Year's season goes by without that embattled corner turning into a party. Dance classes and membership meetings continue, and time and again Cepeda is back at the microphone to rally new rounds of support in defense of the casita.[6] A copy of the brochure from the Experimental Gallery's opening exhibit has its place on the wall inside, one memorable but not particularly consequential page in the life-story of "urban cultural alternative," Rincón Criollo.

Collage featuring the Joe Cuba band and the Drifters at the Apollo Theatre (1967)

(Photo by Doc Anderson; Courtesy of Willie Torres)

5

"Cha-Cha with a Backbeat"

SONGS AND STORIES OF LATIN BOOGALOO

"BANG BANG"

"Let's just try it out, Sonny. If it doesn't work, I'll buy you a double." Jimmy Sabater remembers the night he kept coaxing his bandleader, Joe Cuba, to play a new number he had in mind. It was 1966 at the Palm Gardens Ballroom in midtown Manhattan, and the house was packed. "It was a Black dance," Jimmy recalls, "*de morenos, morenos americanos de Harlem* and stuff, you know, they had Black dances one night a week there and at some of the other spots. So that night we were playing selections from our new album, *We Must Be Doing Something Right*, that had just come out, the one with 'El Pito' on it, you know, 'I'll never go back to Georgia, never go back . . .' The place was packed, but when we were playing all those mambos and cha-chas, nobody was dancing. So at the end of the first set, I went over to Joe Cuba and said, 'Look, Sonny' (that's his nickname), 'I have an idea for a tune that I think might get them up.' And Joe says, no, no, no, we got to keep on playing the charts from the new album. Then toward the end of the second set, I went on begging him, and said, 'Look, if I'm wrong, we'll stop and I'll buy you a double.' So finally he said OK, and I went over to the piano and told Nick Jimenez, 'Play this' . . . Before I even got back to the timbal, the people were out on the floor, going 'bi-bi, hah! bi-bi, hah!' I mean mobbed!" As Joe Cuba himself recalls, "Suddenly the audience began to dance side-to-side like a wave-type dance, and began to chant 'she-free, she-free,' sort of like an African tribal chant and dance."[1]

The new tune by the Joe Cuba Sextet was "Bang Bang." Within weeks it was recorded and released as a single which soon hit the national *Billboard* charts and stayed there for ten weeks, one of the few Latin recordings ever to reach that level of commercial success. It even outdid "El Pito," which the year before had also made the charts, and the album on which "Bang Bang" appeared, *Wanted: Dead or Alive*, was a huge hit as well. It was the heyday of Latin boogaloo, and Joe Cuba's band was at the height of its popularity. The year 1966 also saw the closing of the legendary Palladium Ballroom, an event marking the definitive end of the great mambo era in Latin music which had already been waning since the beginning of the decade. And, looking ahead to developments to come, it was some six years later at that very same Palm Gardens venue, by then called the Cheetah Club, that the Fania All-Stars were filmed in performance in the making of the movie *Nuestra Cosa* (Our Latin Thing), which is sometimes regarded as the inauguration of "salsa." Between the mambo and salsa, in the brief period spanning the years 1966–1968, the boogaloo was all the rage in the New York Latin community and beyond. It was both a bridge and a break, for with all the continuities and influences in terms of musical style, the boogaloo diverged from the prevailing models of Latin music in significant ways.

Jimmy Sabater's story about the making of "Bang Bang" helps explain the social function of boogaloo, while the song itself is characteristic of its style and musical qualities. As neighbors and coworkers, African Americans and Puerto Ricans in New York had been partying together for many years. For decades they had been frequenting the same clubs, with Black and Latin bands often sharing the billing. Since the musical revolution of the late 1940s, when musical giants like Mario Bauzá, Machito, and Dizzie Gillespie joined forces in the creation of "Cubop" or Latin jazz, the two traditions had come into even closer contact than ever, with the strains of Afro-Cuban *guaguancó*, *son*, and *guaracha* interlacing and energizing the complex harmonic figures of big band and bebop experimentations. For African Americans, that same midcentury mambo and Cubop period corresponded to the years of rhythm and blues, from the jump blues of Louis Jordan to the shouters and hollerers and street corner doo-woppers of the 1950s. Scores of American popular tunes of those years bore titles, lyrics, or musical gimmicks suggestive of the mambo or cha-cha, while many young Puerto Ricans joined their African American and Italian partners in harmonizing the echo-chamber strains of doo-wop love songs and novelty numbers.[2]

With all the close sharing of musical space and tastes, however, there were differences and distances. African American audiences generally

appreciated and enjoyed Latin musical styles, yet those who fully understood the intricacies of Afro-Cuban rhythms and came to master the
challenging dance movements remained the exception rather than the
rule. Most Black Americans, after listening admiringly to a set of mambos and boleros, will long for their familiar blues and R&B sounds and,
by the mid-1960s, it was of course soul music. Popular Latin bands thus
found themselves creating a musical common ground by introducing the
trappings of Black American culture into their performances and thus
getting the Black audiences involved and onto the dance floor. "Bang
Bang" by the Joe Cuba Sextet, and Latin boogaloo music in general, was
intended to constitute this meeting place between Puerto Ricans and
Blacks, and by extension, between Latin music and the musical culture
of the United States.

"Bang Bang" begins with a short piano vamp, which is then immediately joined by loud, group handclapping and a few voices shouting excitedly
but unintelligibly, and then by a large crowd chanting in unison, "bi-bi, hah!
bi-bi, hah!" The chant is repeated four times, increasing each time in intensity and accompanied throughout by the repeated piano lick, handclapping, and shouting, which is then supplemented by Jimmy Sabater on timbales, all the while building up to the resounding chorus "bang bang!" This
refrain phrase is introduced by the solo vocal, then repeated over and over
by the group chorus while the solo—none other than the legendary Cheo
Feliciano—goes off into a kind of *skat soneo* or adlib, blurting out random
phrases, mostly in Spanish, very much in the improvisational style of the
son montuno. This lead vocal interacts with the choral "bang bang" and with
the bongo bells (played, it turns out, by Manny Oquendo), and throughout
the song resounds in indirect and playful dialogue with another solo voice
line, in English, carried by Willie Torres, mostly exhorting the crowd and
the band with slang phrases like "come git it" "sock it to me," "hanky
panky," and the like. Somewhere in the middle of the four-minute recording is the line, "Cornbread, hog maw, and chitlins," repeated several times
and then teased out with Spanish comments like "comiendo cuchifrito" and
"lechón, lechón!" The last half of the song involves three or four false end-
ings, as over and over the irresistible rowdy clamor is rekindled by the same
piano vamp, with the solo vocal exchanges taking on a more and more gos-
sipy and jocular tone.

Though some changes were obviously required for the studio recording
of the tune, "Bang Bang" remains very much a party. Like many other pop-

ular songs of boogaloo, it reenacts a bawdy happening at the peak of its emotional and sexual energy, with instrumentals and vocals playing in full and wild association with the crowd. Joe Cuba recalls, thinking mainly of "Bang Bang," that "when I recorded in those days I always left a big boom mike overhanging above all the musicians to put in a little live effect." The musical texture of the song is a patchwork of noises, emotive outbursts, cries of glee, short musical phrases, and the recurring, abiding counterpoint of the crowd chorus and the leitmotiv piano lick. The lyrics, though of no consistent narrative or dramatic significance, nevertheless do have a meaning, which is the interplay of Black and Latin festivity and culture, the playful mingling of African American phrases and cultural symbols with those from Puerto Rican daily life. Musically this same message is carried across with the collage-like mixing of familiar trappings from mambo and R&B styles. The perspective is clearly that of the Latino, and Latin music is the main defining sound of the piece; but the traditional features and structuring principles of the Afro-Cuban model are consistently overridden by their conjoining with qualities from the R&B and soul traditions. The overall effect of the recording is one of collective celebration, gleeful partying where boundaries are set not so much by national and ethnic affiliation, or even language or formalized dance movements, but by participation in that special moment of inclusive ceremony.

As "Bang Bang" illustrates, the defining theme and musical feature of boogaloo is precisely this intercultural togetherness, the solidarity engendered by living and loving in unison beyond obvious differences. Its emergence coincided with the historical moment of the Civil Rights movement and the coming-of-age of the first generation of Puerto Rican youth born and raised in New York City. Latin music expert and producer René López calls boogaloo "the first Nuyorican music," and a consensus has gathered in concurrence with that description. It is the sound that accompanied the teenage years of the Young Lords and of the Nuyorican poets in the later 1960s; Piri Thomas's groundbreaking novel *Down These Mean Streets* was published in 1967. Like those experiences, it attests to the guiding, exemplary role of African American culture and politics for that generation of Puerto Ricans growing up in New York. "Bang Bang" is an explosion of excitement arising from that cultural conjunction, the linking of Puerto Rican backgrounds with the African American influences so prevalent in all aspects of social life, including of course their music and dance.

"Lookie Lookie"

Latin boogaloo burst onto the scene in 1966, the year that saw the recording not only of "Bang Bang" but of the other best-known boogaloo tunes as well. Johnny Colón's "Boogaloo Blues," Pete Rodríguez's "I Like It Like That," and Hector Rivera's "At the Party" all hit the record stores in 1966–67 and made overnight stars of many of the young musicians in El Barrio and in the clubs throughout the New York area. Much to the concern, and even hardship, of the established bandleaders from the 1950s and early 1960s, it was the young boogaloo musicians who seemed to come out of nowhere who were suddenly hot—getting top billing, selling the most records, and receiving enthusiastic requests for airplay. The standbys, on the other hand, notably Tito Puente and Charlie Palmieri (Eddie's brother), suddenly found themselves in dire straits. As Joe Cuba recalls, with boogaloo the career of his band, which had been around for over ten years by then, was catapulted into the national and international spotlight; now they were sharing shows and touring with big-time performers like the Supremes, the Temptations, Marvin Gaye, James Brown, and the Drifters, and traveling widely. They had a long and successful run at the Flamboyán Hotel in Puerto Rico, where boogaloo also caught on like wildfire. The most popular band in Puerto Rico in those years, El Gran Combo, brought out an album with six of the twelve cuts listed as boogaloos, and included the immensely popular "Gran Combo's Boogaloo." The fever then held on for another year or two, longer than most of the dance crazes of those years, and even the disdainful holdouts among the more sophisticated musicians, like Eddie Palmieri and Tito Puente, came around to recording their own boogaloos. It was a time when, as many of the musicians attest, you could not *not* play boogaloo and expect to draw crowds and get recording contracts.

Jimmy Sabater got that piano lick which served as the fuse for "Bang Bang" from a tune by Ricardo (Richie) Ray. "Bang Bang," for all its symbolic interest in responding directly to African American tastes and for all its commercial success, was not the first boogaloo tune, nor did it even mention the word in its lyrics. Who was the first one to use the term, or to start making Latin music explicitly called boogaloo? Several musicians involved at the time point in the direction of Richie Ray, whose two albums *Se Soltó* (On the Loose) and *Jala Jala y Boogaloo* drew immediate attention when they came out on Alegre in 1966 and 1967. Evidently, when Pete Rodríguez, Johnny Colón, and other boogaloo bands were introducing their new sides under that designation, Richie Ray had already made the term and associated musical styles familiar to dance and listening audiences. Discussions of origins always stir up debate and dissension, but if Richie Ray wasn't in fact the first he is certainly responsible for giving music called boogaloo a certain standard of fascination and quality, which little of what followed was able to live up to.

The experienced bassist and cognoscente Andy González for one doesn't even think of Richie Ray as a boogaloo musician. For González, Ray's band was a straight-up mambo and *son montuno* act, and like a lot of other groups they just took up boogaloo when it was the thing to do. While it is true that Ray and his vocalist Bobby Cruz had a broad repertoire and a career that outlasted the boogaloo era, the group did make its mark with those two albums, and the boogaloo tunes included are at least of the caliber of the other more traditional numbers. More importantly, there is in these recordings, perhaps more than anywhere else in Latin boogaloo, some statement about what the music is about and how it fits in relation to other, more familiar Latin rhythms. "Danzón Bugaloo," "Guaguancó in Jazz," "Azucaré y Bongo," "Lookie Lookie," "Richie's Jala Jala," "Colombia's Boogaloo" and "Stop, Look, and Listen" constitute a body of songs that provides a rich sense of the compatibility and kinship of traditional Afro-Cuban sounds with various strains of African American music. When standby vocalist and composer Willie Torres says repeatedly that for him boogaloo was a further experiment at moving Latin music in the direction of jazz, he might have had Richie Ray, and perhaps Johnny Colón, foremost in mind.

Unlike most of the young musicians coming up, Ray was formally trained at the piano, was gratefully indebted to the great Noro Morales, and had some years of experience playing with famed jazz trumpeter Doc Cheatham. Cheatham in fact stayed with Ray through the boogaloo years, and it is his trumpet that lends a special quality to songs like "Mr. Trumpet Man"—probably the most famous of all of Ray's tunes from that era—and "Lookie Lookie." More than the trumpet parts, though, it was Ray's own work on piano that established the primacy of that instrument in threading the typically patchwork fabric of the boogaloo format, thus giving it an anchor in the *jaleo* and *montuno* so emblematic of Latin dance music but with a subtle trace of the blue note. As in "Bang Bang" the repeated piano vamp occurs in continual counterpoint to the vocal and other instrumental lines and serves as a constant reminder of the syncopated and rhythmic grounding of the Afro-Cuban tradition. With all the admixture of prevailing pop styles of contemporary American music (not to mention the so-called British invasion), most conspicuously represented perhaps by Motown and the Beatles, Richie Ray's boogaloos emphasize musically that the perspective within that fusion is that of the Puerto Rican Latino in New York. But, interestingly in a tune like "Colombia's Boogaloo," it is the voice of the Latino who has gained something of value from New York, referring to boogaloo as "el nuevo ritmo," that he wants to share with his fellow Latin Americans. On his imagined visit to Colombia he brings with him "guanguancó, mambo y bolero" because "it comes from the heart" ("me sale del corazón"), but he also bears "el rico boogaloo," the refrain being "boogaloo, boogaloo, yeah, yeah."

In fact, the "jala jala" seems to be Ray's own adaptation of still another new dance fad, in this case one introduced by El Gran Combo in Puerto Rico, and as is clear from its spelling (it's not "hala hala"), it was intended as a more strongly Latin-accented version of the boogaloo or within the boogaloo category. The signature tune "Richie's Jala Jala" is actually about returning to Puerto Rico, where people enjoy the move and sound of the new rhythm, which is basically a *guaracha* jazzed up with some trumpet and piano work ("en Puerto Rico la gente goza más, . . . jala jala pa' vacilar"). Perhaps the most programmatic of these early boogaloos is the appealingly simple "Lookie Lookie," with its insistent refrain, "Lookie lookie, how I do the boogaloo," sung with an obvious Spanish accent. Again it is a kind of show-and-tell, this time indirectly through something he heard in Mexico but again indicating the diffusion of boogaloo to Latin America and its origins in New York; the brief narrative of the English lyric goes, "Down in old Mexico, just a few days ago, as I walked down the street, a little boy said to me, I will show you señor, what I learned in New York . . ." Maintaining a basic Latin feel throughout, the song unfolds in three parts: a slow, narrative first half, then a short repeat section at double the tempo, and a finale featuring an open, airy trumpet solo (by Doc Cheatham) with timbal and piano accompaniment. Though the mix varies from part to part, the overall effect of the tune is one of seamless affinity and mutuality between the *son montuno* and jazz idioms. If Richie Ray doesn't go down as the founder of Latin boogaloo, he certainly served as its representative in Puerto Rico and Latin America; his international orientation and frequent tours made of him, as one of his best songs is titled, "El Señor Embajador."

But as Richie Ray recalls, the key idea motivating him, Bobby Cruz, his brother Ray Maldonado (whence the name Richie Ray), and the other musicians in their group at the time was "crossover." Recognizing how much American audiences liked Latin music, they were intent on finding ways of making it even more accessible, and of course expanding their market range, by combining the Cuban rhythms with familiar pop sounds in the air in those years. In addition to echoes of the Beatles and Motown, for example, the opening tune on the breakthrough *Se Soltó* album, "Danzón Boogaloo," is actually a playful Cubanized version of "Whipped Cream" by Herb Alpert and the Tijuana Brass. Among the proliferation of dance crazes of the 1960s, they were particularly aware of the sweeping popularity of the twist, and Richie Ray even suggests that Chubby Checker used the word "boogaloo" in several of his songs. In the years prior to their boogaloo releases, the band spent long stints playing in the hotels in the Catskills, carefully trying out such crossover possibilities, choosing their songs, and developing arrangements.

With all their calculations, though, it was a more spontaneous situation in live performance that Richie Ray recalls as their first contact with boogaloo. After their apprenticeship in the Catskills, they started to play in the major venues around New York City, such as the Village Gate and the Palm Gardens. It was a night at Basin Street East when they noticed the public, mostly Blacks and Latinos, dancing a step they had never seen before. When they spoke with their friends in the crowd, they were told that the dancers were combining Latin moves with steps from the boogaloo and that "they go real well together." The bandmembers then took to observing the dance moves closely and fitting the rhythms and other musical qualities to the movements. As in the case of "Bang Bang," it was the interaction between music and dance cultures, and between performers and public, that was of formative importance in the emergence of Latin boogaloo, and which in Richie Ray's case resulted in the songs in boogaloo style that brought them to the height of their popularity.

PRELUDES IN BOOGALOO

But the roots of boogaloo run deeper than its presumed founding act, even if it is of the accomplishment shown by Richie Ray and his group, with its creative mingling of jazz and rock flavors into a range of traditional Cuban styles, all in the name of boogaloo. Indeed, without using the word, "Bang Bang" and "El Pito" are closer to the core of what boogaloo is about, musically and socially, than anything in the Richie Ray and Bobby Cruz repertoire of those years. The bawdiness, the strong presence of funk and soul music, the abrupt break with some tradition-bound conventions of Latin style, all figure centrally in most boogaloo and point more clearly to the musical influences that set the stage for that brief yet dramatic transition in Latin music of the mid-1960s period. After all, Jimmy Sabater got the inspiration for "El Pito" (which in 1965 might well have preceded the songs on Richie Ray's *Se Soltó* album) not from Ray's piano but from basic motives of "Manteca." Jimmy was thinking of Machito and Dizzie Gillespie and their historic recording of the tune that became the cornerstone of Latin and jazz fusion. Even the words of "El Pito" ("I'll never go back to Georgia") were spoken by Dizzy at the beginning of the "Manteca" recording and comprise a phrase that Jimmy associates more than any other with African American experience and expression. What appealed to him most for the purposes of "El Pito" was the perfect fit between the rhythm of that spoken phrase and the cadence of Latin musical phrasing: "Never go back to Georgia, never go back." It was all this, Jimmy comments, "and none of us had ever been to Georgia."

Puerto Rican musicians during the boogaloo era, whether newcomers or those with years of experience, were all formed during the illustrious mambo period of the 1950s. All of them, even those who venture furthest into non-Latin musical fields, acknowledge their indebtedness to the "Big Three," and speak with awe and unqualified gratitude of the crowning achievements of the Machito, Tito Rodríquez, and Tito Puente orchestras, especially in their unforgettable home at the Palladium. Mambo, *guaguancó, son guajira, guaracha,* bolero, cha-cha-chá, all performed at the peak of their potential, was the music that nourished and inspired Latin musicians during the 1950s and throughout the 1960s and beyond. Both major crazes of that decade—the charanga-pachanga fever of the first half and the boogaloo of the second—arose and faded in the afterglow of the Palladium years.

But the new generation of Latinos emerging in the 1960s, including the musicians then in their 'teens and twenties, was reared on another musical culture as well. While surrounded by a full range of Latin styles at home, on the radio, and in family and neighborhood occasions, many young Puerto Ricans in the 1950s and early 1960s were listening to and singing doo-wop and other rhythm and blues and rock and roll sounds. While the "older" musicians associated with boogaloo, those then in their thirties, had earlier performed with or in association with the bands of the mambo era, the younger ones typically recall that their favorite music when growing up ("*our* music") had been R&B and other forms of African American popular song, especially doo-wop. Influential boogaloo composers and performers like Tony Pabón of the Pete Rodríguez band, Johnny Colón and his vocalists Tito Ramos and Tony Rojas, in addition to Bobby Marín, King Nando, and countless others were members or sometimes founders of doo-wop groups even before they connected, or reconnected, with Latin music. Bobby Marín speaks authoritatively of the Puerto Ricans involved in some of the major doo-wop acts, beginning with the three who formed the Teenagers with Frankie Lymon, and who evidently composed some of his biggest hits. For King Nando it was the Drifters who was his favorite group after he arrived from Puerto Rico in the 1950s, and for Jimmy Sabater it was the Harptones, though his all-time "king," of course, was Nat King Cole.

Two musical languages thus coexisted in the world of the boogaloo musician—that of his cultural and family heritage and that of life among peers in the streets and at school. The challenge was, how to bring these two worlds together and create a new language of their own. King Nando tells of how as a teenager raised on doo-wop and early rock and roll he once went to the Palladium and heard Tito Rodríguez play "Mama Guela." "From then on," he recalls of this moment in 1961, "I Latinized all my R&B arrangements."[3] The musical career of Johnny Colón, whose band gained fame with its 1967 recording of "Boogaloo Blues," began when he formed and sang with the East Harlem doo-wop group the Sunsets. For Colón, boogaloo was above all "a kind of bridge, a way for the young, R&B-reared Latino musicians and fans to link back with their musical heritage." This musical linkage took many forms, and only some of it was called boogaloo; the boogaloo repertoire actually ranges along a continuum from basically Latin sounds and rhythms with the trappings of African American styles on one end, to what are R&B, funk, and soul songs with a touch of Latin percussion, instrumentals, Spanish-language lyrics or inflections. The only proviso for it to be part of the world of boogaloo is that both musical idioms be present, and that both the Latino and the African American publics find something of their own to relate to.

Though foreshadowed by similar trends in the Cubop and Latin jazz of the previous generation, the crosscultural fusions characteristic of the boogaloo period differed in significant ways. For one thing, the Latin musicians of the boogaloo period had both traditions—the Latin and the African American—acting as active forces in their experience from the beginning of their musical efforts, while with few exceptions there was in the 1940s and 1950s still a divide between Latin and African American musicians in terms of background familiarity. Furthermore, boogaloo involved the mixing of Afro-Cuban style with the vernacular, blues, and gospel-based currents of African American music, the R&B and soul sounds that saturated the airwaves and enlivened broadly popular settings of the 1960s period, selling to broad markets not even approximated by any jazz offerings. It was the dance and party music of the wide American and international public that the boogaloo fusion took as the most direct partner of the popular Latin sounds, such that aside from the most immediate connection to African American styles, boogaloo involved the engagement of Latin Caribbean music with the pop music market to a degree unprecedented in previous periods. Salsa personality Izzy Sanabria considers Latin boogaloo "the greatest potential that we had to really cross over in terms of music."[4]

While mambo and doo-wop thus form the dual heritage from the 1950s that went into the making of boogaloo, there are more immediate precursors, from the early 1960s, that anticipate many of the features of Latin boogaloo and help to understand in a broader context the fad that was to hold sway in the Latin music field later in the decade. That context may be thought of as New York Latin music of the 1960s, the period before the advent of salsa, in chronological terms, or in such musical expressions as "Latin soul," the whole range of Latin–African American fusions of which boogaloo is a part. Before boogaloo hit the scene, for example, there was Latin music in English, connecting to soul and funk rhythms and sounds (as well as jazz), based on improvised conversation or party noise, and with sales capable of cracking the national charts. In songs like Willie Torres's "To Be with You," Ray Barretto's "El Watusi," Mongo Santamaría's "Watermelon Man," and Eddie Palmieri's "Azúcar," all recorded in the early 1960s, many of the identifying ingredients of Latin boogaloo are already present, and at a level of musical achievement seldom surpassed during the boogaloo years. They were, along with Tito Puente's "Oye Como Va," the most popular Latin recordings of those years, and all involved an inflection of Latin traditions in the direction of African American R&B and soul sounds. They are among the "classics" of Latin soul (excepting perhaps Puente's, where the association is based more on Santana's Latin rock cover version of 1969), and thus prefigure in varied ways the whole gesture of boogaloo.

"To Be with You" has been called the "all-time classic Latin Soul ballad," and there are few New York Latinos around from the early 1960s who would dispute that judgment.[5] What may appear surprising is that such stature is accorded a song performed entirely in English, and which evidences far more "soul" than "Latin." It was written in the early 1950s by Willie Torres and Nick Jiménez, a team responsible for composing some of the first pieces of Latin dance music in English, starting with a version of "I've Got You Under My Skin" in cha-cha tempo, and the very popular "Mambo of the Times."[6] Torres, reflecting on those early crossovers, feels there was a need for English lyrics, not only in order to reach non-Latino audiences but among the New York Latinos of the day as well. "You have to remember," says Torres, whose musical career extends back to the early 1940s, "that most of us were Nuyoricans, born here, bred here. Machito and them, they were like the anchor, but as it kept going, most of the kids, their Spanish was limited, like mine. I spoke Spanish at home because I had no choice. But as far as having a great knowledge of it, I didn't. So I got with Joe," he continues, referring to bandleader Joe Cuba, and he might have added Nick Jiménez, Jimmy Sabater, Cheo Feliciano, and the others. "He was of my era, too. So we said, let's do this in English, and it worked out." It is thus clear that long before the boogaloo era, as exemplified by the early years of the Joe Cuba Sextet, there was already a major bilingual and English-dominant Latin music community in New York.

Torres never got to record "To Be with You" with the Joe Cuba band, though he sang it before countless hotel and club audiences through the 1950s, beginning with a memorable debut at the Stardust Ballroom in 1953. Torres even recorded the tune on the *Manisero* album of the Alegre All-Stars, where producer Al Santiago labeled it a "bolero gas." But Torres had left the Joe Cuba group in 1956, and so it was Jimmy Sabater, the lead English vocalist of the band at the time, who came to immortalize the song in the 1962 pop single. Its inclusion in the 1967 *Steppin' Out* album draws the song into association with boogaloo, with which it has mainly its penchant for English lyrics in common. But it is, no doubt, Latin soul, of the Nat King Cole with a slight Latin accent variety. The "Latin" musical accents of this R&B love ballad are also muted, with bolero tempo and bongo slaps playing off against the vocal harmonies and crescendos that carry the romantic feeling of the song. As tailored as the sound is to an American ballroom setting, Torres is quick to recall that "To Be with You" is actually an interpretation of an old bolero, "Nunca (No Te Engañé)," and that he himself often sang it in Spanish, as "Estar Contigo."

Willie Torres did get to be "El Watusi," though. "You remember that song 'El Watusi'?" he asks. "Well, you're looking at him. For real, I'm the other voice. Not the deep one that does most of the talking, but the other one, el watusi himself, the one he's talking about, and to. Ray Barretto, who did the tune, got me to be the other voice, to just grunt a few words in response to the deep one, the one who's talking about el watusi as the biggest and baddest in all of Havana: 'Caballero, allí acaba de entrar el watusi. Ese mulato que mide siete pies y pesa 169 libras . . . El hombre más guapo de La Habana.' That deep Cuban-sounding voice was Wito Cortwright, the guy who used to be second voice and *güiro* player in Arsenio Rodríguez's band. We were the voices. And so I am el watusi."

Few beyond Willie Torres's own circle would know that he was the voice of the fearsome neighborhood tough guy, but Ray Barretto's 1962 recording went on to hit the Top Twenty on the U.S. pop charts in 1963, peaking at number three in May of that year. It thus became the first recording by a Latin band to reach that milestone, and stands to this day as the greatest commercial success, still unsurpassed in Barretto's long and varied career. "El Watusi" was originally the B-side novelty number intended to accompany the more accomplished "Charanga Moderna" as part of the raging charanga-pachanga craze in New York Latin music. But it was "El Watusi"—that odd, charanga-flavored sample of braggadocio in tough-talking Cuban street Spanish—that caught on and set the stage for the boogaloo phenomenon in other ways. Here it is obviously not the bilingual or English lyrics, nor the admixture of R&B sounds, though there can be no doubt that there were many African Americans among its fans. In this case it is the spontaneous, conversational nature of the voices and the general rowdy crowd atmosphere that anticipates songs like "El Pito," "Bang Bang," "At the Party," and others in the boogaloo mode. The handclapping, which accompanies the unchanging bass beat throughout the tune, became a hallmark of Latin boogaloo, as did (in many cases) the free and open song structure. "Lyrics?" Willie Torres recalls, laughing. "We made it all up as we went along."

But the fluke hit "El Watusi" prefigured the boogaloo craze in other ways as well, an association underlined by Willie Rosario's popular 1968 recording of "Watusi Boogaloo." The commercial success of this tune by a Latin band hitting the charts was itself proof that it was possible to play around with Latin sounds and have a hit. But there were other reasons for the appeal of this zany Spanish rap with the charanga flute beyond its musical novelty which also point to a relation with boogaloo. For the watusi was also one of the most popular dances in the same year as the release of Barretto's recording, especially after the release of the smash hit "Wah Watusi" by the Orlons, which was high on the charts for thirteen weeks, peaking at number five, in the previous year. The dance craze itself was introduced by the Vibrations with their 1961 hit "The Watusi," which in turn is based on the similar tune "Let's Go, Let's Go, Let's Go," by Hank Ballard and the Midnighters (the group, incidentally, which sang the original version of "The Twist" in 1959, a year before Chubby Checker's historic cover version). The word *watusi*, then, along with its sundry undefined connotations and connection to a well-known dance move, was in the air when "El Watusi" came out, such that Barretto's recording, in a musical language totally unrelated to the American watusi, rode the wave of that catchy familiarity of the moment.

Clearly, Latin boogaloo was similarly implicated in the prevailing dance crazes and pop categories in its time a few years later. Though there is no certainty as to its place of origin—Chicago and New York being the main contenders—it is established that the boogaloo was "the most successful new dance of 1965–66," the very years of the emergence of Latin boogaloo, quickly overshadowing the jerk, the twine, and the monkey of the previous season.[7] The first of the many boogaloo records, according to this version, was "Boo-Ga-Loo" by the Chicago dance/comedy/singing duo Tom and Jerrio, who got the idea from seeing the dance done at a record hop. "The record, released on ABC, was a huge, million-selling hit for the pair in April 1965." A slew of boogaloo recordings then followed (including the Flamingos' "Boogaloo Party"), many of which became moderate hits on the soul and funk markets. Another account of Black boogaloo, less oriented toward city of origin and pop charts and more toward musical force, identifies as the quintessential sound that of classic soul tunes like "Mustang Sally" and "In the Midnight Hour," both of which were made popular by Wilson Pickett. It was Pickett, too, who recorded the huge 1967 hit "Funky Broadway." Whether boogaloo is defined by these recordings, some more memorable than others, or the peculiar dance move, which "had a totally new look compared to previous dances, and its popularity crossed over to whites,"[8] it is clear that boogaloo was the foremost name for funky soul music at that moment in its history, and that Latin boogaloo took its name and direct crossover impulse from that immediate source. Though closer musically to its African American namesake than was "El Watusi," Latin boogaloo evidences the same process of mass popularity through association, and on a far more influential scale.

But neither "To Be with You" nor "El Watusi" exemplified or foreshadowed the main musical quality of Latin boogaloo, which is the fusion of Afro-Cuban rhythms with those of funk. That accomplishment is most directly attributable to Mongo Santamaría and Willie Bobo, and most familiar to general audiences in another chart-setting hit of the times, Mongo's "Watermelon Man," listed nationally in August 1963. Some would even consider "Watermelon Man," written by Herbie Hancock, to be "the original boogaloo," but here the reference is specifically musical. For beyond the adlibbed, conversational atmosphere in the vocals—a few grunts, animal sounds, and exhortations—Mongo's tune has the sound, the rhythmic feel of the Latin-funk fusion, most notably in the percussive backbeat on the timbales and other, mostly Afro-Cuban elements of the rhythm section. While the moaning brass sound is more in the Latin jazz idiom for which Mongo is famous, the rhythmic texture of the piece is closer to that of R&B, and it is the pronounced backbeat that anticipates the signature effect of Latin boogaloo.

Though it was Mongo's recording of "Watermelon Man" that drew broad attention to this musical possibility, there were other musicians who shared this early Latin-funk field with him and who personified more directly the Puerto Rican–Black American rhythmic fusion. One was obviously Willie Bobo, the black Puerto Rican born William Correa in Spanish Harlem who was Mongo's protegé since the late 1940s. "I was his interpeter," he said of his relation to the great Cuban drummer Mongo, and "in return he showed me the different shades of sounds the drum is capable of producing."[9] In tunes like the significantly titled "Fried Neck Bones and Some Home Fries," Bobo stands squarely at the crossroads of Afro-Cuban and African American cultures, with a particularly sharp nose for funk. At the other side of the Latin-Black divide is Pucho, the African American Henry Lee Brown from Harlem who formed the Latin Soul Brothers, comprised of African American musicians and famous for, among other things, their 1967 recording "Boogaloo on Broadway." It is Pucho, in fact, who remembers Willie Bobo circulating among the musicians smelling for funk. Pucho recalls that his band was, along with Mongo's and Willie Bobo's, one of the top three Latin-funk acts in the years before boogaloo, his own group serving as the training ground for the other two, which surpassed his in prominence. He played timbales, one of various African Americans from Harlem who mastered the instrument according to the recollection of Benny Bonilla, the *timbalero* for the Pete Rodríguez band. During the mid-1960s Pucho would typically make Latin boogaloos by taking known soul hits of the time (he mentions "Mustang Sally" and "In the Midnight Hour," among others) and "put[ting] Latin rhythms to them." And it was Pucho, the deft *timbalero* for the Latin Soul Brothers, who coined his own catchphrase for the music of Latin boogaloo—"cha-cha with a backbeat."

Ironically, the Latin musician who stood most prominently at the threshold of boogaloo was the one who held it in the most utter disdain. For it was Eddie Palmieri, who to this day regards boogaloo as the most tragic retrogression in New York Latin music, whose bold creativity brought Latin music into the 1960s and opened the eyes and ears of the musicians of the boogaloo era to what Latin music could be like for their own generation. The admiration for him among musicians associated with Latin boogaloo is unanimous. Palmieri's La Perfecta, with five excellent albums since 1963, was the hottest Latin band around by the mid-1960s when boogaloo hit the scene. He had top billings everywhere, and with Manny Oquendo on timbales, Barry Rogers and the Brazilian José Rodrigues on the trademark trombones, and Palmieri's ingenious arrangements, he set the standard for sheer musicianship and audience appeal, among Latins and audiences of many other nationalities. In fact, in another foreboding of boogaloo's social appeal, Palmieri had a huge, enthusiastic following among African Americans.

The origin of one of Palmieri's biggest hits of those salad years, "Azúcar," directly prefigures the making of vintage boogaloo songs like "Bang Bang" and "I Like It Like That." " 'Eddie, play some sugar for us,' Blacks would yell at him time and again. 'Sugar' was the word they invoked whenever they wanted a fiery up-tempo Palmieri tune. Palmieri wrote 'Azúcar' (Sugar for You) and it attracted an even larger number of Blacks to his dances."[10] This is but one example of Palmieri fashioning the qualities of Latin music in response to an African American dance public, just as the Joe Cuba, Richie Ray, Pete Rodríguez, and other groups were to do in the subsequent boogaloo phase.

Though a proto-boogaloo model in this sense, however, and preceding the vintage hits in popularity by only a few years, Palmieri has never had a kind word for anything related to boogaloo. He scorned the amateurishness, the banality, and especially the retreat from serious and creative adaptations of Afro-Cuban models being developed in those years after the blockade of

Cuban music following the 1959 revolution. "It was like Latin bubblegum," Palmieri recalls. " 'Bang Bang,' what's that? It's like something you find in a Frosted Flakes box. And half the musicians didn't even know what side of the instruments to play out of." Aside from his musical judgment, which was shared by many, including many of those associated with boogaloo, Palmieri was of course thinking of the disastrous impact the boogaloo craze had had on established musicians such as his brother Charlie and of course Tito Puente, Machito, and even Tito Rodríguez. The top billings and frequent bookings they had grown accustomed to were suddenly in jeopardy, and their recordings vastly outsold; ominous changes were afoot in the Latin recording and broadcast fields. Though he accepts the recognition, Palmieri considers himself among the victims of boogaloo rather than a benefactor, and of course would resist being considered a model of any kind for what was for him the boogaloo "epidemic."

"¿Qué qué, Eddie Palmieri, boogaloo?" Such is the first line of "¡Ay Qué Rico!," a boogaloo by Eddie Palmieri. The lead voice is Cheo Feliciano's, while on bass is the legendary Israel "Cachao" López doing a shing-a-ling (a string-based variant on boogaloo), on a recording from 1968, when boogaloo fever was already beginning to subside. The final irony of the Palmieri-boogaloo story is that it was Eddie Palmieri, the staunchest antagonist of everything boogaloo, who composed and led what is arguably the best boogaloo recording of them all. "¡Ay Qué Rico!" is bawdy, festive, conversational, and has all the trappings of Latin boogaloo sounds. Its special attraction in the boogaloo repertoire is that its playful irony seems to be directed at itself—as if it is saying, "You want boogaloo, *here's* boogaloo!"—and of course its consistent musical excellence. That and another number on Palmieri's important *Champagne* album of 1968, "The African Twist," show Palmieri fully in the spirit of Latin funk. Another play with pop styles, "The African Twist" was written and sung by an African American woman, Cynthia Ellis, in a style reminiscent of Motown. In these tunes it is clear that Palmieri was not spending his time berating boogaloo, but taking it to another level.

"I LIKE IT LIKE THAT"

"Eddie Palmieri was the headliner," recalls Benny Bonilla, the *timbalero* for Pete Rodríguez y Su Conjunto. "They needed a cheap band to open up for him, so they heard about us. So the booking agents, I remember it was two West Indian guys, came to hear us at one of our gigs, and they liked us. So they asked us for a short recording to help promote the dance on the radio. We looked at each other and said, 'Recording? We ain't got no recording.' And they said, no problem, we'll book a studio, just do a short spot, one minute, and we'll use that." Pete Rodríguez and his bandmembers started groping around for something to play and couldn't come up with anything. Then Benny Bonilla remembers Tony Pabón, the group's trumpeter, vocalist, and composer, saying "Let's try this." He taught Pete how to do that piano vamp, and started adlibbing: "Uh, ah, I like it like that." The spot was played on the radio and, according to Benny, "the phone at the station started ringing off the hook."

"I Like It Like That" was recorded in 1966, in a full studio session for Alegre, and the Pete Rodríguez orchestra became an overnight sensation in El Barrio and around the city. The group had been around awhile, since the end of the 1950s, but mostly as openers, a backup band with low billing beneath all the major attractions: Machito, Tito Puente, Tito Rodríguez, El Gran Combo, Johnny Pacheco, Orquesta Broadway. They even played on the closing nights of the Palladium, all of which featured the likes of Eddie Palmieri, Vicentico Valdéz, and Orquesta Broadway. "We didn't have the best band," Benny Bonilla admits. "We had no training or anything. We were out there to have fun." Unlike the Joe Cuba Sextet or even Richie Ray, the other possible initiators of Latin boogaloo, the Pete Rodríguez band had not established itself before the advent of boogaloo. Its recognition began and ended with the boogaloo craze, making it, of all the major groups, the boogaloo band par excellence.[11] And "I Like It Like That," by far their greatest hit and known to the world through cover versions, movie soundtracks, and Burger King commercials, might well be considered the quintessential song of Latin boogaloo.

The musical inspiration of the *conjunto* was Tony Pabón. Though Pete Rodríguez was the bandleader and played piano, and Benny Bonilla was important on the timbales, it was Pabón who wrote and arranged most of the songs (including all of the popular ones), sang many of them, and was always there on trumpet. "Tony was a rock and roller," recalls Bonilla, who was a good ten years older than Pabón. In addition to covering all the Latin sounds, he sang doo-wop, loved jazz, and seemed to be open to many musical styles. His turn to boogaloo illustrates this lively eclectic interest and jibes perfectly with the stories of the Joe Cuba and Richie Ray groups, though it leaves open the issue of origins. Whichever was the "first" Latin band to play boogaloo, they all turned to that style in response to African

American dance audiences and tastes. "In early 1966," Pabón recalls, "we kept getting repeated requests from dancers to add a little soul to the music. At the time nothing similar to the Boogaloo was being played, nor was the word Boogaloo used. Pete asked me to write music that would please the promoters of the dances. A week later I heard Peggy Lee singing 'Fever.' I wrote a tune inspired by the bass lines of 'Fever' and I called it 'Pete's Boogaloo.' We introduced the phrase ooh-ah, ooh-ah. Symphony Sid introduced it on the radio. Sid told us there were calls for the tune so we decided to continue with the new sound."[12]

Whether it was the first one ever written or performed, "Pete's Boogaloo" was the first Latin boogaloo song to be played on the radio. It is the lead-off tune on their first album, *Latin Boogaloo*. It is not a particularly interesting piece, with the boogaloo-style handclapping, rowdiness, and backbeat inserted as a section between rather standard *montuno* and mambo fare, and the song's title unwisely calling attention to Pete's uninspired work on piano. And there is nothing of Peggy Lee or "Fever" but the bass lines, and even they are hardly discernible. Nevertheless, with "I Like It Like That," and generally the tunes on the second album (of which it is the title song), the group comes into its own. Tony Pabón's compositions "El Hueso," "Micaela" and "3 and 1" from that album, and then "Oh, That's Nice" and "Here Comes the Judge," are among the group's hits of those years, and they all seem to draw on tunes or phrases from R&B and other popular tunes of the time. "I got four gold records while Pete got the money from royalties," Pabón mentions. "So I left the band to form La Protesta in 1970."[13]

"I Like It Like That" has all the trappings of Latin Boogaloo: the opening piano lick, the handclapping and ever-present chorus throughout, the raucous laughter and shouting, the adlibbed conversation and goofy comments, the ecstatic buildups and restarts, the intertwining of *montunos* and mambo rhythms with R&B-style backbeats, and vocals with lyrics in English. Interestingly, it is here that the slow bass figure on piano reminiscent of "Fever" is foregrounded, and it plays off well against the upbeat tempo of most of the tune. (It is worth mentioning that "Fever" was first recorded by Little Willie John back in 1958 and was written by the prolific and sadly unsung R&B composer Otis Blackwell from Brooklyn, who also wrote songs made famous by Elvis Presley and Jerry Lee Lewis.) Again, as in "Bang Bang," Hector Rivera's "At the Party," and countless other tunes of the genre, "I Like It Like That" exudes a wild, festive party atmosphere—a *bembé*—and the music incites and participates in the fun. From the excitement and energy in Tony

Pabón's lead voice, it sounds as though the musicians are out there dancing with the crowd, instruments and all. And as in "Bang Bang" and "At the Party," the chorus includes voices of women and children, adding to the inclusive and participatory spirit of the occasion.

What is different about "I Like It Like That," among the best-known Latin boogaloos, is the lyrics, and particularly the refrain. While the male swagger and dance exhortations are commonplace, here there is a specific reference to boogaloo and an emphasis on the contribution of Latin rhythms: "Let me say this now," the song begins, "here and now let's get this straight / Boogaloo, baby, I made it great / Because I gave it the Latin beat / You know, child, I'm kind of hard to beat." The claim is not repeated, but the point is made—without the "Latin beat," boogaloo would not be what it is—and this is reinforced by the flow of the song, which seems to move continually in the direction of the blaring trumpets, piano *montunos*, and the free-wheeling interplay of *soneo* and chorus so familiar to lovers of Latin music. The refrain, which is also the title of the song and of the album (*A Mi Me Gusta Así*), remains the most memorable feature of all—for it is the domain of the chorus, of everyone involved, repeated over twenty times, and all the while improvised, played with, and built up to. More than "bang bang," "lookie lookie," or "at the party," it is a playful, catchy phrase with multiple entendres. It signals personal joy and pleasure ("like"), but the indefinite "it" and "that" leave the specific reference open, whether it be to the song itself, the way the band is playing (the "Latin beat"), the dance moves, the party spirit, sex, rum, marijuana, whatever. Like the song itself, the phrase signals a kind of seductive ambiguity.

Interestingly, the phrase "I like it like that" was not new to Tony Pabón's song. Like the "Fever"-inspired bass figure, it was in the air during those years, especially in the world of R&B. In 1961 a song by that title rose to number two on the national charts and was on people's lips everywhere: "Come o-o-o-o-n, let me show you where it's at / The name of the place is . . . I like it like that." The original was composed and sung by Chris Kenner, a New Orleans songwriter whose other big hit, covered by several groups and immortalized by Wilson Pickett, was "Land of a Thousand Dances." In 1964 "I Like It Like That" was covered by the Miracles, reaching number 27, and in the following year Michael Rodgers got it onto the charts again. There is no saying whether Tony Pabón was humming Kenner's song in any of its versions when he made up his tune for the Pete Rodríguez band, and of course he uses it in a different way, adding an infectious melodic lilt. But it is clear that the phrase was by then a familiar part of pop music lore, as contagious as "get a job" or "gee whiz." In fact, in "Land of a Thousand Dances," "I like it like that" is even mentioned as one of the "thousand dances" proliferating at the time, along with the twist, the hully gully, and the others. Moreover, the refrain plays a similar role in Pabón's song to that in Kenner's original and then in the various covers. The 1961 recording was produced by the great Allen Toussaint, who also leads it off with a syncopated piano lick in the style of Professor Longhair or Huey "Piano" Smith. One of the notable characteristics of Toussaint's many productions, according to one account, was "the use of ingenious hook lines, often delivered at a pause at the end of a chorus. Two superior examples of this device became hits in spring 1961: Ernie K-Doe's 'Mother-In-Law' and Chris Kenner's 'I Like It Like That.' "[14] In Toussaint's production of Kenner's song, it should be noted, as in Pabón's, it is the chorus that blares out the phrase rather than the solo in response to the chorus, as it is in "Mother-In-Law."

While no deliberate reference can be ascertained in the use of the same hook-line in the manner of Toussaint and New Orleans R&B, the parallels are striking and point up the affinities among Afro-Caribbean–based musical idioms. Tony Pabón was of course sensitive to such affinities, and he could count on the same awareness in his experienced percussionist, Benny Bonilla. By the time he got to the boogaloo days, Bonilla had already played timbales in a range of bands, and at countless gigs, many of them for non-Latino audiences. Along with his early training on congas, bongos, and the timbal, he and other of the Latin percussionists also had ongoing contact with many African American drummers in Harlem and picked up American-style percussive techniques. While in the late 1950s Black musicians were coming to master the Latin timbal (such as Pucho, but Bonilla also mentions Art Jenkins and Phil Newsome), Latin *timbaleros* like himself and Jimmy Sabater were picking up on ways to use their instrument in the manner of an American snare drum, for the "American effect." In his countless gigs at hotels and lounges, he often had to play fox trots and other traditional American rhythms along with the mambos and cha-chas. He tells of how they used to put a set of keys on the drum to get that brush and cymbal sound. And of course he talks about the hallmark 2/4 backbeat found in Latin boogaloo. Almost imperceptibly, it is this flexible timbal that modulates the energy of "I Like It Like That," as Sabater did with the Joe Cuba band, moving it through the slower vocal parts, then setting up the buildups and kicking in with full backbeat when the band and chorus are letting all the stops out. The biculturalism of Latin boogaloo is contained in the timbal, the only stick drum commonly used in Latin music and brought center stage by master *timbaleros* like Manny Oquendo and of course Tito Puente.

"Boogaloo Blues"

Sex, drugs, and rock 'n' roll. Latin Boogaloo thrived during the years of the 1960s counterculture, the heyday of flower power, hippies, psychedelic drugs, and sexual liberation. Young people were listening to the Beatles, the Rolling Stones, and Jimmi Hendrix as they milled in their publicized "be-ins." "Boogaloo Blues," the only one of the major hits of Latin boogaloo to use the word *boogaloo* in its title, touched on many of these chords of appeal to the youth culture of the times, and its market. The song is an acid trip, an orgasm, a loud party, a brooding reverie, a taunt and seduction, all to a fusion of bluesy jazz piano, R&B vocalizing, and outbursts of *montunos* and Latin rhythms. Like most other boogaloo tunes, it is a seemingly disheveled patchwork of musical modes and tempos, the only structuring principle being the repeated movement from slow handclapping and bass beginnings to a buildup and climax of energy, and then a restart and new buildup. Yet, as representative as it is taken to be of Latin boogaloo as a phenomenon, "Boogaloo Blues" is in some ways idiosyncratic among the best-known recordings of the genre, in part because here the lyrics tell a story.

Tito Puente said the song sounded like a Coca-Cola commercial. The judgment of "el Maestro" may be harsh, and must have been discouraging to Johnny Colón and his youthful bandmembers. But there can be no doubt that the song is to a significant degree a fabrication of the recording industry. Despite the creativity and sincerity of the musicians, who did want to put out a new kind of sound in tune with their times, the intervention of experienced record producers and radio disk jockeys proved decisive in the construction of the song, and in its immediate popularity.

The story of "Boogaloo Blues" begins at Los Guineitos, an after-hours club on the second-floor loft of a building in East Harlem. In earlier years it had been the storage place for bananas (*guineos*) sold at the many Italian produce stores in the neighborhood. On weekends the upstairs storage loft came to serve as a late-night club owned by two brothers from the neighborhood, who lent it out as a rehearsal space during the week. That night in 1965 the influential record producers George Goldner and Stan Lewis were there, at the invitation of Johnny Colón, to see if they were interested in the band's material for recording on their Cotique label. Johnny was improvising some blues figures on piano, with the band and lead vocalists Tito Ramos and Tony Rojas then segueing into a rendition of the Latin standard "Anabacoa." Goldner and Lewis told them that they liked the piano intro and suggested that for the recording they follow through on the bluesy feeling and drop the "Anabacoa" part. Tito Ramos then composed lyrics to match the piano part, and the result was "Boogaloo Blues." As the bandmembers remember it, Goldner and Lewis embraced each other when they heard it. The band went on to play its new song to avid fan reception, first at a local church dance, then in the prestigious dance spot, the Colgate Gardens. Within months of the recording, and with the help of repeated airplay by deejay Symphony Sid, a close friend of Goldner and Lewis, "Johnny Colón, Tito Ramos and Tony Rojas were popular celebrities in Black and Spanish Harlem."[15]

The members of Johnny Colón and His Orchestra all grew up within blocks of the Banana Club, as the produce loft was called in English. They were young, even younger than the Pete Rodríguez group; the band was not even formed until 1964, when Pete Rodríguez was already getting billings at the major spots and with the leading names in Latin music. As teenagers in the 1950s, they all sang doo-wop—Johnny as leader of his own group, and Tito and Tony with many of the impromptu streetcorner harmonizers around Central and East Harlem. Johnny Colón, the bandleader, was most active in promoting the group's chances for recognition, and sought out the right people in the music industry. When Goldner and Lewis caught wind of them, the veteran doo-wop and rock and roll producers for the influential Roulette label sensed that the group, with its dual upbringing in Latin and R&B styles, might be ideal for their new Cotique venture. For Cotique (as the name reveals, an offshoot of the Tico label which Goldner had recently left) was to specialize in Latin boogaloo. With the Johnny Colón band they had a group of youngsters who not only had the right cultural mix but who knew little or nothing about music as a profession, or as a business. What did they know about cutting out the "Latin part" of the song and its Spanish lyrics, if the producer doesn't like it? Who were they to refuse to stay in the blues, R&B "groove" if George Goldner, that old hand at picking up on emerging tastes and markets, says it "won't work"?

Here was a band, then, that could be made for and of the boogaloo craze, who could make a big-selling record just by tapping the many sources of energy and attraction alive at the moment, give it a Latin flair for added excitement, and call it boogaloo. As vocalist Tony Rojas recalls, "Boogaloo Blues" was written not so much to appeal to Black dance audiences, as was the case with Latin boogaloo in its first and most definitive impulse, but "to please the record producers. We wanted to do what they wanted, or thought was right." Of course he and his closest partner, composer and lead singer Tito Ramos, were well aware of the drug and free-sex culture of the day; they had no qualms about considering themselves part of it in some ways, and knew that young people in El Barrio were also into it. But they also knew that the big-time producers and promoters would warmly welcome their sultry lyrics about sex in the park ("take it off, take it *all* off") and their taunting, stoned-out choruses, "LSD has a hold on me" and "1–2–3, I feel so free."

In addition to the susceptibility to commercial exploitation, because of its narrative lyrics "Boogaloo Blues" also best exemplifies the thoroughly male and sexist perspective of much of boogaloo music. Like most other pop music fads, whether of those years or at any stage, as performance Latin boogaloo amounts to an extended masculinity ritual, with virtually no women involved in any aspect of the musical scene beyond that of chorus and audience, and with the sexual playfulness of the songs uniformly from a masculine point of view. More than a string of off-color incitations and double entendres, "Boogaloo Blues" is a story of sexual conquest, totally orchestrated by the commanding presence of the male solo voice. He is all power and self-confidence, while the "girl," "that one girl who cried and cried," is voiceless, confused, spaced-out, and ultimately helpless in the face of his irresistible advances. Though it is she who defines the acronym—"L" is for love, "S" for strong, and "D" for dynamic—she does so only through the words of the chorus, and those magical words are descriptive of him and of her feelings for him. Even compared to the Beatles' "Lucy in the Sky with Diamonds," the psychedelic anthem that served as an obvious model here, "Boogaloo Blues" is unequivocally phallic in its imagery. When coaxing her into letting her guard down, the male lead asks, "Baby, why are you so blue? Don't you like my boogaloo?," where the word "boogaloo" itself stands rather blatantly for his penis, as the composer had fully intended.

But for Tito Ramos and the other members of Johnny Colón's band, their signature song was most of all about freedom, the overcoming of "hang-ups" and the transgression of moral and cultural limits. Speculating as to why the song was so popular among Puerto Rican audiences, Tony Rojas claims that in El Barrio LSD evoked not so much the drug itself as a vague fascination with liberation and carefree youthfulness associated with the counterculture. For the musicians, this breaking of barriers and defiance of cultural norms was also what the music itself, Latin boogaloo, was all about. "It wasn't straight Latin, it wasn't straight American," they state, but was a pushing of the conventions of each by use of the other. The patchwork-like, stylistically intermingling texture of the tune matched its multiple reception among diverse audiences, with people dancing Latin style, American style, or just moving to the groove in whichever way they felt most comfortable. Tony recalls shows when most of the audience was just swaying to the song. The song's opening lines—"I remember that time, when the world was mine, and as I sing this same tune, which we call the boogaloo blues"—set the story into a strange kind of nostalgia for the present, as though the ecstasy of the moment were already an old tune from days gone by. With its mammoth sales, like the other big boogaloo hits outstripping by many times previous sales of any other Latin music, "Boogaloo Blues" was a crossover dream come true. It might not have sold too many Coca-Colas, but it sure sold a lot of records.

By the end of 1967, within a year of its rise to instant stardom, the Johnny Colón orchestra had already disbanded. While the bandleader himself went on to musical achievement by forming the successful and long-lived East Harlem Music School and a range of further musical endeavors, Tito and Tony soon organized TNT, another Latin Soul band that enjoyed big hits with their songs "Mr. Slick" and "Meditation." According to Johnny Colón, "Boogaloo Blues" is still selling to this day, boosted by its rerelease on compact disk and its inclusion in recent anthologies. The musicians see it as the centerpiece of a revival of Latin boogaloo thirty years after its heyday. But compared with its "competing song," as they refer to "I Like It Like That," to today's ears their big hit appears dated and locked into the clichés of its historical moment. Its bluesy piano intro is not only too long—it extends a full 1:20—but shows none of the tightness and inventiveness of a Richie Ray, not to mention an Eddie Palmieri. At nearly seven minutes, the song itself is too long as well, and despite its deliberately free organizational structure and storytelling lyrics, ultimately disjointed and rambling. To give due credit to the musicians, who are to this day bursting with talent and ingenuity, other numbers on their 1967

Boogaloo Blues album showed a more successful execution of both Latin and R&B stylistic possibilities, as did several of the later efforts by TNT. But the sway of the market, which so largely determined the structure and preferred context of "Boogaloo Blues" and fashioned it into such a block-buster hit, is also responsible for the identification of the group with that one song. And it occurred by the use of the category boogaloo, even though the song itself is only partially representative of that musical phe-nomenon and its stylistic trappings.

"Gypsy Woman"

The boogaloo fever and marketing potential, while bringing important and timely innovations to Latin music of the day, spawned a whole crop of new musicians and groups, all responding to the opportunity to combine their two musical heritages, Latin and African American. Some were adept and experienced musicians and composers who managed to record sizable hits, like Hector Rivera with his "At the Party." Rivera provided a range of bands, including Joe Cuba's and Eddie Palmieri's, with many of their compositions and arrangements, and "At the Party" was on *Billboard*'s charts for eight weeks in 1966–67, peaking at number 26. Though he brought in seasoned musicians for the recording, notably Cachao on bass and Jimmy Sabater on timbales, and though he boasts of using an African American singer, Ray Pollard, for the R&B vocals, "At the Party" has a derivative effect when heard today, not quite matching the freshness and playfulness of "Bang Bang," resonating too closely with Sabater's other big seller "Yeah Yeah," and lack-ing the infectious hook-line refrain and shifting tempos of "I Like It Like That." Rivera himself never liked or used the term *boogaloo*, and he is sure-ly right in claiming far more interests and accomplishments than are im-plied in it. But given the influence of commercially motivated tastemakers in stamping performers and their acts, he is known to posterity primarily by that one tune, and by his association with the boogaloo period.

But the rash of Latin boogaloo bands was comprised mostly of newcom-ers, young singers and novice instrumentalists who jumped on the band-wagon and, for better or worse, made their musical start and left their mark. Singers like Joey Pastrana and Ralfie Pagán, for example, enjoyed immense popularity in El Barrio at the time, and are remembered fondly for their soulful ballads infused with Latin rhythms and typically trailing off into or interspersed with Spanish lyrics. King Nando (Fernando Rivera), the guitarist and singer from El Barrio famous for his shing-a-lings, captivated audiences in the summer of 1967 with his composition "Fortuna," a slow, grinding number inspired by memories of his native Puerto Rico. The Lebrón Brothers, a family-based group from Brooklyn, were another creation of George Goldner's boogaloo hit-making machine, though before being named (by Goldner) they had minor hits on their own with tunes like "Tall Tales" and "Funky Blues." Yet they were also casualties of the same process, and like so many of the other youthful acts of the time, they remember the experience with a note of bitterness. Speaking of Goldner and their best-known album, the group's spokesman Angel Lebrón comments that "when we recorded 'Psychedelic Goes Latin' . . . , we didn't get paid for it. Despite the propaganda that was printed then, the boogaloo bandleaders were the hottest bands at the time. The boogaloo era came to an end when we threatened to rebel against the package deals."[16] Beyond these examples, young musicians with evident potential and genuine popularity, there were other groups who appear to have been made for the occasion, bearing bubblegum-sounding names like the Latin-aires and even the La-Teens. But this gimmicky nomenclature can be deceiving, as a forgotten group like the Latin Souls produced some impressive a capella songs, and there is no telling how many of the selections of the Hi Latin Boogaloos, organized by Gil Suarez, might have survived oblivion were it not for the vagaries and interested selectiveness of the commercial gatekeepers. The Coquets, a pair of African American woman singers who did backup for Joey Pastrana, might also have made a contribution to the repertoire of Latin soul vocalizing.

But of all these upstarts from the boogaloo era, the one who stands apart and who has enjoyed a long though difficult career since, is surely Joe Bataan. His first recording, "Gypsy Woman," was an immediate and lasting hit among Black and Puerto Rican audiences when it was released in 1967, the midst of the Latin boogaloo era. Yet neither that song, a Latinized cover of Curtis Mayfield's huge 1961 hit with the Impressions, nor any of his many other compositions, are considered boogaloo, nor has he ever wanted them to be. "I don't like the word, never did," Bataan comments. "In fact I hate it. I consider it insulting and always have. My own music, and most of what's called boogaloo, is for me Latin soul." He sometimes refers to it as "La-So" for short, and after salsa set in, he takes credit for coining the term "salsoul," which was then popularized as the name of a briefly successful record label.

Though raised in El Barrio and a well-known figure in the street gangs there during the late 1950s and early 1960s, Bataan was not of Puerto Rican ethnic parentage. "My father was Filipino and my mother was African American, and my culture is Puerto Rican," as he explains it. His childhood associates were as much African American as Puerto Rican, and his music, which he undertook after spending years in prison, has tended to have greater appeal among Blacks and Whites than among strictly Latino audiences. If the music of the Latin boogaloo period made up a continuum from Latin to R&B, Bataan's is clearly on the Black side of the spectrum. But he has always been an extremely eclectic composer and performer, drawing ideas and experiments from a wide range of sources. And far more explicitly than any of the young barrio musicians of the time, he was inspired in his creations by his own experience and from life in the streets. Even a reluctant admirer like bassist Andy González, who had little regard for the music itself, had to admit that "if you want to know what was going on in the streets, listen to the songs of Joe Bataan."[17]

Bataan's life in music is a story of survival and determination, and provides further insight into the machinations of the industry. "Music was my salvation," he says. "At 15 I began a five-year sentence at Coxsackie. One day after a guard's lecture shook me up I decided I was going to learn a skill and stay out of prison. . . . Through trial and error I learned to play the piano. I imitated Eddie Palmieri's style, he was my man. . . . In 1965 I organized a band and [promoter] Federico Pagani got us steady gigs."[18] The band consisted of very young kids from the neighborhood, with little or no musical experience. When his singing of "Gypsy Woman" caused an enthusiastic response from the audience, he continues, "Pagani referred me to Goldner. After I sang 'Gypsy Woman' for him, he told me in a polite way, 'It's great, but let someone else sing it. You do not have a masculine voice.'" Bataan was furious, offended perhaps more in his masculinity than his musicianship, and was determined to get even. "I signed a contract with [famed deejay] Dick 'Ricardo' Sugar, who in turn introduced me to Jerry Masucci of Fania after he heard me sing at the Boricua Theater. I signed with Fania and recorded 'Gypsy Woman' in 1967."[19]

Bataan explains the popularity of his music, created as it was with so little professional training or support, to be the public's identification with his realistic themes taken from everyday life in society, and not just the parties and good times. Well-known early tunes like "What Good Is a Castle," "Poor Boy," and "Ordinary Guy," he says, "were bestsellers because I was

singing about me, my life, my experiences. . . . Mr. Goldner once told me
that my songs were sad. Suddenly I realized it was true. There never was
much happiness in my life. I rarely used the word love. Many people identified with my songs because they also experienced the same pain, day after
day."[20] Even his first hit, "Gypsy Woman," an upbeat dance tune overtly
about admiring love for an exoticized woman, is also tinged with a tone of
sadness, partly due to Bataan's own unpretentious, "ordinary guy" voice
with its characteristic flattening at the end of each line. Without being
gloomy or morose, his songs do not typically revel in the kind of ecstasy
and enthusiasm notable in most songs identified with Latin boogaloo.
They seem like the sounds left after the party is over, or coming from outside the party looking in. Their effect is not to dampen the festive atmosphere—thousands of young people have partied to his music over the
years—but they tend to remind the revelers of the hard, cold world around
them in everyday life. Their musical simplicity and apparent lack of sophistication are thus deceptive, and in no way negate the emotional depth
and homespun creativity of his fusions of Black and Latin cultural idioms.
Joe Bataan stands as the social conscience, and with his contributions to
the formation of later styles like disco and rap, the continuation of Latin
boogaloo as a cultural impulse of the 1960s.

BYE BYE BOOGALOO

"The Boogaloo didn't die out. It was killed off by envious old bandleaders, a
few dance promoters and a popular Latin disc jockey." By 1969, just three
years after its explosive entry onto the New York music scene, Latin boogaloo
was gone, and most musicians involved, young and older, agree with King
Nando's explanation of its rapid demise. "We were the hottest bands and we
drew the crowds. But we were never given top billing or top dollar. The
Boogaloo bandleaders were forced to accept 'package deals' which had us
hopping all over town . . . one hour here, one hour there . . . for small change.
When word got out we were going to unite and no longer accept the package
deals, our records were no longer played over the radio. The Boogaloo era was
over and so were the careers of most of the Boogaloo bandleaders."[21]

Not everyone bemoaned its passing in equal measure, of course, or
views it in such conspiratorial terms. The boogaloo was, after all, just another dance fad on the American pop scene and thus destined to a fleeting
life span and instant oblivion. Latin boogaloo was more than that, as it

marked an important intervention in the history of Latin music as well, and served as an expression of Puerto Rican and African American cultures in those pivotal years of their experience in New York. But in the name of boogaloo, rather than the broader Latin soul concept, the style was doomed to fade, as a new generation of young Latinos came to seek out something that they, too, could call their own. The "next big thing" for Latin music in New York went by the name of *salsa*.

"Boogaloo was eclipsed? Yeah, I guess so. And you know, thank God, in a way." Willie Torres, the veteran vocalist and composer in whose career boogaloo was just a phase, was relieved when the fever subsided, though he qualifies his judgment when he recalls the sheer fun they had playing music in those years. "Un vacilón," he says, "it was a goof." He himself didn't go on past boogaloo, leaving the music business in 1970 to take a job driving a bus with New York City's Municipal Transit Authority. But he is comforted to think that the proven musicians, abruptly sidelined by the boogaloo craze, did have a chance to come back and prove their longevity. "Sure, a lot of promising young talent got blocked, but look at Cheo Feliciano, Eddie Palmieri, Tito Puente, Ray Barretto, Larry Harlow . . . They and a lot of other greats survived the craze and went on to greater heights than ever." For Willie Torres, the main responsibility for the eclipse of boogaloo in the name of salsa, aside from the musicians themselves, was Fania Records. Though the category "salsa" did not come into currency until 1972, it was Fania that shook New York Latin music loose of the boogaloo and went on to define the sound of the 1970s to world audiences.

Boogaloo, shing-a-ling, jala jala—none of that was part of the package, nor was the fusion with R&B or the street origins of the music. The boogaloo musicians were not named to the Fania All-Stars, and none was present on that historic night at the Cheetah when "Our Latin Thing" was filmed. Not that Fania has been consistent in excising these sounds, having been the first to record Joe Bataan, Willie Colón, and other initiates. Fania's invaluable 1983 anthology '60's Gold, which includes many of the boogaloo classics, is evidence that the company was anything but conspiratorial in its marketing strategy. But Izzy Sanabria, sometimes called "Mr. Salsa" for his role as man-about-town master of ceremonies and publisher of *Latin New York* magazine, points to Fania in drawing the relationship between musical tastes and potential economic gain. "What destroyed it," he says, speaking of Latin boogaloo, "was a movement by Fania. And what happened was, Puente and the others, who were not with Fania at the time, put down the Latin Boogaloo because the kids were off clave. I mean eventually Puente recorded the Boogaloo. But you see, they were not on clave. They were not perfectly syncopated. But they were singing English lyrics. And this music became extremely popular. . . . So this was eventually eased out, in order to return to the more typical, correctly played music, supposedly. They were critical of all these kids. I mean Tito Puente used to describe Willie Colon as a kiddie band. Which it was."[22]

Because of the broad visibility achieved by salsa in the intervening years, the musician most widely (though mistakenly) associated with the inner-city, streetwise spirit of boogaloo is surely Willie Colón. Born in 1950, Colón was perhaps too young in the boogaloo days to participate and never recorded any boogaloos, either in name or in musical style. But his first album, *El Malo*, came out in 1967, during the height of boogaloo, and achieved great success. Though the musicianship of the "kiddie band" was widely scorned by knowing musicians, that and subsequent releases featured album covers establishing his identity as a "bad" street tough. Of course, Ray Barretto's 1967 album *Acid* was also a major hit of that year, which along with his all-time 1962 hit "El Watusi" makes him another Fania stalwart bearing a continuity with the boogaloo era. As is Larry Harlow, along with Johnny Pacheco perhaps the musical mastermind behind Fania, who dabbled—unsuccessfully—with boogaloo during those years. But it is Willie Colón, along with his vocalist Hector Lavoe whom many of the boogaloo musicians remember from the streets, that, justifiably or not, represents the bridge between the boogaloo era and the advent of salsa. As part of the Fania stable, he then went on to become "more and more of a force in this business," as Sanabria concludes, much to the "amazement" of Tito Puente.

But the "movement by Fania," its effort to establish a certain range of identifiable stylistic possibilities for its "salsa" concept, was more intent on change than continuity, at least with the immediate past. The emphasis would be on "roots," continued recovery and reworking of Afro-Cuban traditions in their varied combinations with jazz. English lyrics were out, as was any strong trace of R&B or funk. The rich legacies of Arsenio Rodríguez, Orquesta Aragón, Machito, Arcanio, and the whole *guaguancó*-son-mambo tradition took precedence over any experimentation with American pop styles. Even traditional Puerto Rican music, though always secondary to the Cuban, served as sources, as in the *danzas, aguinaldos, seises,* and plenas in a few of the landmark albums by

Eddie Palmieri and Willie Colón from the salsa period. Explicit musical references to the African roots of the music were typically via Cuba and the Caribbean, even in stereotypical terms as in one of Colón's biggest hits, "Che Che Colé."[23] The African American connection with the New York Latino community receded in prominence, at least in terms of vernacular musical styles. Willie Colón even raises the all-Spanish lyrics to a matter of principle, saying that "the language was all we have left. Why should we give in on that one?"[24] A point that is perhaps easier to insist on when you can count on the likes of a Tite Curet Alonso, the prolific Puerto Rican songwriter who composed many of Colón's most memorable lyrics.

"The Boogaloo might have been killed off," notes Latin music historian Max Salazar, "but Latin Soul lived on."[25] With a broader understanding of the musical and social experience called boogaloo, or salsa for that matter, and disengaging it from those commercially created categories, it becomes possible to see the continuity and coherence of the Latin–African American musical fusion in clearer historical perspective. Many of the musicians themselves preferred the idea of Latin soul all along, even during the peak of boogaloo's popularity, and the term may be seen to embrace musical styles both before and after the rise and fall of boogaloo, perhaps even including much of what has been called salsa. With the help of his guiding concept of "Afro-American Latinized rhythms," Salazar is able to identify an entire lineage of musical follow-through on the impulse of boogaloo, an inventory that includes not only direct holdovers from the era like Louie Ramírez, Bobby Marín and his Latin Chords, and Chico Mendoza, but unexpected standbys like Johnny Pacheco, Mongo Santamaría, and the Fania All-Stars, along with non-Caribbean Latinos like Santana and Jorge Dalto.

Dislodged from the power of Fania's formative influence, the term *salsa* itself can be thought of in more expansive and inclusive terms, and as is necessary a full twenty-five years after its "founding," can also be conceived in its various stages and tendencies. Maybe, as Tito Ramos suggests, boogaloo should be considered part of what he calls "salsa clásica" (as against the "salsa monga," "lame salsa," of more recent years), and its repertoire a significant inclusion among the "oldies" of the genre. Certainly the music radio programming in Puerto Rico and other parts of Latin America present it in that way, as do some of the recent anthologies of Latin music from the 1960s and 1970s. The sounds of Pete Rodríguez, Joe Cuba, and Richie Ray are still adored in countries like Colombia and Venezuela, and there no sharp distinction is made between those old favorites and what is called salsa.

In retrospect perhaps it is true, as is claimed by some commentators, that the most important influence of Latin boogaloo was not even in the Latin music field but on Black American music, it having been "one of the single most important factors in moving Black rhythm sections from a basic four-to-the-bar concept to tumbao-like bass and increasingly Latin percussive patterns."[26] That may be the case, but of course that impact started well before boogaloo, and it should be no reason to understate the change which that eclipsed era brought to Latin music, even if mainly by negative example. Growing out of a time of "strong Puerto Rican identification with Black politics and culture," cultural critic George Lipsitz has it, Latin boogaloo "led organically to a reconsideration of 'Cuban' musical styles . . . as, in fact, *Afro*-Cuban and . . . a general reawakening of the African elements within Puerto Rican culture. Condemned by traditionalists as a betrayal of the community, Latin Bugalú instead showed that the community's identity had always been formed in relation to that of other groups in the U.S.A."[27] Whatever musical elements of boogaloo might have been left behind, the social context of which it was an expression, the historical raison d'être of Latin soul, has only deepened through the years.

A Latin boogaloo revival? Many of the musicians speak of a rekindled interest on the part of the present generation, and the huge success of Tito Nieves' 1998 *I Like It Like That* album, which also contains still another cover of "Bang Bang," is an obvious indication. They also point to the enthusiasm of fans in Puerto Rico, Latin America, Western Europe, and Japan. In England it is now classified, along with kindred styles, as "Latin Acid" or "Acid Jazz," and much is included under that umbrella, from rereleases of Hector Rivera and Mongo Santamaría's old material to the work of Pucho and other African American musicians in the Latin groove. *The Latin Vogue, Nu Yorica: Culture Clash in New York City*, and *¡Sabroso! The Afro-Latin Groove* are some of the compilations of recent years, and all of them include Latin boogaloo classics and related and more recent material. The Relic label has even issued a collection titled *Vaya!!! R&B Groups Go Latin*, which comprises twenty tunes by doo-wop and R&B groups from the 1950s who mixed in mambo and other Latin rhythms, starting with the Crows' "Gee" and the Harptones' "Mambo Boogie" in 1954.

But a renewal of the spirit of boogaloo in our time, and a recuperation of some of the musical experiments seemingly left by the wayside, will need to be forward-looking and not just nostalgic. With the emergence of hip-hop in the late 1970s and 1980s, another common space was forged for joint African American and Latino musical expression, and again it was Black and Puerto Rican youth from New York City who created and laid first claim to that new terrain. As with boogaloo, it is again the African American dimension that appears most visible, but the Latino input can also be established.[28] Commercially successful acts like Mellow Man Ace and Cypress Hill introduced such fusions of rap and Latin sounds in the early 1990s, as have rappers in Puerto Rico and the Dominican Republic. Current salsa stars like La India and Marc Anthony were reared on rap and house and got their starts there, while salsa musicians as far-ranging as Manny Oquendo's Libre, El Gran Combo, and Tito Rojas have turned to rap techniques and collaborations to diversify their repertoire. Salsa in English, a long-standing crossover goal, is attempted with increasing frequency, though until now with minimal musical success. Surely it is in the context of such experiments, as the adjacent and kindred Black and Latino cultures continue to intermingle, that the spirit of Latin boogaloo may live on in the years ahead. Jimmy Sabater, the all-time master of "cha-cha with a backbeat," has that spirit in mind when he says, "Boogaloo? Boogaloo for me was basically an early form of rap."

Rick Rodriguez and Anthony Boston of Latin Empire (1992)

(Photo by Máximo R. Colón)

6

Puerto Rocks

RAP, ROOTS, AND AMNESIA

By the early 1990s, hip-hop had finally broken the language barrier. Though young Puerto Ricans from the South Bronx and El Barrio have been involved in breakdancing, graffiti writing, and rap music since the beginnings of hip-hop back in the 1970s, it is only belatedly that the Spanish language and Latin musical styles came into their own as integral features of the rap vocabulary. By the mid-nineties, acts like Mellow Man Ace, Kid Frost, Gerardo, and El General became household words among pop music fans nationwide and internationally, as young audiences of all nationalities came to delight in the catchy Spanglish inflections and the *guaguancó* and merengue rhythms lacing the familiar rap formats. Mellow Man Ace's "Mentirosa" was the first Latino rap record to go gold in the summer of 1990; Kid Frost's debut album *Hispanic Causing Panic* instantly became the rap anthem of La Raza in the same year; Gerardo as "Rico Suave" has his place as the inevitable Latin lover sex symbol; and El General has established the immense popularity of Spanish-language reggae-rap in the Caribbean and Latin America.

Who are these first Latin rap superstars and where are they from? Mellow Man Ace was born in Cuba and raised in Los Angeles, Kid Frost is a Chicano from East L.A., Gerardo is from Ecuador, and El General is Panamanian. But what about the Puerto Ricans, who with their African American homeboys created hip-hop styles in the first place? They are, as usual, conspicuous for their absence, and the story is no less startling for all its familiarity. Latin Empire, for example, the only Nuyorican act to gain some exposure among wider audiences, is still struggling for its first major record deal. Individual emcees and deejays have been scattered in well-known groups like the Fearless Four and the Fat Boys, their Puerto Rican backgrounds all but invisible. Even rap performers from Puerto Rico like Vico C, Lisa M, and Rubén DJ, who grew up far from the streets where hip-hop originated, enjoy greater commercial success and media recognition than any of the Puerto Rican b-boys from the New York scene.

This omission, of course, is anything but fortuitous and has as much to do with the selective vagaries of the music industry as with the social placement of the Puerto Rican community in the prevailing racial-cultural hierarchy. As the commercialization process involves the extraction of popular cultural expression from its original social context and function, it seems that the "Latinization" of hip-hop has meant its distancing from the specific national and ethnic traditions to which it had most directly pertained. But instead of simply bemoaning this evident injustice, or groping for elaborate explanations, it is perhaps more worthwhile to trace the history of this experience from the perspectives of some of the rappers themselves. For if New York Puerto Ricans have had scant play within the "Hispanic rap market," they have one thing that other Latino rappers do not, which is a history in hip-hop since its foundation as an emergent cultural practice among urban youth.

Such an emphasis is not meant to imply any inherent aesthetic judgment, nor does it necessarily involve a privileging of origins or presumed authenticity. Yet it is easy to understand and sympathize with the annoyance of a veteran Puerto Rican deejay like Charlie Chase when faced with the haughty attitudes he encountered among some of the rap superstars from the Island. "The thing about working with these Puerto Rican rappers," he commented, reflecting on his work producing records for the likes of Lisa M and Vico C, "they are very arrogant! You know, because they are from Puerto Rico, and I'm not, right? I feel kind of offended, but my comeback is like, well, yeah, if you want to be arrogant about that, then what are you doing in rap? You're not a rapper. You learned rap from listening to me and other people from New York!"[1] Actually this apprenticeship was probably less direct than Charlie Chase claims, since they more likely got to know rap through the recordings, videos, and concert appearances of Run DMC, LL Cool J, and Big Daddy Kane than through any familiarity with the New York hip-hop scene of the early years.

Where did those first platinum-selling rappers themselves go to learn the basics of rap performance? Again, Charlie Chase can fill us in, by remembering the shows he deejayed with the Cold Crush Brothers back in the early 1980s. "When we were doing shows, you know who was in the audience? The Fat Boys. Whodini. Run DMC, L.L. Cool J, Big Daddy Kane. Big Daddy Kane told me a story one time, he said, 'You don't know how much I loved you guys.' He said, 'I wanted to see you guys so bad, and my mother told me not to go to Harlem World to see you guys perform because if she found out I did she'd kick my ass!' And he said, 'I didn't care, I went. And I went every week. And I wouldn't miss any of your shows.' That's how popular we were with the people who are the rappers today."

To speak of Puerto Ricans in rap means to defy the sense of instant amnesia that engulfs popular cultural expression once it is caught up in the logic of commercial representation. It involves sketching in historical contexts and sequences, tracing traditions and antecedents, and recognizing hip-hop to be more and different than the simulated images, poses, and formulas the public discourse of media entertainment tends to reduce it to. The decade and more of hindsight provided by the Puerto Rican involvement shows that, rather than a new musical genre and its accompanying stylistic trappings, rap constitutes a space for the articulation of social experience. From this perspective, what has emerged as "Latin rap" first took shape as an expression of the cultural turf shared, and contended for, by African Americans and Puerto Ricans over their decades as neighbors, coworkers, and "homies" in the inner-city communities. As vernacular cultural production prior to its commercial and technological mediation, hip-hop formed part of a more extensive and intricate field of social practice, a significant dimension of which comprises the long-standing and ongoing interaction between Puerto Rican and Black youth in the shared New York settings. Not only is the contextual field wider, but the historical reach is deeper and richer as well: the Black and Puerto Rican conjunction in the formation of rap is prefigured in important ways in doo-wop, Latin boogaloo, Nuyorican poetry, and a range of other testimonies to intensely overlapping and intermingling expressive repertoires. Thus when Latin Empire comes out with "I'm Puerto Rican and Proud, Boyee!" they are actually marking off a decisive moment in a tradition of cultural and political identification that goes back several generations.

I have gained access to this largely uncharted terrain by way of conversations and interviews with some of the protagonists of Puerto Rican rap. Early hip-hop movies like *Wild Style* and *Style Wars*, which documented and dramatized the prominent participation of Puerto Ricans, sparked my initial interest and led to a burst of research (which hardly anyone took seriously at the time) and a short article published in various English and Spanish versions in the mid-1980s. At that time, the only adequate written consideration of Puerto Ricans had to do with their role in the New York graffiti movement, as in the excellent book *Getting Up* by Craig Castleman and an important article by Herbert Kohl. Steven Hager's *Hip-Hop* includes a valuable social history of youth culture in the South Bronx and Harlem at the dawn of hip-hop, with some attention to the part played by Puerto Ricans in graffiti, breakdance, and rap music.[2] Otherwise, and since those earlier accounts, coverage of Puerto Rican rap has been limited to an occasional article in the *Village Voice* or *Spin* magazine, generally as a sideline concern in discussions of wider style rubrics like "Hispanic," "Spanish," or "bilingual" rap. Primary evidence of a historical kind is even harder to come by, since Puerto Rican rhymes were never recorded for public distribution and many have been forgotten even by their authors.

CHASIN' THE FLASH

Charlie Chase calls himself "New York's Number One Puerto Rican DJ," and that's how he's been known since back in the seventies when he was blasting the hottest dance music on the waves of WBLS and in the early eighties when he was deejay for the legendary Cold Crush Brothers. When he says "Number One," he means not only the best but also the first: "When I started doing rap, there were no Hispanics doing it. If there were I didn't know about it. Anyway, I was the first Hispanic to become popular doing what I did. I was a deejay."

Charlie was born in El Barrio in the 1950s, and though his family moved a lot it was always from one Puerto Rican and Black neighborhood to another. "I grew up in Williamsburg from the age of two to nine. I moved to the Bronx, on Brook Avenue and 141st, !que eso por allí es candela! I grew up there from ten to about thirteen, then I moved back to Brooklyn, over in Williamsburg, Montrose Avenue, por allá on Broadway. Then we moved back to the Bronx again, 161st and Yankee Stadium. From there we went to 180th and Arthur, and from there it was Grand Concourse and 183rd, then Valentine and 183rd, then back to 180th. I mean, we moved, man! I've been all over the place, and it's like I've had the worst of both worlds, you know what I mean?"

Charlie's parents came from Mayagüez, Puerto Rico. Though family visits to the Island were rare, that Puerto Rican background remained an active influence throughout his upbringing. At home he was raised on Puerto Rican music. "You see I always listened to my mother's records. She was the one who bought all the Latin records. She bought them all. She bought Tito Puente, she was into trios, el Trio Los Condes." Even his career in music seems to have been handed down to him as part of that ancestry. "I come from a family of musicians. My grandfather was a writer and a musician; he played in bands. So did my father; he played in trios. So I kind of followed in their footsteps. My father left me when I was ten and I never learned music from him; he didn't teach me how to play instruments. For some reason or other, it must have been in the blood, I just picked up the guitar and wanted to learn."

Charlie makes clear that he didn't start off in rap or as a deejay. "I'm a bass player. I played in a Spanish ballad band, merengue band, salsa band, rock band, funk band, Latin rock band. I produced my first album at the age of sixteen and it was a Spanish ballad album. We played with the best, Johnny Ventura, Johnny Pacheco, Los Hijos del Rey, Tito Puente. The name of the group was Los Giramundos." So it turns out that Charlie Chase, famed deejay for the Cold Crush Brothers, started off gigging in a Latin band when he was fifteeen years old and could have had a whole career in salsa. "Yeah," he recalls, "but there was no money in it. There were a lot of people being ripped off. . . . I said, man, I want to do something else." Fortunately, he did have somewhere to turn, for alongside his inherited Latin tradition there was his dance music and R&B. Talking about his transition to deejaying he remembers: "I was a music lover. I grew up listening to WABC, Cousin Brucie, Chuck Leonard, all of these guys, and I was always into music. In school I would always have the radio on. It was always a big influence in my life and then I turned into a musician. I started playing with the band, and then a few years later I got into deejaying, and then the deejaying was making more money for me than the band."

It all seems to make sense, I thought, but what about that name? What's a Puerto Rican doing with a name like Charlie Chase? "My name was Carlos," he said. "Charlie is a nickname for Carlos." Fine, I said, but what about Chase? "Chase?" he repeated, hesitantly. "There is a story behind that which I never told anybody, and I don't know if I want to say it. Because when this person reads this, he is going to be so souped." (Little was I to know how much this little story has to say about the situation of young Puerto Ricans in the early days of rap.) "I made up my name because of Grandmaster Flash. Flash is a friend of mine. I first saw Flash doing this, cutting and all of this, and I saw that and I said, aw, man, I can do this. I was deejaying at the time, but I wasn't doing the scratching and shit and I said, I can do this, man. I'll rock this, you know. And I practiced, I broke turntables, needles, everything. Now 'Chase' came because I'm like, damn, you need a good name, man. And Flash was on top and I was down here. So I was chasing that niggah. I wanted to be up where he was. So I said, let's go with Charlie Chase."

There's no telling how "souped" Grandmaster Flash will get when he finds out, but his friend and main rival (along with Grandmaster Theo) back in the days, grew up as Carlos Mandes. "It's Mandes," Charlie emphasized, "m-a-n-d-e-s. Not Méndez." Whatever the origin of his Puerto Rican name, ever since he started chasing the Flash Carlos Mandes has been known, by everyone, as Charlie Chase. He doesn't even like it when "Mandes" appears on the records he wrote. "Nobody knows my name was Carlos Mandes. They'd laugh. They'd snap on me."

Charlie might think that Mandes sounds corny now, but at the time the problem was that it didn't fit. He never tires of telling about how difficult it was to be accepted as a Puerto Rican in rap, especially as a deejay, and because he was so good. "A lot of Blacks would not accept that I was Spanish. You know, a lot of times because of the way I played they thought I was Black, because I rocked it so well." As a deejay he was usually seated in back, behind the emcees and out of sight. In the beginning, in fact, his invisibility was a key to success. "I became popular because of the tapes, and also because nobody could see me. Since they thought I was Black, you know, because I was in the background." Even when they saw him, he says that "they still wouldn't believe it. They are like, 'no, that's not him! That's bullshit! That's not him!' A few years went by and they accepted it, you know. I was faced with a lot of that. You know, being Hispanic you're not accepted in rap. Because to them it's a Black thing and something that's from their roots and shit."

"What the fuck are you doing here, Puerto Rican?" Charlie remembers being faced with that challenge time and again when he went behind the ropes, among the rappers, at the early jams. He had to prove himself constantly, and he recalls vividly the times when it took his homeboy Tony Tone from DJ Breakout and Baron to step in and save his skin. "I turn around and see him breaking on them and I hear what he's saying and I'm like, oh shit!" As tough as it got, though, Charlie knew very well that he wasn't out of place. "I was the type of kid that, you know, I always grew up with Black people. . . . My daughter's godfather is Black. He's like my brother, that guy."

But the best proof was that Charlie was with the Cold Crush Brothers, who were all Black. "We all grew up in the streets, man. It's like a street thing. Once you see that the guy is cool, then you're accepted, everything flows correctly." And it's not that Charlie just did everything like the other brothers, to fit in. Aside from his "mancha de plátano," those indelible earmarks of the Puerto Rican, he had his own personal style about him that he wasn't about to give up just to be one of the boys. He remembers about Cold Crush that "the only thing was, it was a trip when it came to the dressing bit. You see, I don't dress like the average hip-hopper and never did. They wanted to wear Kangols, Martin X, and these British walkers and all that stuff at the time, and I was like, that's not me, fellas. That's not me, man. At that time, I combed my hair back in a DA." Not only did he refuse to fit the mold, but Charlie's insistence helped the group arrive at the look that helped to establish their immense popularity in those years. "We came up with a look that everybody copied afterwards, which we all felt comfortable with. It was the leather and stud look, which we popularized in rap and through that look we became hard."

Besides, as alone as he was sometimes made to feel, Charlie knew that he wasn't the only Puerto Rican who was into rap. "Hispanics always liked rap, young Puerto Ricans were into it since the beginning. I wasn't the only one who felt the same way about music like that. There were plenty of them, but they didn't have the talent, they just enjoyed it. Me, I wanted to do it, you know. Forget it, there were plenty of people. I mean, when you grow up in the streets, it's a street thing, man." In its street beginnings, Puerto Ricans were an integral part of the rap scene, and not only as appreciative fans. Though their participation in production and performance was submerged (far more so than in breaking and graffiti), they were an essential and preponderant presence in the security crews that, in the gang environment, made the whole show possible. "It was rough, man," Charlie recalls. "All of my crew, the whole crew, were Spanish, maybe two or three Black guys. They were all Spanish, and when we jammed we had bats. If you crossed the line or got stupid, you were going to get batted down, alright? And that was that. That was my crew, they would help me with records, they were security. The guys in my group were Black, but the rest of the guys, security, were Hispanic. . . . People'd be like, yo, those are some wild Spanish motherfuckers. Don't mess with them, man."

But with a little coaxing Charlie will even call to mind some other Puerto Rican rappers from those days. There was Prince Whipper Whip and Ruby D (Rubén García) from the Fantastic Five, OC from the Fearless Four with Tito Cepeda, Johnny who was down with Master Don and the Def Committee. "Then there was this one group," Charlie recalls, "that wanted to do Latin rap songs, way back. And they had good ideas and they had great songs, but they just didn't have enough drive, you know? They had a great idea, they had a routine. They had these crazy nice songs, but they just weren't ambitious enough. . . . Robski and June Bug, those were the guys." Years before anybody started talking about "Latin rap," Robski and June Bug were busy working out Spanglish routines and even rendering some of the best rhymes of the time into Spanish. "They took our songs and translated them into Spanish. They blew our heads, man! It was weird, because they actually took everything we said and turned it into Spanish and made it rhyme. And they did a good job of it."

But in those days using Spanish in rap was still a rarity, especially in rhymes that were distributed on tapes and records. It wasn't only lack of ambition that prevented Robski and June Bug from making it, " 'cause at that time," Charlie says, "a lot of people were doing it underground, but they couldn't come off doing it, they couldn't make money doing it. The people that did it, did it in parties, home stuff, the block, they were the stars in their ghetto." But Charlie himself, "chasing the Flash," was with the first rap group to be signed by CBS Records, the first rap group to tour Japan, the group that played in the first hip-hop movie, *Wild Style*. At that level, rapping in Spanish was still out of the question. Charlie explains what it was like for him to face this constraint, and gives a clear sense of the delicate generational process involved in the entry of bilingualism into commercially circumscribed rap discourse. "I always stressed the point that I was Hispanic doing rap music, but I couldn't do it in Spanish, you understand? But that was my way of opening the doors for everybody else to do what they're doing now. You see, there are certain degrees, certain levels and steps that you have to follow. And being that I was there at the very beginning, that was the I way I had to do it, that was my contribution. I feel sorry that I couldn't do it then, but I want to do it now and I'm making up for it, because now I can. . . . I wanted everybody to know that I was Spanish, rocking, ripping shit up. In a Black market."

At that early stage in negotiating Puerto Rican identity in rap, the key issue was not language but what Charlie calls "the Latin point of view";

pushing rhymes in Spanish was not yet part of the precarious juggling act. "For me it's the Latin point of view. You see, what I emphasize is that I'm Hispanic in a Black world. Not just surviving but making a name for myself and leaving a big impression. Everything that happened to me was always within the Black music business, and I always was juggling stuff all of the time, because I had to be hip, I had to be a homeboy. But I also had to know how far to go without seeming like I was trying to kiss up or something, or 'he's just trying to be Black.' When you deal with the people I deal with, especially at a time when rap was just hard core and raw, you're talking about guys who were *títeres*, you know, tough guys. I had to juggle that. I had to play my cards correct."

If Spanish wasn't yet part of the "Latin point of view," the music was, especially the rhythmic texture of the songs which is where as the deejay Charlie was in control. He remembers sneaking in the beat from the number "Tú Coqueta," right "in the middle of a jam. I'm jamming, I throw that sucker in, just the beat alone, and they'd go off. They never knew it was a Spanish record. And if I told them that they'd get off the floor." Even the other rappers couldn't tell because the salsa cuts seemed to fit in so perfectly. "It was great! I would sneak in Spanish records. Beats only, and if the bass line was funky enough, I would do that too. Bobby Valentín stuff. He played bass with the Fania All-Stars, and he would do some funky stuff." As a bassist in Latin bands, Charlie knew the repertoire to choose from.

But he also knew that he had to walk a fine line and that he was ahead of his time, not only for the R&B-savvy rappers but for Latin musical tastes as well. In fact it was because of the resistance he faced from the Latin musicians, and not only the better pay, that Charlie decided to leave Los Giramundos and go into rap full time. "Sometimes I'd go to gigs and in between songs I'd start playing stuff from rap music and the drummer would like it too, and he'd start doing some stuff. And sometimes people would get up to dance to it and the rest of the guys in the band would get furious at us, and they would say, 'What are you doing? If you're not going to play a song, don't do it.' They would break on me. They didn't want that stuff." Not that Charlie didn't try to interest Latin musicians in mixing some elements of rap into their sound. He especially remembers working on a record concept with Willie Colón. "He could have had the first Latin hip-hop record out and it would have been a hit. It was a singing rap. He was singing, right, there was a little bit of rap, and I was scratching. I did the arrangements. What happened was, the project was being held and held and held. What happened? He put out the record, an instrumental! He took out all the raps, then he overdubbed. Killed the whole project. He slept on it."

But as Charlie learned early on, when it comes to the emergence of new styles in popular music it's all a matter of timing. He himself had trouble relating to the use of Spanish in rap when he first heard it on record. Back in 1981 the group Mean Machine came out with the first recorded Spanish rhymes in their "Disco Dream," a side that deeply impressed some of the present-day Latino rappers like Mellow Man Ace and Latin Empire when they first heard it, though that was some years after it was released. But Charlie knew Mean Machine when they started and recalls his reaction when "Disco Dream" first came out. "It was strange, and it was new. At first I didn't jive with it because I was so used to and I myself got so caught up in that whole R&B thing that when I heard that, it didn't click with me. And I was like, 'Naw, this is bullshit!.' " But with time tastes changed, as did Charlie's understanding of himself and his own role. "And then," he goes on, "something made me realize one day that, wait a minute, man, look at you, what are you? You don't rap like they do, but you're Hispanic just like them, trying to get a break in the business. And I said, if anything, this is something cool and new."

Seen in retrospect, Mean Machine was only a faint hint of what was to become Latino rap in the years ahead. The Spanish they introduced amounted to a few party exhortations rather than an extended Spanish or bilingual text. Charlie draws this distinction, and again points up the changing generations of Latino presence in rap.

"The way that they did it was not like today. Today it's kind of political, opinionated, and commercial, and storytelling. What they did was that they took a lot of Spanish phrases, like 'uepa' and 'dale fuego a la lata, fuego a la lata,' stuff like that, and turned them into a record." However perfunctory their bilingualism and fleeting their acclaim, Mean Machine's early dabbling with Spanglish rhymes did plant a seed. Puerto Rock of Latin Empire attests to the impact "Disco Dream" had on them: "They didn't continue. After one record, that was it. I know them all, we keep in contact. Mr. Schick came out with, 'Tire su mano al aire / Yes, means throw your hands in the air / y siguen con el baile means / dance your body till you just don't care.' And then it ended up with, 'Fuego a la lata, fuego a la lata / agua que va caer.' So we were like bugging! We were more or less doing it but in English and got crazy inspired when we heard that record. We was like, Oh, snap! He wrote the first Spanish rhyme! We was skeptical if it was going to work, and when we heard the record we were like, it's going to work."[3]

The disbelief and strategic invisibility that surrounded Latino participation in rap performance in the early years gave way to a fascination with something new and different. Charlie sees this process reflected in the changing fate of his own popularity among hip-hop audiences. "It was kind of complicated," he recalls. If at first he became popular because "nobody could see me," he later became even more popular because "everyone found out I was Hispanic. And it was like, 'yo, this kid is Spanish!' and 'What? Yo, we've got to see this!' " Once he began to feel this sense of curiosity and openness, a new stage appeared in rap history, and Charlie was quick to recognize its potential, commercially and politically. He tells of how his enthusiasm caught the attention among some of the Latin musicians, especially his friend Tito Puente, who seemed to be fondly reminded of their own breakthrough a generation before. "These guys, they love it. Because for one, it's for them getting back out into the limelight again, you know, in a different market. . . . The musicians are very impressed to see that somebody like me wants to work with them in my style of music. And when I tell them about my history they are very impressed because in their day, when they came out, they were the same way. When Tito Puente came out, he was doing the mambo and it was all something new. It was all new to him, too. So he can relate to what I'm doing. And for him it's almost like a second coming."

After the decade it has taken for Puerto Rican rap to come into its own, Charlie now feels that the time is right for the two sides of his musical life to come together, and for full-fledged "salsa-rap" to make its appearance. "For this next record I want to do a project, where I want to get all the East Coast rappers together, I want to get POW, I want to get Latin Empire, I want to get a few other guys that are unknown but that are good. I want to join them, I want to bring in Luis 'Perico' Ortíz, I want to bring Tito, I want to bring Ray Barretto, you know. Bring them to handle all the percussion stuff and then my touch would be to bring in the rap loops, the beats, the bass lines, the programming. I'll program and also arrange it. And they will come in, Luis 'Perico' would do the whole horn section, Tito would come in and handle all the percussion section, and Ray Barretto would handle the congas. And I would get my friend Sergio who is a tremendous piano player, a young kid, he's about twenty-four, twenty-five now, he works for David Maldonado. I just want to kick this door wide open, once and for all, and that's the way I'm going to do it."

As ambitious as such a project may sound, bringing together Puerto Rican musicians across musical traditions is only half of Charlie's strategy for promoting Latino unity. For "if any Hispanics want to make it in this business," he claims, "they've got to learn to pull together, no matter where you're coming from, or it's not going to work. It's not going to work, man. Kid Frost on the West Coast right now, he's got a little thing going. He and I are working around a few things. He's got his Latin Alliance on the West Coast. I've got a lot of Latin people who work with me on this. I'm trying to form something here where we can merge, cover the whole United States. That's the best way we can do it, if we unify."

Yet with his repeated emphasis on Latino unity, Charlie has more than commercial success in mind. His own experience, he now feels, leads him to set his sights on the political and educational potential of his musical efforts. "Because what I did, I had to unite with Black people to get my success and become Charlie Chase, 'New York's Number One Puerto Rican DJ.' Ironically, I did it with Black people. Which proves, man, that anybody can get together and do it. If I did it with Black people, then Hispanics can do it with Hispanics and do a much better job. That's my whole purpose right now. I mean, I have made my accomplishments, I have become famous doing my thing in rap, I have respect. Everybody knows me in the business. I have all of that already, man. I've tasted the good life, I've toured the world, I've done all of that. Now I want to do something meaningful and helpful. Hopefully, because a lot of kids are being steered the wrong way."

PUERTO ROCKS

Moving into the 1990s, then, the prospects and context have changed for Latino rap. Hugely popular albums like *Latin Alliance, Dancehall Reggaespañol* and *Cypress Hill* have been called a "polyphonic outburst" marking the emergence of "the 'real' Latin hip-hop." Kid Frost's assembly of Latin Alliance is referred to as "a defining moment in the creation of a nation-wide Latino/Americano hip-hop aesthetic." Unity of Chicanos and Puerto Ricans, which has long eluded politicos and admen, is becoming a reality in rap, and its potential impact on the culture wars seems boundless: "Where once the folks on opposite coasts were strangers, they've become one nation kicking Latin lingo on top of a scratch', samplin' substrate. . . . There is no question that we are entering an era when the multicultural essence of Latino culture will allow for a kind of shaking-out process that will help define the Next Big Thing."[4] Not only is the use of Spanish and bilingual rhyming accepted, but it has even become a theme in some of the best-known rap lyrics, like Kid Frost's "Ya Estuvo," Cypress Hill's "Funky Bi-lingo," and Latin Empire's "Palabras." Latino rappers are cropping up everywhere, from the tongue-twisting, "trabalengua" Spanglish of one Chicago-Rican group to the lively current of Tex-Mex rap in New Mexico and Arizona.[5] And it's not only the rappers themselves who have been building these bicultural bridges: Latin musical groups as varied as El Gran Combo, Wilfredo Vargas, Manny Oquendo's Libre, and Los Pleneros de la 21 have all incorporated rap segments and numbers into their repertoire.

But while he shares these high hopes, a seasoned veteran of "the business" like Charlie Chase remains acutely aware of the pitfalls and distortions involved. After all, he had witnessed firsthand what was probably the first and biggest scam in rap history, when Big Bad Hank and Sylvia Robinson of Sugar Hill Records used a rhyme by his close friend and fellow Cold Crush brother Grandmaster Cas on "Rapper's Delight" and never gave him credit. The story has been told elsewhere, as by Steven Hager in his book, but Charlie's is a lively version. "This is how it happened. Hank was working in a pizzeria in New Jersey, flipping pizza. And he's playing Cas' tape, right? Sylvia Robinson walks in, the president of Sugar Hill. She's listening to this, it's all new to her. Mind you, there were never any rap records. She says, 'Hey, man, who's this?' He says, 'I manage this guy. He's a rapper.' She says, 'Can you do this? Would you do this on a record for me?' And he said, 'Yeah, sure. No problem.' And she says, 'Okay, fine.' So he calls Cas up and says, 'Cas, can I use your rhymes on a record? Some lady wants to make a record.' You see what happened? Cas didn't have foresight. He couldn't see down the road. He never imagined in a million years what was going to come out of that. He didn't know, so he said, 'Sure, fine, go ahead.' With no papers, no nothing. And it went double platinum! Double platinum! 'Rapper's Delight.' A single. A double platinum single, which is a hard thing to do."

Charlie doesn't even have to go that far back to reflect on how commercial interests tend to glamorize and, in his word, "civilize" rap sources. He tells of his own efforts to land a job as an A&R (artist and repertoire) person with a record label. "All of this knowledge, all of this experience. I have the ear, I'm producing for all of these people. I mean, I know. You cannot get a more genuine person than me. I can't get a job." The gatekeepers of the industry could hardly be farther removed from the vitality of hip-hop. "I go to record labels to play demos for A&R guys that don't know a thing about rap. They talk to me and they don't even know who I am. White guys that live in L.A. Forty years old, thirty-five years old, making seventy, a hundred thousand a year, and they don't know a thing! And they're picking records to sell, and half of what they're picking is bullshit. And I'm trying to get somewhere and I can't do it."

As for promoting bilingual rap, the obstacles are of course compounded, all the talk of "pan-Latin unity" notwithstanding. "Not that long ago," Charlie mentions, "Latin Empire was having trouble with a Hispanic promoter at Atlantic Records who wouldn't promote their records. You know what he told them? (And he's a Latino.) He told them, 'Stick to one language.' And that's negative, man. You're up there, man, pull the brother up." And of course it's not only the limits on possible expressive idioms that signal a distortion but the media's ignorance of rap's origins. *Elle* magazine, for example, announced that Mellow Man Ace "has been crowned the initiator of Latin rap," their only evident source being Mellow Man himself: "I never thought it could be done. Then in 1985 I heard Mean Machine do a 20-second Spanish bit on their 'Disco Dream.' I bugged out." And the Spanish-language *Más* magazine then perpetuated the myth by proclaiming that it was Mellow Man Ace "quien concibió la idea de hacer rap en español" ("whose idea it was to do rap in Spanish").[6]

The problem is that in moving "from the barrio to *Billboard*," as Kid Frost puts it, Latino rappers have faced an abrupt redefinition of function and practice. The ten-year delay in the acceptance of Spanish rhymes was due in no small part to the marketing of rap, through the eighties, as a strictly African American musical style with a characteristically Afrocentric message. Charlie Chase confronted this even among some of his fellow rappers at the New Music Seminar in 1990 and appealed to his own historical authority to help set the record straight. "I broke on a big panel. Red Alert, Serch from Third Base, Chuck D, the guys from the West Coast, these are all my boys, mind you, these are all of my friends. So I went off on these guys because they were like 'Black this, and Black music', and I said 'Hold it!' I jumped up and I said, 'Hold up, man. What are you talking about, a Black thing, man? I was part of the Cold Crush Brothers, man. We opened doors for all you guys.' And the crowd went berserk, man. And I grabbed the mike and I just started going off. I'm like, 'Not for nothing, man, but don't knock it. It's a street thing. I liked it because it came from the street and I'm from the street. I'm a product of the environment.' I said that to Serch, I pointed to Serch, 'cause that's his record from his album. And I said, 'Yo, man, rap is us. You're from the street, that's you man, that's rap. It ain't no Black, White or nothing thing, man. To me, rap is colorblind, that's that!' The niggahs were applauding me and stuff. I got a lot of respect for that."

Latin Empire has had to put forth the same argument in explaining their own project. As Rick Rodríguez aka "Puerto Rock" puts it, "When it comes to hip-hop I never pictured it with a color." They too are a "product of the environment" and see no need to relinquish any of their Puerto Rican background. "Our influence," Puerto Rock says, "is the stuff you see around you. Things you always keep seeing in the ghetto. But they don't put it in art. It's streetwise. The styles, the fashions, the music is not just for one group. Everybody can do it. But too many Puerto Ricans don't understand. There's a big group of Latinos that's into hip-hop, but most of them imitate Black style or fall into a trance. They stop hanging out with Latin people and talking Spanish. I'm proving you can rap in Spanish and still be dope." Puerto Rock's cousin and partner in Latin Empire, Anthony Boston aka MC KT, has had to deal even more directly with this stereotype of rap, as he is often mistaken for a young African American and was raised speaking more English than Spanish. KT's rhymes in "We're Puerto Rican and Proud!" serve to clarify the issue:

> I rarely talk Spanish and a little trigueño
> People be swearin' I'm a moreno
> Pero guess what? I'm Puertorriqueño.
> Word 'em up.
> All jokes aside, I ain't tryin' to dis any race
> and

> *Puerto Rock*
> He'll announce everyplace . . .

> *M.C. KT*
> That I'll perform at, so chill, don't panic
> It is just me, Antonio, another deso Hispanic.

To drive the point home, the initials KT stand for "Krazy Taino": "It's fly," Puerto Rock comments. "With a 'K,' and the 'r' backwards like in Toys-R-

Us. In our next video he's going to wear all the chief feathers and that. Nice image. With all the medallions and all that we've got. Like in Kid Frost in his video, he wears the Mexican things. That's dope, I like that. Tainos have a lot to do with Puerto Ricans and all that, so we're going to boost it up too. Throw it in the lyrics."

But KT didn't always signal the Puerto Rican cultural heritage, and in fact the derivation of their names shows that their struggle for identity has been a response against the stereotyped symbolism of rap culture. "MC KT is his name because before Latin Empire we were called the Solid Gold MCs. KT stood for karat, like in gold." The group gave up the faddish cliché Solid Gold because they had no jewelry and didn't like what it stood for anyway. When they started, in the early eighties, "We worked with a few different trend names. We started off with our name, our real names, our nicknames. Like Tony Tone, Ricky D, Ricky Rock, all of that. Everything that came out, Rick-ski, every fashion. Double T, Silver T, all of these wild Ts." After trying on all the conformist labels, Rick finally assumed the identity that was given him, as a Puerto Rican, in the African American hip-hop nomenclature itself; he came to affirm what marked him off. "And then I wound up coming up with Puerto Rock," he explains, "and I like that one. That's the one that clicked the most. The Puerto Ricans that are into the trend of hip-hop and all that, they call them Puerto Rocks. They used to see the Hispanics dressing up with the hat to the side and all hip-hop down and some assumed that we're supposed to just stick to our own style of music and friends. They thought rap music was only a Black thing, and it wasn't. Puerto Ricans used to be all crazy with their hats to the side and everything. So that's why they used to call the Puerto Ricans when they would see them with the hats to the side, 'Yo, look at that Puerto Rock, like he's trying to be down.' They used to call us Puerto Rocks, so that was a nickname, and I said, 'I'm going to stick with that. Shut everybody up.'"

The name the group's members chose to replace Solid Gold was arrived at somewhat more fortuitously, but equally reflects their effort to situate themselves in an increasingly multicultural hip-hop landscape. "Riding around in the car with our manager, DJ Corchado, we were trying to think of a Latin name. We was like, the Three Amigos, the Latin Employees, for real, we came up with some crazy names. We kept on, 'cause we didn't want to limit ourselves, with Puerto Rican something, yeah, the Puerto Rican MCs. We wanted Latin something, to represent all Latinos. So we was the Two Amigos, the Three Amigos, then we came up with many other names, Latin Imperials, Latin Alliance. And then when we were driving along the Grand Concourse my manager's car happened to hit a bump when I came out with the Latin Employees. Joking around, we were just making fun and when the car hit the bump my manager thought I said 'Empire.' I was like, what? Latin Empire! I was like, yo, that's it! As soon as they said it, it clicked. It's like a strong title, like the Zulu Nation."

Groping for names that click, of course, is part of the larger process of positioning themselves in the changing cultural setting of the later eighties. The decision to start rhyming in Spanish was crucial and came more as an accommodation to their families and neighbors than from hearing Mean Machine or any other trends emerging in hip-hop. "In the beginning it was all in English and our families, all they do is play salsa and merengue, they thought you were American. They considered it noise. "Ay, deja ese alboroto,' 'cut out that racket,' you know. We said, 'Let's try to do it in Spanish, so that they can understand it, instead of complaining to us so much.' They liked it. They was like, 'Oh, mi hijo.' " And when they tried out their Spanish with the mostly Black hip-hop audiences, they were encouraged further. "We used to walk around with the tapes and the big radios and the Black people behind us, 'Yo, man, that sounds dope, that's fly!' They be like, 'yo, I don't understand it, man, but I know it's rhyming and I hear the last word, man, that's bad' they be telling us. We was like, oh, snap! Then I used to try to do it in the street jams and the crowd went crazy."

Acceptance and encouragement from the record industry was a different story, especially in those times before Mellow Man Ace broke the commercial ice. Atlantic did wind up issuing "We're Puerto Rican and Proud," but not until after "Mentirosa" went gold, and then they dragged their feet in promoting it. Since then, aside from their tours and the video "Así Es la Vida" which made the charts on MTV Internacional, Latin Empire has been back in the parks and community events. They believe strongly in the strong positive messages of some rap and have participated actively in both the Stop the Violence and Back to School campaigns. They pride themselves on practicing what they preach in their antidrug and antialcohol rhymes. They continue to be greeted with enthusiastic approval by audiences of all nationalities throughout New York City, and on their tours to Puerto Rico, the Dominican Republic, and, most recently, Cuba.

Their main shortcoming, in the parlance of the business, is that they don't have an "act," a packaged product. As the author of "The Packaging of a Recording Artist" in the July 1992 issue of *Hispanic Business* suggests,

"To 'make it' as a professional recording act, you must have all the right things in place. Every element of what a recording act is must be considered and exploited to that act's benefit. The sound, the image, the look—all these factors must be integrated into a single package and then properly marketed to the public." In the packaging and marketing process, the artists and the quality of their work are of course secondary; it's the managers, and the other gatekeepers, who make the act. The article ends, "So while quality singing and a good song are the product in this business, they don't count for much without strong management."7

The pages of *Hispanic Business* make no mention of Latin Empire, concentrating as they do on the major Hispanic "products" like Gerardo, Exposé, and Angelica. What they say about Kid Frost is most interesting because here they are dealing with a Latino rapper who is "on his way to stardom in the West Coast Hispanic community" and cannot be expected to "lighten up on who he is just to get that cross-over audience." Clearly the main danger of the artist crossing over is not, from this perspective, that he might thereby sacrifice his focus and cultural context, but that he could lose out on his segment of the market. "It's so tempting for an artist to do that once they've gained acceptance. But you risk losing your base when you do that and you never want to be without your core audience. That's why we work as a team and always include our artists and their managers in the packaging and marketing process."8

Latin Empire's members can't seem to get their "act" together because they remain too tied to their base to endure "strong management." Their mission, especially since rap "went Latin," is to reinstate the history and geography of the New York Puerto Rican contribution to hip-hop and counteract the sensationalist version perpetrated by the media. In some of their best-known numbers like "El Barrio," "Mi Viejo South Bronx" and "The Big Manzana," they take us deep into the Puerto Rican neighborhoods and back, "way back, to the days of *West Side Story*," when the New York style originated. Tracing the transition from the gang era to the emergence of the "style wars" of hip-hop, they tell their own stories and dramatize their constant juggling act between Black and Latino and between Island and New York cultures. In another rhyme, "Not Listed," they "take hip-hop to another *tamaño* [level]" by emphasizing the particular Puerto Rican role in rap history and countering the false currency given new arrivals. They end by affirming these ignored roots and rescuing the many early Puerto Rican rappers from oblivion:

Y'all need to see a médico
but we don't accept Medicaid
we don't give no crédito
we only give credit where credit is due
we got to give it to the Mean Machine
and the other brothers who were out there
lookin' out for Latinos
some kept it up, some chose other caminos
but we can't pretend that they never existed
cause yo, they were out there, just not listed.

In another of their rhymes Latin Empire's members address the music
business itself, lashing out at the counterfeits and subterfuges facing them
in their "hungry" battle for a fair record deal. Some of "Kinda Hungry"
sounds like this:

Yeah that's right I'm hungry,
in other words, yo tengo hambre.
Those who overslept caught a calambre.
Fake mc's hogging up the posiciones,
but all we keep hearing is bullshit canciones.
Don't be feeding mis sueños.
You might be the head of A&R but I want to meet the dueños.
So I can let 'em know como yo me siento
and update 'em on the Latino movimiento
'cause I'm getting tired of imitadores
that shit is muerto, that's why I'm sending you flores,
En diferentes colores.
I'm like an undertaker . . .
I still don't understand how they allowed you to make a
rap record que no sirve para nada.
I'll eat 'em up like an ensalada.
Speakin' about food you want comida?
Na, that's not what I meant,
what I want is a record deal en seguida
so we can get this on a 24 track
put it out on the market and bug out on the feedback.
Huh, tú no te dabas cuenta,

a nigga like me is in effect en los noventas.
Straight outta Vega Baja
the other candidates?
I knock 'em out the caja, knock 'em out the box
because I'm not relajando I truly feel it's time
I started eliminando mc's givin' us a bad nombre.
I can't see TNT nor my righthand hombre
the Krazy Taino sellin' out,
there's no way, there's no how,
that's not what we're about.
We're all about looking out for my gente,
here's some food for thought, comida para la mente.

With all their "hunger" for recognition, members of Latin Empire also feel the burden of responsibility for being the only Nuyorican rap group given any public play at all. They realize that, being synonymous with Puerto Rican rap, they are forced to stand in for a whole historical experience and for the rich variety of street rappers condemned to omission by the very filtering process that they are confronting. A prime example for them of the "not listed" is the "right hand hombre" mentioned here, MC TNT. Virtually unknown outside the immediate hip-hop community in the South Bronx, TNT is living proof that hard-core, streetwise rhyming continues and develops in spite of the diluting effects and choices of the managers and A&R departments. Frequently, Puerto Rock and KT have incorporated TNT into many of their routines, and his rhymes and delivery have added a strong sense of history and poetic language to their presentations.

Like Puerto Rock, TNT (Tomás Robles) was born in Puerto Rico and came to New York at an early age. But in his case, childhood in the rough neighborhoods on the Island figures prominently in his raps, as in this autobiographical section interlaced with samples from Rubén Blades's salsa hit "La Vida Te Da Sorpresas":

Este ritmo es un invento
Cuando empiezo a rimar le doy el 100 por ciento
No me llamo Chico, o Federico
Dónde naciste? Santurce, Puerto Rico
Cuando era niño no salía 'fuera
porque mataban diario en la cantera

Esto es verdad, realidad, no un engaño
mi pae murió cuando yo tenía seis años
La muerte me afectó con mucho dolor
pues mi mae empaquetó y nos mudamos pa' Nueva York
cuando llegué era un ambiente diferente
pero no me arrepentí, seguí para frente
y por las noches recé a Dios y a la santa
porque en mi corazón el coquí siempre canta.

[This rhyme is an invention / When I start to rhyme I give it 100 percent / My name isn't Chico or Federico / Where were you born? /
Santurce, Puerto Rico / When I was a boy I didn't go out / 'cause
there were killings / in the quarry every day / This is true, reality, not
a hoax / my father died when I was six / his death caused me a lot of
pain / well my mother packed up and we moved to New York / when I
arrived it was a very different atmosphere / but I didn't regret it, I moved
ahead / and at night I prayed to God and the holy mother / because in
my heart the *coquí* frog always sings."]

By the late 1970s, as an adolescent, TNT was already involved in the gang
scene in the South Bronx and took part in the formation of Tough Bronx Action and the Puerto Rican chapters of Zulu Nation. By that time he was already playing congas in the streets and schoolyards and improvising rhymes.
When he first heard Mean Machine in 1981, he recalls, he already had note-
books of raps in Spanish, though mostly he preserved them in his memory.

TNT also goes by the epithet "un rap siquiatra" ("a rap psychiatrist"): in
his lively, storytelling rhymes he prides himself on his biting analysis of
events and attitudes in the community. He responds to the charges of gang-
sterism by pointing to the ghetto conditions that force survival remedies
on his people. "Livin' in a ghetto can turn you 'to a gangster" is one of his
powerful social raps, and in "Get Some Money" he addresses the rich and
powerful directly: "he threw us in the ghetto to see how long we lasted / then
he calls us a little ghetto bastard." His "Ven acá tiguerito tiguerito," which
compares with anything by Kid Frost and Latin Alliance in sheer verbal ingenuity, captures the intensity of a combative street scene in El Barrio and is
laced with phrases from Dominican slang. His programmatic braggadocio is
playful and ragamuffin in its effect, yet with a defiance that extends in the
last line to the very accentuation of the language:

Soy un rap siquiatra un rap mecánico
óyeme la radio y causo un pánico
te rompo el sistema y te dejo inválido
con un shock nervioso te ves bien pálido
no puedes con mi rap
aléjate aléjate
tómate una Contact y acuéstate
o llame a los bomberos que te rescaten.

[I'm a rap psychiatrist, a rap mechanic hear me on the radio and I cause
a panic / I break your system and I leave you an invalid / with a nervous
shock you look pretty pale / you can't deal with my rap / go away, go
away / take a Contac and go to bed / or call the firefighters to come
rescue you.]

By the mid-1990s, at twenty-five, MC TNT was already a veteran of
Spanish rap battles, still "unlisted" and awaiting his break, yet constantly
working on his rhymes and beats every moment he can shake off some of
the pressure. He is the closest I have run across to a rapper in the tradition
of Puerto Rican plena music, since like that of the master *pleneros* his work
is taking shape as a newspaper of the barrios, a running, ironic commen-
tary on the untold events of everyday Puerto Rican life. When all the talk
was of referendums and plebiscites to determine the political status of
Puerto Rico, TNT had some advice for his people to contemplate:

Puerto Rico, una isla hermosa,
donde nacen bonitas rosas,
plátanos, guineos y yautía,
Sasón Goya le da sabor a la comida.
Y ¿quién cocina más que la tía mía?
Pero el gobierno es bien armado,
tratando de convertirla en un estado.
Es mejor la dejen libre (asociado?).
Cristóbal Colón no fue nadie,
cruzó el mar con un bonche de salvajes.
Entraron a Puerto Rico rompiendo palmas,
asustando a los caciques con armas.
Chequéate los libros, esto es cierto,

pregúntale a un cacique pero ya está muerto.
¿Cómo él descubrió algo que ya está descubierto?
Boricua, ¡no te vendas!

[Puerto Rico, a beautiful island / where there are pretty roses, /
plantains, bananas, and root vegetables,/Goya seasoning gives the food
flavor / And who cooks better than my own aunt? / But the government
is well armed, / trying to convert it into a state / It's better to leave it free
(associated?) / Christopher Columbus was nobody, / he crossed the sea
with a bunch of savages, / they entered Puerto Rico destroying the palm
trees, / terrifying the Indian chiefs with their weapons. / Check out the
books, this is true, / ask one of the Indian chiefs but they're already
dead. / How could he discover something already discovered? /
Puerto Rico, don't sell yourself!]

Like other Latino groups, Puerto Ricans are using rap as a vehicle for affirming their history, language, and culture under conditions of rampant
discrimination and exclusion. The explosion of Spanish-language and bilingual rap onto the pop music scene in recent years bears special significance in the face of the stubbornly monolingual tenor in today's public discourse, most evident in the crippling of bilingual programs and services
and in the ominous gains of the "English Only" crusade. And of course
along with the Spanish and Spanglish rhymes, Latino rap carries an ensemble of alternative perspectives and an often divergent cultural ethos
into the mainstream of U.S. social life. The mass diffusion, even if only for
commercial purposes, of cultural expression in the "other" language, and
above all its broad and warm reception by fans of all nationalities, may help
to muffle the shrieks of alarm emanating from the official culture whenever mention is made of "America's fastest-growing minority." Latin rap
lends volatile fuel to the cause of "multiculturalism" in our society, at least
in the challenging, inclusionary sense of that embattled term.

For Puerto Ricans, though, rap is more than a newly opened window on
their history; rap *is* their history, and Puerto Ricans are an integral part in
the history of hip-hop. As the "Puerto rocks" themselves testify in conversation and rhyme, rapping is one of many domains within a larger field of
social and creative practices expressive of their collective historical position
in the prevailing relations of power and privilege. Puerto Rican participation in the emergence of hip-hop music needs to be understood in direct,

interactive relation to their experience in gangs and other forms of association among inner-city youth through the devastating blight of the seventies. "Puerto rocks" are the children of impoverished colonial immigrants
facing even tougher times than in earlier decades. They helped make rap
what it was to become, as they played a constitutive role in the stylistic definition of graffiti writing and breakdancing.

In addition to these more obvious associations, the formative years of
rap follow closely the development of both salsa and Nuyorican poetry, expressive modes which, especially for the young Puerto Ricans themselves,
occupy the same creative constellation as the musical and lyrical project of
bilingual and bicultural rap. Musically, rap practice among Puerto Ricans
is also informed by the strong antecedent tradition of street drumming
and, at only a slight remove, their parallel earlier role in styles like doo-wop,
boogaloo, and Latin jazz. In terms of poetic language, Spanglish rap is em-
bedded in the everyday speech practices of the larger community over the
course of several generations, and even echoes in more than faint ways the
tones and cadences of lyrics typical of plena, bomba, and other forms of
popular Puerto Rican song.

Like these other contemporaneous and prefiguring cultural practices,
the active presence of Puerto Ricans in the creation of rap bears further
emphatic testimony to their long history of cultural interaction with African Americans. Hip-hop emerged as a cultural space shared by Puerto Ricans and Blacks, a sharing that once again articulates their congruent and
intermingling placement in the impinging political and economic geography. It is also a sharing in which, as the story of rap reveals, the disso-
nances are as telling as the harmonies, and the distances as heartfelt as the
intimacy. The Puerto Ricans' nagging intimation that they are treading on
Black turf and working in a tradition of performative expression most directly traceable to James Brown and Jimmy Castor, the dozens and the
blues, makes rap into a terrain that is as much contested as it is coinhab-
ited on equal terms. Jamaican dubbing, with its strong Caribbean resonance, serves as a bridge in this respect, just as reggae in more recent
years is helping to link rap to otherwise disparate musical trends, especially in its reggaespañol dancehall versions. In the historical perspective
of Black and Puerto Rican interaction, rap is thus a lesson in cultural negotiation and transaction as much as in fusions and crossovers, especially
as those terms are bandied about in mainstream parlance. If multiculturalism is to amount to anything more than a wishful fancy of a pluralist

mosaic, the stories of the "Puerto rocks" show that adequate account must be taken of the intricate jostling and juggling involved along the seams of contemporary cultural life.

What is to become of Latino rap, and how we appreciate and understand its particular messages, will depend significantly on the continuities it forges to its roots among the "Puerto rocks." Recuperating this history, explicitly or by example, and "inventing" a tradition divergent from the workings of the commercial culture, makes for the only hope of reversing the instant amnesia that engulfs rap and all forms of emergent cultural discourse as they migrate into the world of pop hegemony. Charlie Chase, TNT, and the other "Puerto rocks" were not only pioneers in some nostalgic sense but helped set the social meaning of rap practice prior to and relatively independent of its mediated commercial meaning. That formative participation of Latinos in rap in its infancy is a healthy reminder that the "rap attack," as Peter Toop argued some years ago now, is but the latest outburst of "African jive," and that the age-old journey of jive has always been a motley and inclusive procession. And as in Cuban-based salsa, the Puerto Rican conspiracy in the present volley shows how creatively a people can adopt and adapt what would seem a "foreign" tradition and make it, at least in part, its own. To return to the first "Puerto rock" I talked with in the early 1980s, I close with a little rhyme by MC Rubie Dee (Rubén García) from the South Bronx:

Now all you Puerto Ricans you're in for a treat,
'cause this Puerto Rican can rock a funky beat.
If you fall on your butt and you start to bleed,
Rubie Dee is what *all* the Puerto Ricans need.
I'm a homeboy to them 'cause I know what to do,
'cause Rubie Dee is down with the black people too.9

Special supplement, New York Newsday *(October 1991)*

7

⚔

Pan-Latino/Trans-Latino

PUERTO RICANS IN THE "NEW NUEVA YORK"

One of the most dramatic and visible changes in the face of New York City since the mid-1970s has been the growing diversity of its Latino presence. Of course, Puerto Ricans have never been the lone Spanish-speaking group here; earlier chapters of that history, as told by chroniclers like Bernardo Vega and Jesús Colón, abound with accounts of Cubans, Dominicans, Spaniards, Mexicans, and many other "Hispanos" making common cause with Puerto Ricans in everyday life and in social struggles on many fronts. But over the decades, and especially with the mass migration of the 1950s, Puerto Ricans have so outnumbered all other Latinos as to have served as the prototype (or archetype, but certainly the stereotype) of Latino/Hispanic/"Spanish" New York. Increasingly since the 1920s, and indelibly with influential milestones like Leonard Bernstein's *West Side Story* and Oscar Lewis's *La Vida,* the overlap has been nearly complete, the terms "Latin New York" and "Puerto Rican" ringing virtually synonymous in the public mind.

By the 1990s that image—based of course on unambiguous demographic realities—has waned significantly, especially as the media and many research efforts tend to find greater delight in the novelties and anomalies of "other," more exotic newcomers than in the quotidian familiarity of Puerto Ricans. And yet, all sensationalism aside, the growth—quantitative and qualitative—of the Dominican community, especially in New York City and in urban Puerto Rico, has indeed been nothing short of sensational; the political and cultural consequences of this, for New York, the Dominican Republic, Puerto Rico, and perhaps most of all for the Puerto Rican community in New York, are already highly visible and promise to increase over time. The "Mexicanization" of New York has also proceeded apace, especially in the 1990s; in fact, for some years the proportional arrival rates from the Mexican state of Puebla may even exceed those from the Dominican Republic. Add to these the huge numbers of Colombians, Salvadorans, Ecuadorians, Panamanians, Hondurans, Haitians, Brazilians, and the "new" New Yorkers from nearly every country of Latin America and the Caribbean, and it is clear why "Latinos in New York" no longer rhymes with Puerto Rican.

This momentous pan-Latinization over the course of a single generation makes it necessary to rethink the whole issue of Puerto Rican culture and identity in the United States. How does Puerto Rican/Nuyorican (self-) identification and cultural history interface with and elude the pan-ethnic "Latino" or "Hispanic" label, which has by now become stock-in-trade of most media, government, commercial, social science, and literary-cultural "coverage," and to which Puerto Ricans themselves have constant recourse in extending their political, cultural, and intellectual reach in accord with changing social realities? For while we may be appropriately critical and even suspicious in the face of the catchall categories, a contemporary analysis of Puerto Rican culture and politics in New York necessarily invokes a more embracing term and idea like *Latino* to refer to what is clearly some ensemble of congruent and intertwining historical experiences. Most of the deliberation over the Latino/Hispanic concept thus far has been nationwide (that is, all of the United States) in reference, or with a mind to areas (mostly cities) witnessing ample interaction among more or less equally sizable Latino groups (Chicago being the first example to come to mind, though Los Angeles and Miami have also seemed pertinent). But in many ways it is New York that has become the pan-Latin city par excellence. And it is perhaps here, in the "new," post-Nuyorican Nueva York, that the Latino concept of group association stands its strongest test.

THE NEW MIX

The first signs of imminent change can be traced to the early 1960s. The aftermath of the 1959 Cuban Revolution brought a huge new influx of Cuban exiles, many of them settling in the New York area. The death of Trujillo in 1961 marked an easing of the restrictive emigration policies which had prevailed in the Dominican Republic throughout the Trujillo era (1930–1960). Pressing economic conditions and ongoing political contention (especially the civil war and U.S. military invasion in 1965) have propelled growing numbers of Dominicans to the United States ever since, the overwhelming majority of them (by 1990 a full two-thirds) to New York City.

But what is considered the single most important factor to usher in the "new immigration" was the change in the U.S. immigration law in 1965, which put an end to the national origins quota system, in effect since the 1920s, favoring northern and western Europeans. This policy shift, which placed a 120,000 ceiling each for Asia and the Western Hemisphere, literally opened the floodgates to a massive immigration from many parts of Asia and most countries of Latin America and the Caribbean. True to its long-standing historical role, New York City has continued to be a favored destination for these new arrivals, and the figures for the post-1965 period are indeed telling. "In the past two decades," it was reported in 1987, "more than a million immigrants have settled in New York City, most from the West Indies, Latin America, and Asia. . . . According to the 1980 census, 80 percent of the Asian-born, 82 percent of the Jamaican-born, and 88 percent of the Trinidadian-born residents in the New York metropolitan area had arrived since 1965."[1] That was how things stood a decade before the 1990 count, which recorded an even greater multiplication of new arrivals.

New New Yorkers from Spanish-speaking countries, increasingly referred to in official parlance as "Hispanics," figure prominently in this demographic explosion, and their numbers are true to the pattern. With the exception of Puerto Ricans and Cubans, representation from nearly all countries of Latin America and the Spanish Caribbean has increased geometrically over the decades since 1960. Already numbering nearly a million according to official count by 1960, the size of the composite New York Latino population has more than doubled by 1990 to make up a full fourth of all New Yorkers, equal in proportion to African Americans. National groups with only a minor presence of one or two thousand in 1960 (such as Salvadorans, Guatemalans, Hondurans, and Peruvians) have grown to around 20,000 by 1990, while the ranks of Colombians, Ecuadorians, and Mexicans have swelled to well over 50,000 each within the thirty-year period. The most dramatic increase, of course, is among the Dominicans, who at 13,293 represented 1.7 percent of the city's Latino population in 1960; by 1990, Dominican New Yorkers totaled 332,713 or 18.7 percent of Latinos in New York, making them by far the largest Latino community after the Puerto Rican.[2]

But while the legislative change of 1965, and for the sake of statistical contrast the 1960 census, may serve as convenient signposts for marking off the "old" from the "new" immigration period, the most dramatic demographic leaps among New York Latino groups actually occur a decade later and thereafter. The "New Nueva York," as *New York Newsday* titled a lengthy supplement on the city's Latinos in 1991, is really a phenomenon of the 1980s and 1990s, though trends did point clearly in that direction by the later 1970s. Referring to the overall Latino population, it is true that growth has been roughly the same per decade since 1960. But when it comes to the diversification of New York's Latinos, and the emergence of the "pan-Latino" face by which the city is now recognized, the last quarter of the twentieth century makes for a more accurate time frame. For, to begin with, it was in the 1970s that the Puerto Rican migration, having reached a benchmark around 1970, leveled off significantly. Puerto Ricans continued to arrive by the thousands, but their numbers were more than offset by a continually growing return migration and diasporic dispersion in the United States itself. Relative to many other Latino groups, and to the composite Latino population, the proportion of Puerto Ricans has been on a steady decline: over 80 percent in 1960, Latin New York is now only half Puerto Rican, with a full 10 percent drop in the 1980s. Cuban New Yorkers, after doubling in size in the post-Revolution 1960s, has been declining substantially ever since; long, and still in 1970, the city's second largest Hispanic group, they were far surpassed by Dominicans during the 1970s; by 1980 there were twice as many Dominicans as Cubans, and by 1990 over six times as many. By 1990, in fact, Cubans no longer even counted among the five largest Latino groups in the city: while in 1980 they were still a comfortable third, by the latest official tabulation they have come to be outnumbered by Colombians, Ecuadorians, and Mexicans, with Salvadorans, Panamanians, and Peruvians ranging not too far behind.

This radical reconfiguration of the Latino mix in New York is of course a highly complex, conjunctural process, with layers and levels of explanation as diverse as the range of Latin American nationalities to have come to reside in the city in the present generation. Rather than one "Latino" story of arrival and settlement in New York, there are clearly Cuban, Puerto Rican, Dominican, Salvadoran, and Colombian stories, each of them bearing varied and sometimes jarring internal narratives of their own. But the stories all converge in "Nueva York," achieving full hemispheric representation (including even that crucial Mexican component) by 1990. The common locus of new social experience and identity formation is New York City, just at a time when it is being christened a "global city" in the contemporary sense.[3]

It is in the story of present-day New York City, the restructurings of the Big Apple (some would say its rotting, squashing, or slicing) in accord with its global geoeconomic role, that it is possible to find a common thread in the intricate "Latino" weave, or at least a framework in which to interpret the huge and diverse Latino presence in some more encompassing way. From this perspective, the history of the "new" immigration, and particularly the story of Latinos settling in New York, takes on a different range and contour. Rather than stretching from 1965 to the present, the changeover from "old" to "new" immigration has comprised two periods, corresponding to two phases in the restructuring of the city's economy since midcentury, with the turning point being marked by the fiscal crisis of the mid-1970s. The first phase (1950–1975, but especially since the early 1960s) amounted to the "dashed hopes" of Puerto Ricans; the second (since 1975) is characterized by their "re-placement" in both senses of the word: to other places, and by other groups.

When Puerto Ricans began flocking to New York by the tens and hundreds of thousands in the late 1940s and early 1950s, hopes were high, and expectations only reasonable, that over time they would find their place in the local economy. There would be gaps to fill in the city's postwar labor market, the thinking went, and adequate employment opportunities for newcomers, which in those years meant predominantly Puerto Ricans and African Americans. "Assuming continued regional vitality and an effective educational system, there was no a priori reason to doubt the likelihood of successful incorporation of these groups into the economic mainstream."[4] The shared historical experience between "Latinos" and African Americans warrants particular emphasis: New York's "Negroes and Puerto Ricans" were, after all, the "newcomers" in Oscar Handlin's influential 1959 book of that title.[5]

But "continued regional vitality," presupposing as it does for the "global city" continued national and international economic vitality, was decidedly not in the offing. The stagnation that set in by the late 1950s, combined with the disastrous aftermath of the Operation Bootstrap experiment, dashed whatever hopes Puerto Ricans might have held to strike a more stable and favorable foothold in New York life. "For Puerto Ricans the principal outcome of this period was labor force displacement, manifested in a sharp decline in labor force participation and a rise in unemployment from 1960 to 1970."[6] In 1976, in what amounts to a stocktaking of this phase, the United States Commission on Civil Rights released its alarming report, *Puerto Ricans in the Continental United States: An Uncertain Future*, which put Puerto Ricans on record as the exception to the rule of immigrant incorporation and advancement.[7]

The second phase, beginning in the mid-1970s, brought a continuation of these developments but at more intense levels and in different ways. Unemployment levels among Puerto Ricans magnified, as stable jobs in both the corporate and public sectors became ever scarcer. Public employment opportunities, which had expanded consistently since midcentury and absorbed increasing numbers of Puerto Rican and African American workers, were curtailed sharply as a result of the fiscal crisis of 1975–76, with Puerto Ricans being the heaviest casualties in this cutback. The replacement of relocated corporations by service industries and light manufacturing harbored little hope, as both "established a new profile of occupations and labor process" largely inaccessible to African Americans and Puerto Ricans. The reorganization of light manufacturing since the mid-1970s in particular spelled the large-scale "re-placement" of Puerto Ricans by more recent immigrants, mostly other Latinos: "The labor force attached to the earlier manufacturing complex, which had been displaced to a significant extent, was not redeployed into the newly evolving sector. The growth of the new sector was dependent on a lower cost of labor, a condition met by the use of new sources of immigrant labor." And further: "It is a considerably revamped manufacturing sector [in which Puerto Ricans have had a historically high representation], dependent on lower labor costs, that has largely absorbed Dominican labor," though it is added that "since the mid-1980s, the garment industry has suffered a new period of decline."[8]

"Decline within decline"—the title of the article cited—seems an apt description of what New York City's ethnic queue has held out for much of its huge Latino population in recent decades, at least when it comes to its fit into a sharply fluctuating labor market. For the critical socioeconomic hardships confronting New York's "new" Latinos in the 1990s are an extension, a further stage, in a local, regional, and global restructuring process extending back to the 1950s, and experienced at its onset by an overwhelmingly Puerto Rican population. In important ways, it was adjustments in the city as postindustrial command center that propelled the demographic movements leading to its most recent repeopling. The emergence of a "pan-Latino" New York comes in the wake of a prior, and precedent, move to import and incorporate Puerto Ricans.

Whatever the parallels and differences, though, the pan-ethnic diversity of the current Latino population is in large measure a reflex of major structural shifts as manifest in the regional political economy of the "global city." The history of this adjustment extends back to the immediate postwar years and has entailed a paradigmatic change in the immigrant experience, from the "old," mainly European, to the "new." Viewed in its full trajectory, the Latinization of New York centers on the congruences and contrasts between Puerto Ricans and the other Latino groups, individually and as a composite. For Puerto Ricans are not only "still the largest and oldest" of the New York Latino populations, a frequent and fitting rejoinder to the usual relativistic fanfare about the city's pan-Latino "melting pot." With a century of experience here, New York Puerto Ricans actually straddle the "old" and the "new," while their emigration en masse in the 1950s and 1960s was clearly the first wave of the "new," non-European flow. Rather than just one more among the many Latino groups, receding in relative prominence as the others expand and dig in, the Puerto Rican community remains at the crux of any consideration of Latinos in New York, the historical touchstone against which much else that follows must be tested.

Within present-day public discourse it is the embattled concept of "Latino" or "Hispanic" that is once again at issue, and by extension the policy and practices of "pan-ethnic" categorization. Over the same generation in which New York came to join Chicago, Miami, Houston, and Los Angeles as "pan-Latino" cities on a contemporary scale, the terms *Latino* and *Hispanic* have established themselves firmly in everyday U.S. parlance, and the debate over their relative validity and limitations—linking as it does the volatile questions of race and immigration—rages close to the combat zone in the culture wars of our time. Before returning to the "New Nueva York," then, and assessing the new issues of Puerto Rican cultural identity raised by its recent reconfiguration, a critical engagement of that discourse may suggest an appropriate theoretical framework.

ETHNIC–PAN-ETHNIC

The terms *Hispanic* and *Latino* have come into such wide currency since the 1970s, and especially since the official use of "Hispanic" in the 1980 census, that they have the ring of neologisms, fresh coinages for a new, as yet unnamed, presence on the social scene. Historical memory seems to stop short at the 1960s, the heyday of the Chicano and Puerto Rican movements, when it comes to a genealogy of these new-fangled labels. Yet the people thus labeled have been using these and similar terms, in English and Spanish, to identify themselves at least since the 1920s and probably much earlier. Even in New York, compared to the Southwest the younger and smaller of the two major concentrations, there were through those early decades countless organizations, periodicals, movements, and events with "Latino," "Hispano," "Latin," "Spanish," "Spanish-speaking" in their titles, probably as many as there were "Puertorriqueño," "Puerto Rican" or "Boricua."[9] Indeed, what could be more "Latino" in the sense of pan-ethnic solidarity than the Partido Revolucionario Cubano with its "Sección de Puerto Rico," which united the two Caribbean nationalities in joint struggle against Spanish colonialism? The Partido, and its affiliated Club Dos Antillas, which included Dominicans and sundry "others," were active in New York City more than one hundred years ago.

The sense and practice of a "Latino/Hispanic" unity across national lines thus go way back, as does the recognized need for names to designate such tactical or enduring common ground. Even the government bureaucracy was not without its earlier pan-group usage: before "Hispanic," the traditional entry had been "Spanish Origin," with "Spanish/Hispanic origin or descent" cropping up frequently in explanatory memorandums prior to the 1980 Census.[10] And there are continuities between the older and the more recent (self)-identifications, not the least of which is their consistently Eurocentric connotation. Though surely outnumbered by the casualties of time and renaming, there are pan-Latino organizations, newspapers, neighborhoods, and of course people that harken back to the earlier decades and attest to the longevity of the cross-ethnic newborn whose baptism we are now asked to celebrate, or at least acknowledge. As has been well argued, the "racialization" of Latin American and Caribbean peoples in the United States, the "othering" process for which the "Hispanic" label provides an official seal, spans the full twentieth century and, if we extend the frame to include hemispheric relations, much of the nineteenth as well.[11]

What is new, if not the object or act of signification, is the discursive context, the sociohistorical climate in which the (self-)naming is enacted. The quantum growth, diversification, and dispersal of the Latino populations over a single generation are surely at the base of this change, though the many Latino social and cultural movements since the late 1960s also resonate strongly in the new semantic reality. More than the census count itself, it is the echoing cries of Brown Power and the alarm signals about "America's fastest-growing minority" that have set the temper for the present discourse, a collective mood ranging from radical defiance to a national anguish bordering on hysteria. By the 1990s, "Hispanic" and "Latino" are everywhere, the terms like the people themselves having proliferated in numbers and locations, and having assumed an emotional charge and connotative complexity unknown in their previous historical usages.

And the "coverage," in the form of media specials and academic studies, also abounds. In the 1980s and 1990s most major newspapers and magazines dedicated investigative surveys and extensive portraits of the "new Americans" from south of the border, while in the same period dozens of books and hundreds of journal articles have focused on the "sleeping giant" of U.S. cultural and political life. The subject now is the experience not so much of single national or regional groups—Caribbeans, say, or Mexicans and Central Americans—but of the whole composite, the "Hispanic" or "Latino" experience, with an emphasis on commonalities and interactions. The first half of the 1990s alone saw the publication of the following book titles: *Latinos: A Biography of the People*; *Latinos in a Changing U.S. Economy: Comparative Perspectives on Growing Inequality*; *Hispanic Presence in the United States: Historical Beginnings*; *Out of the Barrio: Toward a New Politics of Hispanic Assimilation*; *Ethnic Labels, Latino Lives: Identity and the Politics of (Re)Presentation in the United States*; *The Hispanic Condition: Reflections on Culture and Identity in America*; and even *Everything You Need to Know about Latino History*.

These varied works—and their variety along political, methodological, and stylistic lines could hardly be more thorough—all tend to take the validity of the "pan-" category for granted, and proceed to make their analyses, spin their reflections, and set forth their policy proposals on that basis. Disclaimers and qualifiers abound, of course, and a book like Earl Shorris's *Latinos*, subtitled "a biography of the people," actually harps more on differences among the groups than on their similarities, and the promised story line ends up splintering into what are really "biographies of people." Little critical energy goes to scrutiny of the category itself, and what there is of theoretical options often amounts to a stereotyped counterposition of "Hispanic" vs. "Latino," with no evidence of a consensus as to the preferred term.[12] But there is in all these writings an assumption that the term(s) refer to something real or in the making, whether a demographic aggregate, a voting bloc, a market, a language or cultural group, a "community," or, in Ilan Stavans's grandiloquent phrase, a "condition." Given the xenophobic tenor of mainstream politics in the 1990s, of course, which perceives "Hispanic" and "Latino" most of all as a "problem" ("HisPANIC Causing Panic"), such conceptions are all necessary and contribute to the social construction of a major group identity.

A consensus of these writings would probably settle on "ethnicity" as the concept that most closely approximates the bond among Latinos, and the boundary that marks them off from "others" in U.S. settings. Though the phrase "Hispanic ethnic group" does not always appear as such, the underlying premise throughout is that insofar as they comprise a definable group, Latinos are an ethnicity. But even in work that seems least troubled by lumping Hispanics together—and demographers are no less inclined in this direction than culturalists—there is also an abiding awareness that, if anything, this is an ethnicity of ethnicities, an "ethnic group" that does not exist but for the existence of its constituent "subgroups."

A more circumspect line of thinking therefore refers to Latinos as a "pan-ethnicity," a group formation that emerges out of the interaction or close historical congruence of two or more culturally related ethnicities. The "pan-ethnic" approach, for which writers like David López, Yen Espiritu, and others have done much to establish a place in contemporary social theory,[13] has the distinct advantage for the study of Latinos of centering analysis on the dialectic between the parts and the whole, the discrete national groups and the "Latino" construct. The focus is necessarily on interaction, while the hypostasized social group itself, along with its "discourse," is understood as process rather than as a fixed entity or meaning.

An early instance of such an approach, though predating concepts like pan-ethnicity by over a decade, is Félix M. Padilla's *Latino Ethnic Consciousness: The Case of Mexican Americans and Puerto Ricans in Chicago*. Published in 1985, the book is actually based on case studies from the early 1970s, when Chicago was still the city with the most substantial multi-Latino population, and the two largest groups, Mexican Americans and Puerto Ricans, at that. Padilla's aim was to analyze "the process of Latino/Hispanic ethnic group formation in the city of Chicago."[14] He is interested in the "conditions that have enabled Mexican Americans and Puerto Ricans to transcend the boundaries of the respective nationally and culturally based communities and adopt a new and different collective 'Latino' or 'Hispanic' identity dur-

ing the early years of the 1970s." By studying the "interaction process in-
volving Puerto Ricans and Mexican Americans," he seeks to understand the
emergence of a "Latino or Hispanic ethnic-conscious identity and behavior,
distinct and separate from the groups' individual ethnic identities."

The strength and the weakness of Padilla's book, looked at now with the
advantage of hindsight, is its pragmatism. On the positive side, it takes seriously what should be an imperative of "pan-ethnic" analysis, the study of
the actual social interaction between and among Latino groups. Focusing
on the lived experience of distinct but kindred communities coming together to act, and feel, as one, Padilla avoids cultural essentialism before
that pitfall was being talked about, at least in present-day terms. To this
end, he argues well for an understanding of Latino unity as "situational,"
and "political" in the sense of being grounded in the recognition of shared
social interests.

The problem with this on-the-ground, pragmatic concept of "Latinismo," however, is that it reduces the object of study, "ethnic consciousness,"
to "behavior" (the words are coupled throughout, often as synonyms). And
because the emergent Latino identity is taken in such explicit and deliberate separation from Mexican American or Puerto Rican identity, the
process of pan-ethnic formation is disengaged from the historical trajecto-
ries of each group. The book is notably sparse, in fact, on such background,
and on any sustained attempt to explain how so many Mexicans and Puerto Ricans got to Chicago in the first place. Contrary to his own expressed
political sentiments, and to views about "Latinismo" to appear in his own
subsequent writings,[15] Padilla effectively divorces the formation of pan-
Latino unity from its larger international context, Latin America.

Many of these limitations are averted, and the terms of analysis significantly updated, in Suzanne Oboler's *Ethnic Labels, Latino Lives: Identity and the Politics of (Re)Presentation in the United States* (1995). Here the
hemispheric sensibility is more alive, as would befit a Peruvian American writing in the years when "Latino ethnic consciousness" is being infused with perspectives and experiences from all over "nuestra América." Oboler treats the conceptualization of Latino identity in much
broader theoretical and historical terms than Padilla, and indeed than
other writings on the subject to date. And while expansive, her account
of "the Hispanic condition" wisely avoids the presumptuousness and the
glaring inaccuracies of Ilan Stavans in his book of that unhappy title.[16]
Most important, Oboler is writing after the officialization of "Hispanic"

as a census category and in the midst of its commercial circulation as an item of semantic consumption.

Oboler's major contribution, as her title indicates, is the critical scrutiny of that clash between "labels" and "lives," between imposed and assumed identities. She traces the genesis of and motives behind the newfound "policy" toward Hispanics and relates it to a larger process of "racialization," though her account of these matters is best supplemented by some of the articles in a special issue of the journal *Latin American Perspectives* (1992) on "The Politics of Ethnic Construction," to which Oboler also contributed.[17] In any case, its sharp dramatization of the crisis of Latino "(re)presentation," its inclusive yet critical sense of a fully "pan-Latino" identity, and its sustained attention to gender and class differentiations, make *Ethnic Labels, Latino Lives* an important and welcome advance beyond the methodological and theoretical confines of Padilla's earlier study.

Nevertheless, when it comes to the Latino concept itself, Oboler remains within Padilla's universe of discourse, or at least in close proximity to it. "Ethnicity," as a reliable category of social differentiation, still reigns supreme, as does the inevitable equivocation, when referring to Latinos, about the two "levels" or kinds of ethnic affiliation, the single group and the pan-ethnic. Oboler cautions repeatedly against the lazy relativism and arbitrariness of the ethnic concept and calls for a historical and structural differentiation among the "Latino" groups. At points she even sides with the skeptics, like Martha Giménez and David Hayes-Bautista, and would seem to do away with the "Hispanic" category altogether.[18] But she pulls back from the implications of Giménez's distinction between "ethnics" and "minorities" and, especially in the second, ethnographic half of *Ethnic Labels, Latinos Lives*, lapses into a "Latino" ethnic relativism of her own.

Oboler conducted her fieldwork—her testing ground for the utility of the Hispanic/Latino label—in New York City in 1988–1990, the "New Nueva York." While teaching ESL (English as a second language) classes for a union education program, she interviewed thirteen women and nine men who worked in the garment industry. Her informants, most of them between thirty and sixty, come from nine different Latin American countries. Significant in the sample, aside from the circumscription of age and other important variables, is that only one male informant, "Juan," was Puerto Rican born in New York, and only three of the twenty-two informants were Puerto Rican. There were four Colombians, three Dominicans, three Nicaraguans, and two each from Peru, Honduras, and El Salvador.

Throughout the book, and when introducing her findings, she emphasizes the main crack in the "Hispanic" front, the difference between the Latin American "immigrant populations" and the "more historically established communities of Chicanos and Puerto Ricans" (102). And in concluding her report she reminds us, "Again, the study is not representative of the immigrant populations from Latin America nor of the Puerto Ricans in New York City" (157), though she fails to mention that when doing her fieldwork over 50 percent of New York Latinos were Puerto Rican. Nevertheless, despite her theoretical intentions, the ethnographic part of *Ethnic Labels, Latino Lives* underplays one of the serious perils in using the Hispanic category, a danger that Martha Giménez for one has identified as potentially "racist"; "these labels are racist," Giménez says, "in that . . . they reduce people to interchangeable entities, negating the qualitative differences between, for example, persons of Puerto Rican descent who have lived for generations in New York City and newly arrived immigrants from Chile or some other South or Central American country."[19]

Now Oboler does not exactly "negate" these differences, as is clear from her theoretical caveats and because they are obvious to all but the most casual observer of Latino life in New York. In fact, it is so significant that she even describes her sample as "a small group of twenty-one Latin American immigrants and one U.S.-born Puerto Rican," and when first defining it she seems to have been uncertain about including any Puerto Ricans at all, especially those from the United States (102, 110). And her report itself has repeated recourse to conditionals like, "many Hispanics, regardless of country of origin (and again, with the exception of Puerto Ricans)" or, "leaving aside the U.S.-born Puerto Rican" (111, 122). The irony is that Oboler does not even need these warning signals; her interviews speak for themselves. "Juan," and to some extent "Teresa," two of her Puerto Rican informants, make statements and express views about "Hispanic" identity and U.S. society which stand out markedly among all the testimony. Examples abound, as when Juan says, "I'm American only by accident, because Puerto Rico's a territory of the United States. I don't think it's by choice, because they've got American bases there" (152). Even "Jorge," a Puerto Rican from the Island, responds to the "Latino" category in a way unmatched by the other foreign-born informants: "At the beginning, when I arrived, my boss wanted me to speak English, even though I didn't know the language. I think he thought that I was a Latino" (152, 154).

But most revealing of the divide between New York Puerto Ricans and the other Latino views cited is the lengthy statement by Juan about the contemporary labeling of groups. "White people," he says, "have a name for everybody else. From Whites you came up with the word Hispanics, and spic. I mean, Puerto Ricans never call each other Hispanic. They never called each other spics. . . . They just count all Latin people in one bunch. They do it to the Blacks, too. I mean, come on, they're more than just Blacks. You got your American Blacks, you got your African, your Jamaican; then you got your Puerto Rican blacks; some guys are darker than me. Then you got your Dominican blacks, you got White people that are dark skinned. . . . So you got your Hispanics over here which includes whatever race you want to put in it south of the border. Then you got your Blacks, anything from the Congo down. Then you got your Whites which is Americans" (155). Oboler notes that Juan is voicing his recognition that the ethnic labeling process in the U.S. context involves the conflation of race and nationality, but she does not acknowledge that he is the only one of her informants to pose the issue in those terms, nor does she make anything of this "exceptional" perspective. Rather, she is so intent on drawing out contrasting class and, to a lesser extent, gender positions across national lines that she leaves unanalyzed the blatant singularity of the "Nuyorican" among the many Latino voices in New York.

PAN-LATINO/TRANS-LATINO

Yet this is precisely the most serious challenge facing an analysis of Latino identity in the "New Nueva York": how are we to conceptualize the converging cultural geography of so many "Latino lives," and assess the relative validity of a common identificatory term for all, while still giving adequate analytical weight to the special position and standpoint of the largest, oldest, and structurally different group, the Puerto Ricans? And further, can that qualitative demarcation be drawn without the analysis appearing divisive, or "exceptionalist" to the point of ignoring important commonalities and new lines of solidarity suggested by changing historical circumstances?

In the reigning public and social science view, of course, New York Puerto Ricans have long been viewed or construed as the "exception," the extraneous ingredient in the melting pot or ethnic pluralist stew, salad bowl, or mosaic. The assimilationist thrust involved in ethnic and immigrant analogies has gone accompanied by the social pathologies of the "Puerto

Rican problem": one thinks of Nathan Glaser and Daniel Patrick Moynihan and Oscar Lewis, or in more benign terms, of C. Wright Mills and Father Joseph Fitzpatrick. And again in the 1990s, as the Hispanic giant rouses from its slumber, the Puerto Ricans are still the "exception" to the pan-ethnic rule, the "problem" even among their own kind. Derailed from the path "toward a new politics of Hispanic assimilation," U.S. Puerto Ricans are granted a special chapter all their own ("The Puerto Rican Exception") in Linda Chavez's controversial *Out of the Barrio* (1991). Again the New York Puerto Ricans are stuck in the "barrio," mired in their "culture of poverty," while even the other Latinos are headed for the mainstream. After fifty years of massive presence in New York and other parts of the United States, Puerto Ricans have gone from being left out of the sauce to being left out of the salsa.

Yet even Linda Chavez, from her officialist, neoconservative stance, seems at least dimly aware that a dismissive, blame-the-victim account gets her only so far when it comes to explaining her "exception." Speaking of their nonassimilation into American ways as evident in their apparent political apathy, she notes, "Puerto Rico's status, however, cannot help having some effect on the attitudes of Puerto Ricans toward the political process, particularly since they retain a strong identification as Puerto Ricans first and Americans second, according to public opinion surveys."[20] Despite their much longer presence here than other New York Latinos and, as formal citizens, their closer historical relationship to U.S. society, Puerto Ricans have most stubbornly rejected the hyphen, and Chavez, for many of the wrong reasons of course, stumbles onto the key line of explanation. "Puerto Rico," she remarks, "is neither fish nor fowl politically, neither a state nor an independent nation."[21] By even relating the Puerto Ricans' "exceptional," unassimilable position to the issue of the political status of Puerto Rico, Chavez is acknowledging that the pan-ethnic concept needs to be aligned with a knowledge of transnational relations if it is to include its most notable "exception." As expected, she sidesteps the deeper implications of this wider conceptual field of reference, concluding her cursory remarks on status options with the comforting thought that, "in any event, it is unlikely that a change in Puerto Rico's status will do much to solve the problems that face Puerto Ricans in the United States."[22]

But the association is made, even when the ideological objective is to deny or minimize its pertinence to generalizations about Latinos as a composite group. The bracketing of Puerto Ricans among the Latino aggregate is necessitated by the abiding colonial relationship between the United States and Puerto Rico, which even the most internally focused, U.S. ethnicity-framed discussion of that particular Latino group cannot altogether ignore. Interestingly, Oboler's South American informants voice an awareness of this difference at some points in their conversation. "Soledad" from Colombia, for instance, hearing some of her fellow workers saying they don't know why Puerto Ricans are "separated" from the other groups, volunteers an explanation: "Oh, I do. It's because they're undecided about Puerto Ricans. They don't really know if they're American or if they're Puerto Rican. See, they have a problem with Puerto Ricans because they can't believe that they can be Americans and still speak Spanish. So they catalogue them as Americans for some things, but for others they're Puerto Ricans. When they count for something they're Americans, but when they don't need them to count for anything they're *boricuas*" (140). Soledad does not explicitly attribute the ambiguity she notes in the identification of Puerto Ricans in New York to the machinations of colonial control, but she is clear that the orchestrated ambivalence particular to them results from a political opportunism at levels far transcending the confines of the New York barrios and factory floors. Here again, the full range of the pan-ethnic category implies transnational relations and perspectives.

Soledad also recognizes that such treatment is not so particular to Puerto Ricans after all, but is perhaps only more evident and intense in their case. The "exception" may also be the paradigm. "But in different ways," she concludes her remarks, "they do that with all of us who speak Spanish. You know, if an American is running, he's just doing exercise; but if one of us is running, we've just committed a robbery" (140). With this common experience in view, what would seem to mark off the situation of Puerto Ricans—the direct structured link between their "ethnic" placement and the political reality of their homeland—is actually a more graphic and prominent version of the Latino experience in general. The reason for differentiating, and perhaps privileging, a Puerto Rican perspective when analyzing the pan-Latino concept does not rest, therefore, on an appeal to the size and longevity of the New York community, though a much longer historical view than that provided by Oboler is clearly called for. There is, after all, some solid and heartfelt truth to an angry response like that of *salsero* Willie Colón to the description of Puerto Ricans in *Out of the Barrio*, which he suggests calling "out of left field."[23] "Perhaps Chavez thinks Puerto Ricans have a genetic problem," he notes, and draws a parallel to the pitiful situation of Native Hawaiians.

"Just change Hawaii to Puerto Rico. This is what happens to people who become guests in their own home." Stressing the price Puerto Ricans have paid for their groundbreaking role in the history of Latin New York, Colón goes on: "The fact that, in the east, people tolerate Spanish speakers, the reason there are Spanish newspapers, TV and radio shows, bilingual driver's license tests, and salsa music is because Puerto Ricans gave their hearts and souls to earn their place here. Puerto Ricans created an environment that makes it easy for other Latinos to succeed. I hear many new Latino immigrants say, 'In this country any little job is a profession.' That's because they weren't here when they would beat you with a baseball bat for trying to sell *piraguas* or put you in jail for playing dominoes."

Again, this "we-were-here-first" and "there's-more-of-us" reaction, however valid in responding to the demeaning insinuations of ahistorical pathology, is not enough to account for the "Puerto Rican exception" among Latino groups. A more adequate explanation, which addresses the seeming paradox of Puerto Ricans having more, as citizens, yet accomplishing less than other Latinos, is suggested in the response to Chavez's book by another public figure, Bronx congressman José Serrano: "She . . . blames us for not capitalizing on our citizenship," Serrano remarked. "How do you capitalize on a second-class citizenship? What she doesn't understand is that in the same way slavery's legacy remains with African Americans, colonialism has affected Puerto Ricans."[24] Serrano insists on the long historical view, and on the enduring impact of international power relations on the life and domestic status of Puerto Ricans in U.S. society. Pan-ethnicity only stands up as a reliable group category if it is recognized that each group making up the aggregate is at the same time participating in a transnational community, the example of the Puerto Ricans, as colonial Latino immigrants, being the most salient case in point.

Losing sight of this exception-as-paradigm location of the Puerto Ricans within the pan-Latino geography can lead to serious misconceptions and omissions, as Oboler's "situational" ethnography illustrates. Such blurring abounds, of course, in the more cosmic, essentialist accounts, usually of a journalistic kind, where "lo Latino" appears as a glorious new "race," united by a primordial bond forged of the Spanish language and Catholicism, a glorious spirit on the verge of a cultural takeover of Nueva York. Enrique Fernández, for example, the Cuban American journalist for the *Village Voice*, *Más* magazine, and the *Daily News*, moans that " 'Hispanization' was a figure of speech at the beginning of the decade. Today, it's an astonishing reality. We're already a majority in San Antonio and Miami. Ay, Nueva York! How soon before we need a 'Festival Americano' to meet minority needs?"[25] Differentiations of a socioeconomic or political kind are a matter of indifference for such triumphalist rhetoric, with the "nuestros hermanos boricuas" being but one more condiment in the festive *sancocho*. (That's "boricuas," for Ilan Stavans's information, or "borincanos," but never "Borinquéns.")[26]

But such imprecision in posing the notion of Latino "ethnicity," with its characteristic inattention to particularities and exclusions, is rampant in the abundant empirical work on New York's Latinos as well. Demographic and socioeconomic profiles generally take the "Hispanic" aggregate and other census designations for granted and proceed to amass evidence and generate analysis and policy proposals accordingly. The 1995 report by Fordham's Hispanic Research Center, for example, promisingly titled *Nuestra America en Nueva York: The New Immigrant Hispanic Populations in New York City, 1980–1990*, does disaggregate data findings according to national group; but nowhere does it reflect on the differential placement and historical experience of Puerto Ricans, and it consistently takes "non-Hispanic whites" (NHW) as the only operational control variable.[27] This conflation of "racial," national, and ethnic categories does not seem to concern the researchers, nor does the potential value of comparisons and contrasts with other groups, particularly African Americans and Asian Americans. And as for any resonances of the José Martí vision echoed in their title, *Nuestra America en Nueva York* is without an inkling of a hemispheric, transnational frame of analytical reference.

The same criticism goes to the earlier report by Department of City Planning demographers Evelyn S. Mann and Joseph J. Salvo, "Characteristics of New Hispanic Immigrants to New York City: A Comparison of Puerto Rican and Non-Puerto Rican Hispanics." Though the title of this 1984 paper would suggest a closely focused look at the differences between discrete aggregates (Puerto Ricans and "other Hispanics)," their results prove to be of limited value for their lack of comparison between Puerto Ricans and each of the "other" groups taken separately, and between Puerto Ricans and the entire "Hispanic" aggregate including Puerto Ricans. Further, the explanatory power of their conclusion is minimal, as is evident in their attribution of the reported differences, which they recognize are "wide," to "basic disparities in fertility, labor force participation and most of all family structure and composition."[28] Once again, ideological assumptions and ahistorical treatment of the "Puerto Rican exception" land us right back at the culture of poverty.

Even analysis undertaken from an explicitly Puerto Rican perspective, where one might expect a more historical cast to the Puerto Rican–"other Hispanic" comparison, can fall short of the mark. The 1995 essay, "Understanding Socioeconomic Differences: A Comparative Analysis of Puerto Ricans and Recent Latino Immigrants in New York City," for instance, disappoints not because it fails to foreground the particularities of Puerto Rican experience, but because it slides too easily from a contrastive to a pan-Latino project, the weight of the argument and policy orientation ultimately resting more on a Latino-mainstream contrast than one between Puerto Ricans and "recent Latino immigrants."[29] Admittedly a first stab at that particular topic, the essay does draw the pertinent data into play and is helpful in defining a research and policy agenda on some of the most visible issues raised in assessing Puerto Rican–"other Latinos" relations. But the most pressing of these issues, having to do with questions of race, class, gender, and political positioning, are either muddled or sidestepped in the name of an undefined "unity," "progress," and "integration." Many of these shortcomings, and just how far we are from such an "understanding" of the noted socioeconomic differences, are evident in the essay's final paragraph:

> The severity of most of the socioeconomic indicators presented above challenges researchers, policymakers, and city officials with a sense of urgency; this is not only a problem for the Puerto Rican or Latino communities. Expected growth in the Latino population coupled with a simultaneous stagnation or decline of socioeconomic position has potentially explosive effects for the entire city—as well as for other areas where Puerto Ricans live. While comparisons between Puerto Ricans and other groups are important to understanding how each group is faring, pitting one against the other does nothing to further the progress of any group— and may actually aggravate intergroup conflicts. It is critical for Puerto Ricans to gain entry into different sectors of the city's economy and regain socioeconomic stability. At the same time, however, lessons learned from the Puerto Rican experience in New York City can be useful to successfully integrating other Latino immigrants into the city's mainstream—and charting the progress of future Latino generations. The problems that affect Puerto Ricans have been identified; understanding their origins is the next step toward devising effective solutions.[30]

Perhaps the central question raised in a comparative inter-Latino analysis of present-day New York is the relation between Puerto Ricans and Dominicans, a question that is generally elided because of the frequent official grouping of Dominicans in the "Central and South American" or "Other Hispanic" categories. This absence of Dominicans as a discrete point of comparison is the case in "Understanding Socioeconomic Differences" and the sources provided in that study. Yet it is clearly the Dominicans, already by far the second largest group and rapidly approaching the number of Puerto Ricans by unofficial count, that bear closest resemblance to the Puerto Ricans in terms of both cultural history and socioeconomic placement. The two groups together, sometimes even conjoined within the Latino aggregate because of their common Caribbean background, account for well over 80 percent of the whole and command the public image of the "New York Latino." And in addition to magnitude and cultural affinities, it is in its comparison with the situation of Dominicans that the exceptional yet exemplary Puerto Rican experience finds its most direct counterpoint.

Unfortunately, sociologically grounded treatment of the Dominican community has thus far left this kind of contrastive analysis largely unaddressed. Whether the pitch is for the community's bustling "vitality" and rapid progress or its unequalled "poverty"—and accounts tend to oscillate between those two extremes—the reference point is the Latino population as a whole, or non-Dominican society in general. One study, *Dominican New Yorkers: A Socioeconomic Profile* (1995), for example, marshals ample tabulations comparing Dominicans with "New York City Overall," "Non-Hispanic White," "Non-Hispanic Black," and "Hispanic, Overall," but includes only one parenthetical mention of the Puerto Ricans ("only Puerto Ricans have a greater presence").[31] Among other things, the omission of such group-to-group comparison places in question the authors' repeated claim to "worst-off status" among all New York Hispanics, and on many counts among all New Yorkers.

Of course, the point of these comparative analyses cannot be to establish a socioeconomic pecking-order of the "most oppressed," or "fastest achievers." The main problem, which goes to explain some of the gravest omissions, has more to do with methodology and theoretical perspective than with the unexplored terrain itself. Another essay by some of the same authors, in fact, arrives at a more balanced account of the complex socioeconomic reality of the New York Dominican community.[32] But it is another publication of the CUNY Dominican Studies Institute, Jorge Duany's

Quisqueya on the Hudson: The Transnational Identity of Dominicans in Washington Heights (1994), that suggests an analytical framework appropriate to a useful comparative study between the two groups, and to a differentiated consideration of the New York Latino experience overall. Not that Duany makes much mention of Puerto Rican identity—though he has written widely on the subject from many angles—much less draws out any parallels or contrasts; his strictly local, neighborhood sample focus is, in fact, even narrower than that of many other studies. But by placing the issue of "Dominican York" experience in the context of globalization and the formation of "transnational identities," he speaks in terms that, from a historical standpoint, resonate with parallels to social processes lived through by Puerto Ricans. In addition to the usual "socioeconomic characteristics," Duany offers observations and cites attitudes on political and cultural orientation toward the homeland, assimilation and its resistance, bilingualism and race, and a range of other identity issues long of central interest in the study of Puerto Rican life in New York. And he frames his discussion with reference to concepts of "transnational communities," diaspora, circular and global migration processes, and other constituents of contemporary social theory. When he describes Dominicans, for example, as a "transnational community," "characterized by a constant flow of people in both directions, a dual sense of identity, ambivalent attachments to two nations, and a far-flung network of kinship and friendship ties across state frontiers,"[33] he could just as well be speaking of Nuyoricans, the prototype of that kind of community among Latinos in New York. "Quisqueya on the Hudson," seen in these terms, bears more than a casual resemblance to El Barrio on the East River in the 1950s and 1960s, a parallel also noted by other seasoned observers.[34]

THE COLONIAL "EXCEPTION"

"Mex-Yorkers," the latest group to appear en masse on the city's Latino landscape, are also very much a "transnational community," as creative ethnographic research has established in convincing detail[35] and a visit to the old Puerto Rican neighborhoods of El Barrio or Williamsburgh, Brooklyn, makes palpably evident. Colombians, Ecuadorians, Salvadorans, all of New York's major Latino groups partake of a "transnational sociocultural system" in their everyday lives, "here" or "there," and in their increasingly hybrid forms of self-identification.[36] Individually and as a composite they are more a "diasporic transnation" than anything resembling an ethnic immigrant group. As much as the familiar immigrant narrative may accompany them as they settle into their niches and enclaves, the prospects for their ready or eventual incorporation into New York life remain dim at best under conditions of global economic restructuring. The formation of systemic transnational linkages with economic, political, and cultural dimensions is thus a matter of historical necessity in both locations; they are structured into the very relations between country or region of origin and the United States, and into the very conditions of migration in the first place. In this respect, the transnational quality of the Latino presence in New York follows the pattern set over the course of decades, and in its most intricate way, by the Puerto Rican emigrant experience.

But even as "Latino transnationals," Puerto Ricans remain the "exception" among the New York groups, distinct even from their closest cousins, the Dominican Yorks. This difference is marked off, in a formal sense, by U.S. citizenship, and in the practical social arena, as Congressman Serrano is quick to add, by the second-class nature of that supposedly privileged status. Direct colonial relations, as an uninterrupted legacy and ever-present reality, govern the motives and outcomes of the whole migratory and settlement process, and fix a consistently low ceiling on the group's expectations and opportunities. For Puerto Ricans, the "blessings" of American citizenship have been even worse than mixed. Under the constant sway of colonial machinations, it has been a setup for stigmatization and pathological treatment, more than outweighing, over the long haul, their advantageous exemption from the most pressing of immigrant woes. As Willie Colón has it in the title of a 1989 album, Puerto Ricans are "legal aliens." And other Latinos, most of whom have indeed endured the deathly humiliations of undocumented status, recognize this difference themselves; as a correspondent for the *Christian Science Monitor* reported in a survey of Hispanic communities, "whenever Puerto Ricans came up for discussion, Chicanos and Cubans repeatedly said that Puerto Ricans had an extra burden to bear, in addition to their language, their color, and their poverty. It was, they said, the psychological uncertainty resulting from the limbo which Puerto Rico's commonwealth status had turned out to be. To the average Puerto Rican, the argument goes, commonwealth status means his or her being made a kept man or woman of the U.S."[37]

Puerto Ricans are perhaps most precisely to be considered "colonial emigrants" (or "[im]migrants" as Clara Rodríguez would have it) in the global metropolis, bearing closer congruences, on an international scale, with counterparts like Jamaicans in London, Martinicans in Paris, and Surinamese in Amsterdam.[38] In rebuffing Linda Chavez, Serrano equates the psychological legacy of colonialism for Puerto Ricans with that of slavery for American Blacks, or at least relates them in the same breath as the unmentioned grounding for her shallow diagnosis of the "Puerto Rican exception." And indeed, it is in many ways their long, profound, and complex relation to African Americans, even more than the outward marker of citizenship, that most clearly distinguishes the social position and interactions of Puerto Ricans from those of the other transnational Latino groups in New York. Throughout their century-long sojourn in the Big Apple, and especially since the late 1940s, New York Puerto Ricans have been at close living and working quarters with Blacks, perhaps closer than any other national group in the history of this country. In addition to unprecedented cultural fusions, most social indicators point consistently to Puerto Ricans bearing greater similarities to Blacks than to the other Latino groups, and to the Latino aggregate.[39] Needless to say, because of the gulf between sociodemographic and qualitative-theoretical analysis, little has been made thus far of those potent and demonstrable realities. And the foisting of a "Latino" construct onto the field of identity options has only further clouded the issue.

As different from transnational diasporic communities in general, the colonial emigrant is organically inserted into the racial divide and the cultural and class dynamic of the metropolitan society. Especially since the 1960s, the issue of Puerto Rican identity has been entwined with the social and cultural experience of African Americans, and with the problematics of Blackness and "double consciousness," more so than is likely even for that of the "blacker" Dominican community for some time to come. Similarly, as part of a U.S. national agenda, Puerto Ricans in the United States bear closer historical ties to the Chicano population than do their ancestral cultural kin from Central America, and even their Mixteco neighbors in El Barrio. It is the directness of the colonial tie that thus places U.S. Puerto Ricans both inside and outside of U.S. domestic politics, with interests rooted equally in the struggles for justice and equality in the United States and in the struggles for sovereignty in the Caribbean and Latin America. The sense of ambivalence generally attributed to the "limbo" of commonwealth status has to do with this duality of political focus, this simultaneous grounding on two social fronts. But it is not just a "burden," as their sympathetic fellow Latinos call it, nor does it necessarily spell dysfunction or identity crisis. Strategically, with an unprecedented half of the nationality living on either side, and with the "sides" constantly intermingling because of an unparalleled circular migration, there is no alternative to a multiple identity position.

The adequacy of the embattled "Latino" or "Hispanic" concept hinges on its inclusiveness toward the full range of social experiences and identities, and particularly its bridging of the divergence within the contemporary configuration between recent "Latino immigrant" populations and, for want of a better term, the "resident minority" Chicano and Puerto Rican communities. In the context of the "New Nueva York," the toughest test of "Latinismo" is its negotiation of the varied lines of solidarity and historically structured relations informing Puerto Rican social identity: with other, Francophone or Anglophone Caribbean communities, for example, or with African Americans and Chicanos, or with other colonial migrants in "global cities," or of course with other Puerto Ricans, "over there" on the Island, or "out there" in the diaspora. All of these crucial dimensions of New York Puerto Rican self-identification stretch the "pan-Hispanic" idea in different ways, but must be accounted for if Puerto Ricans are not once again, as was reported back in 1958, to "substitute [the terms *Hispano* and *Latino*] for that of 'Puerto Rican,' because the latter, in more ways than one, has become a 'bad public relations' identification for New York Puerto Ricans."[40] That is, unless the "pan-ethnic" net is cast wide enough across and along language, "racial," class, and geographic lines, the Puerto Rican component too readily equates with the stigmatized, abject implications of the label, the stain of which the "new politics of Hispanic assimilation" must be cleansed.

On the other hand, the influence is of course reciprocal and general, and the perspectives introduced by the new Latino groups are also helping shape the terms of a multigroup identity and social movement. These terms are always provisional and subject to reexamination, as is clear in the ironic reversal of inter-Latino conditions in present-day Chicago, where "Latino ethnic consciousness" was first committed to sociological study by Félix Padilla. By the end of 1995, there were Latino groups calling for a dismantling of the congressional district they had once fought so hard to create. The reason given: that Mexicans and Puerto Ricans are, in their words, "racially different and have little in common beyond their language."[41] (To which, by the way, the president of Chicago's Latino Firefighters Association Charles Vazquez pointedly responded, "To those who say we are 'racially different,' what's the difference between a poor Mexican making minimum wage and a poor Puerto Rican making minimum wage?")[42] Tales of such contention among Latino groups abound, of course, in Los Angeles, Miami, and New York and put the lie to any too facile, wishful, or ominous image of Latinos as a seamlessly knitted tribe or horde. But practical disjunctures do not necessarily invalidate the strategic prospects and formative process of Latino unity. Rather, they point up the need for an eminently flexible, inclusive concept based on a clear understanding of historical differences and particularities.

With such a concept in view, one can only agree with Suzanne Oboler when she argues that "differences in the ways that race and class are understood by more recently arrived Latin American immigrants are important to consider in assessing the issues that contribute toward or hinder the fostering of . . . a 'Latino Culture' in the U.S. context" (16). The lessons and experiences from Latin America and the Caribbean stand to enrich and broaden the cultural and political horizons of those Latinos, notably Mexican Americans and Puerto Ricans, with a longer standing in U.S. barrios and workplaces. They offer grounds for hope that the idea and study of "Latino" might transcend—and transgress—the domestic confines of U.S. public discourse on politics and cultural identity, and engage (or reengage) it to the global processes of which it is a part. This hope is very much alive in the "New Nueva York," as Puerto Ricans—U.S. citizens and increasingly English-speaking—are impelled in the name of Latino solidarity to reassert their commitment to immigrant and language rights, and to embrace the trans-Latino vision of "nuestra América."[43]

Buying fruit, on Third Avenue in El Barrio, East Harlem (1997)
(Photo by Máximo R. Colón)

8

Life Off the Hyphen
Latino Literature and Nuyorican Traditions

The View from the Hyphen

In 1990 literary history was made when for the first time a book by a Hispanic writer won the Pulitzer Prize for fiction, generally considered the most prestigious honor in American literature. *The Mambo Kings Play Songs of Love*, the second novel by Cuban-American author Oscar Hijuelos, tells the story of two musician brothers, Cesar and Nestor Castillo, who arrive from Cuba in 1949 to try their luck on the New York music scene. Though not an untroubled immigrant success story, the Castillo brothers do get their piece of the American Dream when in 1955 they appear in a scene of the *I Love Lucy* show. The book's success, however, was boundless, having been helped along by what has been called "the most highly promoted Hispanic book in history by a major press."[1] Before culminating in the Pulitzer, recognition gathered in approving reviews, extensive exposure, advance sales of foreign rights, and a movie deal. By 1990 the time was right for a Hispanic Pulitzer, and when *Mambo Kings* rose to the top the door was thrown open for the entry of "Latino literature" onto the landscape of mainstream American letters.

The accolades were not at all unanimous, however, even among Latinos, many of whom believe that the book (and its insidious movie version) only repeat and reinforce some of the most nagging stereotypes of Latinos. Besides, the touted Pulitzer has never been regarded as a sure stamp of literary quality, many past awards having gone to books that were quickly forgotten and subject to more qualified reviews once they were read more closely. The Pulitzer board and juries, responsible for finalizing decisions since the first fiction award in 1948, have been composed almost entirely

of white males, predominantly professional journalists, with the first woman, non-white, nonjournalist board member admitted as late as 1980.
Their perspective on literature is reflected in the principles which have
guided the novel prize since its inception in 1917, where it is stated that the
honor will go to the works that best present "the whole atmosphere of
American life and the highest standard of American manners and manhood."[2] When the president of Columbia University Nicholas Butler Mur-
ray assumed his lengthy and influential role in the history of the prizes, the
word "whole" was changed to "wholesome." The primacy of patriotic and
moralistic criteria have led some to the view that "the Pulitzer Prize novels
make a significant if negative contribution to the history of American fiction,"[3] while as early as 1935 Malcolm Cowley already was voicing his objection to the conventionalism and amateurishness of some of the prize-
winners, and to the conservative biases of the prize itself. For Cowley, the
prize implies "a guarantee to the American public that the chosen books
have nothing in them to shatter conventions or shake the state, nothing to
drive the stock market down or interrupt the sleep of virgins."[4]

In the case of *The Mambo Kings Play Songs of Love*, the board and the jury
(composed that year of the president of the Guggenheim Foundation,
writer and critic Diane Johnson, and an English professor from Bowling
Green State University) were divided, some preferring the other finalist, E.
L. Doctorow's *Billy Bathgate*, others not liking either book. Once the prize
had been announced and the movie hit the theaters, the songs of praise for
Hijuelos's work became more muted, and the response of Latino readers
ambivalent at best. While major Latino literature publisher and promoter
Nicolás Kanellos, for example, refers to it as "the best Hispanic book ever
published by a large commercial press," his judgment is qualified when he
notes that "the novel drags in the middle and towards the end, without the
benefit of a hard-driving plot. Its insistence on detailing the culture and
spirit of the times and its repetitive reminiscence are somewhat tiring."[5]
The Latino commentator for the *Village Voice*, Cuban-American Enrique
Fernández, finds many objections to the claim that the book is "well-re-
searched" in its historical references, pointing out some of the many anach-
ronisms and other inaccuracies with regard to Latin music history. He concludes that "something tastes flat," and mentions that "the night Hijuelos's
Pulitzer was announced, [some critical Latino] friends threatened to start a
ruckus outside his house."[6] Perhaps the sharpest critical note is sounded by
the young New York Puerto Rican writer Abraham Rodriguez, who points

to the rampant sexism of the book as one of its most glaring retrogressions: "It took Hispanic women like thirty years to get over that macho bullshit," he says, "and he brings it all back, and they reward him with the Pulitzer. I think he's full of shit."[7]

Though hardly a breakthrough in literary terms, *The Mambo Kings* will likely retain its landmark status if only for its timeliness, the big prize establishing it as the book that inaugurated "Latino literature" as an accepted, English-language component of the multicultural canon, and as an attractive marketing rubric, in the 1990s. Several commentators speak in terms of "before and after" the event, noting the sudden plethora of works by Latinos published by major presses, the new space for Latino listings in catalogues and bookstores, and the promotionals featuring Latino writers—all in the decade since the award.[8] Beyond the expected celebrations, Hijuelos has become the author of choice to write prefaces to the many anthologies of Latino literature, where the inclusion of selections from his own work is all but obligatory.[9] After all, while some of the scenes in his laureled novel may well "interrupt the sleep of virgins," the overall effect is to bolster that "wholesome atmosphere of American life"; like Desi Arnaz, who has a preponderant symbolic role in the novel, it signals a modus vivendi between "Latino" culture and the coziness of the American living room, all the more welcome by our times when the Latino population has grown so alarmingly immense in size and diversity. As "full of shit" as he may be, Hijuelos helped provide the needed handle by winning the Pulitzer, the proof that a Latino book could make it into the long-elusive American mainstream, and the foundational fiction, as it were, of a legitimate, subcanonical concept of "Latino literature."

Not that a literature by U.S. Latinos is new, of course, its history extending back to the beginnings of American letters and encompassing a succession of discernible stages and periods.[10] The decades preceding the first "Premio Pulitzer" saw the publication of many works of Latino fiction and poetry, some of greater significance than *The Mambo Kings*, and even the idea of an embracing, pan-Latino heritage had been promoted by many critics and publishers, notably the Arte Público Press at the University of Houston. What is new about the post-Pulitzer period, in fact, is not so much the writing itself, which has tended to carry forward with the thematic and stylistic concerns of the previous years, but the prevalent notion of a Pulitzer-eligible Latino literature—that is, a literature by U.S Latinos that is compatible with the prescribed "wholesomeness" of American life, a literature that, with all its play on cultural differences, matches up convincingly to the "standards of American manners and manhood." The coronation of *The Mambo Kings* heralded the ascendancy of a Latino literature which, however nostalgic for the old culture and resentful of the new, is markedly assimilationist toward American society and its culture, thus departing from the contestatory and oppositional stance characteristic of much writing by Latino authors in the past. Two prominent Latino critics, speaking specifically of Hijuelos, have referred to it as a Latino literature, and life, "on the hyphen," where the hyphen is embraced as an equal sign.[11]

Gustavo Pérez Firmat, the Cuban-American writer and professor of Latin American literature, entitles his intriguing book *Life on the Hyphen: The Cuban-American Way* (1994). His goal is very specific: to characterize the idiosyncrasy of Cuban culture in the U.S. setting, and to mark off what he refers to as the "one-and-a-half generation," that is, the generation of Cubans like himself, whose formative experience lies midway between those who grew up in Cuba before migrating ("too Cuban to be American") and the second generation, like the author's children, who grew up here and are "too American to be Cuban." Pérez Firmat traces this sequence of adaptations and negotiations between the Cuban and the American as links in what he calls "the-Desi-chain," refractions of Desi Arnaz's TV character Ricky Ricardo, "the single most visible Hispanic presence in the United States over the last forty years."[12] With Desi as the paradigm, and the elaborate discussion of the *I Love Lucy* show comprising the strongest section of the book, *Life on the Hyphen* ranges widely through Cuban-American literature and popular culture, with ample reference to Gloria Estefan and the Miami Sound Machine and to the historical placement of the mambo craze of the 1940s and 1950s. But it is Oscar Hijuelos and *The Mambo Kings*, where the "Desi chain" has the same fictional role as it has for Pérez Firmat's cultural discourse, that is clearly the most direct catalyst and exemplum for the enactment of the distinctively Cuban-American "life on the hyphen." While making due note of the criticisms of the book, and himself noting its many errors and dogged "anglocentrism," Pérez Firmat speaks of the "beguiling richness of the novel" and is obviously taken by this emblematic evidence of his theories of immigrant adaptation over the generations. He even ventures explanations for the book's blatant phallocentrism, and for the multitude of historical and linguistic errors, chalking them up to the task of cultural "translation." In the process, he offers the most extended and insightful interpretation of *The Mambo Kings* to date.[13]

With his subtitle and repeated insistence throughout the book, Pérez Firmat aims to limit himself to the "Cuban-American" way, the particularity of that hyphen, and that instance of Latino immigrant adaptation. But as his reference to Desi as "the single most visible *Hispanic* presence" belies, the agenda of *Life on the Hyphen* is more ambitious than that: his lens may be "one-and-a-half generation" Cuban-American, but the cultural landscape is that of the contemporary United States as a whole. Inspired by a *People* magazine cover story devoted to Gloria Estefan, the book opens by taking this sign of celebrity as "a fair indication of the prominent role that Cuban Americans [no hyphen here] are playing in the increasing—and inexorable—latinization of the United States; by now, few Americans will deny that, sooner or later, for better or for worse, the rhythm is going to get them."[14] Interest is not focused here on the hyphen in "Cuban-American," or the establishment of the neologism "cubanglo" as the most precise designation of Cuban one-and-a-halfers. As an extension of this group-specific discourse, Pérez Firmat is talking about "hyphenation" itself as a bicultural process, a pattern of cultural hybridization. At one point, his musings on Cubano-Americanism issue directly into a broad, three-stage theory of immigrant group experience; though Cuban-American examples prevail, his whole point is to explicate the paradigmatic passage of immigrant cultures and communities from the stages of "substitution" to "destitution" to "institution" in adjusting to the new "home country" and settling in. And among the immigrants, Cuban-Americans of course share their hyphenation with other Latinos, of whose generalized experience it is taken to be a "prominent" example.

It is important to bear these broader fields of validation in mind when addressing what Pérez Firmat regards as the distinctive quality of Cuban-American cultural placement in the U.S. setting. "I realize," he writes, "that mine is not a fashionable view of relations between 'majority' and 'minority' cultures. Contemporary models of culture contact tend to be oppositional: one culture, say white American, vanquishes another, say Native American. But the oppositional model, accurate as it may be in other situations, does not do justice to the balance of power in Cuban America" (6). To "oppositional" he prefers "appositional," for the "balance of power" in this case is defined by "contiguity" rather than "conflict," by "collusion" rather than "collision." This particular case, he contends, puts the lie to other, more "fashionable" views of ethnic relations and culture contact in that the hyphen, the ultimate mark of hybridity, signals equilibrium and not tension. Unlike other "minority" cultures, and at odds with the experience of many other Latino groups, "over the last several decades, in the United States, Cuba and America have been on a collusion course, . . . display[ing] an intricate equilibrium between the claims of each culture" (6). At no point venturing a historical or sociological explanation of this unique and exceptional circumstance, the author nevertheless upholds the representative stature of his case in point. Like his cherished hyphen, Pérez Firmat's analysis "is a seesaw, . . . tilt[ing] first one way, then the other" (6) between exceptionalism and generalization, between the "Cuban-American way" and the "Hispanic condition."

While Pérez Firmat's *Life on the Hyphen* retains a Cuban-American focus despite its forays into broader cultural and theoretical terrains, Ilan Stavans in *The Hispanic Condition* (1995) will do with no such narrow boundaries; he subtitles his book expansively "Reflections on Culture and Identity in America." Here the hyphen—he calls his introductory chapter "Life in the Hyphen"—marks not just the "cubanglo" dilemma, but takes on hemispheric proportions, "the encounter between George Washington and Simón Bolívar,"[15] or even, at a civilizational level, between Shakespeare and Cervantes. Stavans, who arrived in the United States from his native Mexico as late as 1985, has been quick to insert himself into the culture wars, bringing with him an essayistic style comprised of warmed-over Octavio Paz and a postmodernist metaphysics of the border. Despite the constant appeal to the relational aspects and indeterminacy of cultural identities, the "Hispanic condition" as portrayed here rests on decidedly essentialist, and existentialist, assumptions. The sense of "displacement" experienced by Cuban-American exiles, for example, "as a struggle, as a way of life, as a condition, . . . is, and will remain, a Latino signature. . . . To be expelled from home, to wander through geographic and linguistic diasporas, is essential to our nature" (59).

With all his cosmic claims, though, Stavans is mainly interested in the new "Latino literature." In *The Hispanic Condition* and other books, numerous anthologies and countless articles, he has become the most frequent commentator on the subject, and the critic who has been most intent on configuring a Latino literary canon in the 1990s. Though perhaps most familiar with the Mexican American tradition, he nevertheless has ample reference to Cuban-American, Puerto Rican, Dominican, and other Latino writers, and his professional training in Spanish and Latin American literatures allows him to range widely—though often diffusely—over the "Hispanic" literary landscape in the widest sense. Unfortunately, what is gained with this potentially welcome framework of cultural kinship and solidarity is lost in the need for specificity and more rigorous differentiation among the varied group perspectives.

For Stavans, *The Mambo Kings Play Songs of Love* is a "dazzling novel," a "moving account of brotherly love in the New York of the 1950s, which traced the impact and influence of Latin rhythms north of the border" (14, 56). References to the book and the Pulitzer abound in *The Hispanic Condition* (though they are unaccompanied by any extended critical analysis), and along with Sandra Cisneros and Julia Alvarez, Hijuelos clearly takes on canonical status here and in Stavans's other writings.[16] Thinking of Hijuelos he asks the question that centrally concerns him: "What does he as a Cuban-American share with Chicana Sandra Cisneros and Dominican-American novelist Julia Alvarez, author of *How the García Girls Lost Their Accents*, other than an amorphous and evasive ethnic background?"[17] At no point do the intervening issues of class position and accessibility to the newly forming literary market figure in his calculations, which despite his many historical digressions continually revert to an internally cultural unit of discourse. Indeed, though he is groping for inclusive, pan-Latino affinities and associations, Stavans is notably selective in his conception of the Latino canon and the conditions of its formation. He favors, among other variables, the "literary" works, those most reminiscent of and compatible with Latin American literary models, especially those of the "boom."

As for group perspective, though his knowledge of Chicano literature is strongest, he is inclined toward that of the Cuban-American; the present-day "Hispanic condition" is most closely tracked as another link in the "Desi chain." "Arnaz's ordeal," he comments, "as Hijuelos knows . . . , is every Latino's dream of making it big in America. Among Latinos, Cuban-Americans symbolize success and progress, assimilation but self-awareness" (58). What would here seem to be a marking off of Cubans among the other groups—the sense of success and progress, assimilation and upward mobility—is repeatedly treated as the "new" element in all of Latino life; "something essential is changing in the texture of the Latino community," he claims, for "behind the much-publicized images of poverty, drugs and violence, upward mobility is indeed taking place" (189). Like Pérez Firmat, Stavans maintains that what is new, "a different approach to the Latino metabolism," is the demise of the idea of Latino culture as resistance, the replacement, in his words, of "the concept of negative assimilation" (14–15).

Though he shies away from a sense of the Latino hyphen as signaling "collusion," his notion of "collision" is far from the politically grounded resistance historically associated with Latino cultural expression. In league with Latin American magical realism (which he calls "eminently marketable"), Latinos are here presented as "soldiers in the battle to change America from within, to reinvent its inner core" (14–15).

What is "new" about the recent Latino writing, and goes to inform it as a marketing category, is that it seeks to be apolitical, and here the foundational Cuban-American is again joined by Julia Alvarez as the trendsetter: "Hijuelos signals a trend by the new generation of Cuban-American and shies away from politics, as does Julia Alvarez in her fictional study of well-off Dominican girls in the United States" (56). With all his disclaimers and fanciful notions of "implosion," Stavans is talking about crossing over, making it into the mainstream, assimilation. The "explosion of Latino arts" which is "overwhelming the country," and which involves a strange gallery of examples, from William Carlos Williams and Joan Baez to Anthony Quinn and Oscar Lewis (!), means above all a move into the heart of American mass culture. Toward the end of *The Hispanic Condition*, Stavans pauses to wonder what it is all about, whether there is any substantive change involved in all the novelty and hype. "Is the pilgrimage from the periphery to mainstream culture," he asks, "one in which the entire Latino community is embarked? Aren't many being left behind?" (187). It is interesting that Stavans allows himself such second thoughts amidst his flurry of enthusiasm. Unfortunately, these questions find no substantive answers within the conceptual framework in which he conducts his "reflections on culture and identity in America."

LATINO LITERATURE AND CULTURAL CAPITAL

There are few Puerto Ricans in *The Mambo Kings*, and when they do appear it is usually as underworld mobsters, typically garbed in "tan suits." Toward the end of the book, as a kind of afterthought in the endless love life of the protagonist Cesar Castillo, there is Lydia, a working-class Puerto Rican woman whose caring relation to the aging but ever libidinous musician is marred by an undertone of personal opportunism. Otherwise, though, the Latin New York of the first Hispanic Pulitzer is entirely Cuban, even though it is set at a time when Puerto Ricans far outnumbered other Latino groups and was written when the Cuban population in New York had declined to relative insignificance. Even the Latin music scene in New York, which in the 1950s was already largely populated by Puerto Rican musicians, is basically a Cuban affair in Hijuelos's novel, renowned Puerto Ricans like Rafael Hernández, Noro Morales, Tito Puente, and Tito Rodríguez getting frequent mention and an occasional cameo appearance but no formative role in either the music or the narrative. It is worth recalling in this regard that Machito's "Afro-Cubans," the supreme orchestral achievement of the whole "mambo kings" era, were almost all New York Puerto Ricans.

The invisibility of New York Puerto Ricans in their own social habitat, while presumably not the intention of the author, is not casual either, for the cultural world of *The Mambo Kings* is "Latino" in a certain selective sense. Aside from its obvious masculinist and heterosexual emphasis, it is the white, middle-class Latino whose experience and perspectives prevail throughout the book. Though they run into some harder times in New York, the Castillo brothers are from a landowning family in Oriente, not of the status of the Arnaz's of the Santiago elite, but they had their means and prospects, and their domestic help; they can even pass as Ricky Ricardo's cousins. They speak proudly of their Spanish background, their father having migrated from Galicia and stubbornly upheld the noble bloodline. They are cubanos, yes, but above all "gallegos"; they are from the mountains, but fashion themselves more as caballeros than "guajiros." They are "mambo kings," masters of Afro-Cuban music, yet the protagonists' deepest love is not the mambo but "songs of love," the bolero.[18] Unable to ignore the reality of racism that plagued the Latin bands, the white "mambo kings" recall it as indignities suffered by the "black musicians," as though they were a rare and marginal presence on the scene.[19] In general, "blackness," pressing poverty, and other markers of social oppression are "othered" in this evocation of New York Latino life, with the African American, even more thoroughly than the Puerto Rican, being a total nonpresence in the book.

Fully in line with the theoretical orientations of Pérez Firmat and Stavans, the concept of "Latino" in *The Mambo Kings* involves the privileging of privilege. Claiming to represent cultural traits shared by all Latinos, they typically have recourse to language, religion, and a Spanish-inflected *mestizaje* (mixing) while evading differential relations of power among the groups involved. The result is an idea of Latino life based on what might be termed the "highest common denominator," one that highlights motives of success and opportunity and underplays issues of poverty and inequality as extraneous to the dynamics of Latino culture. The "condition" and concerns of middle-class exiles, bearing with them and reproducing the cultural capital inherent in their family lines, becomes the paradigm of the Latino experience. The communities forged of working-class migrations from colonized countries and regions recede into the background of this "Latino" landscape, and often find representation as fearful, hostile, inner-city jungles. The hyphenated Latino—the hyphen standing for equilibrium, "collusion," or even Stavans's wishful "implosion"—is fully compatible with white social identity in the U.S. racial formation, while blackness, especially as embodied by the African American, is typically distanced from the terrain of representative Latino experience.

Latino literature, as that category has emerged in contemporary canon-formation, is circumscribed from this perspective. To begin with, most of the prominent writers, those who appear in the anthologies, publish with major houses, and win literary prizes, are from this background of class and racial privilege. Beyond that, even those whose origins are more humble and disadvantaged, such as Puerto Rican authors Esmeralda Santiago and Judith Ortíz Kofer, tend to thematize their own upward mobility and distance themselves from the crasser aspects of inner-city barrio life, as is evident from their aloof treatment of African Americans. But writers like Dominican American Julia Alvarez, Cuban American Cristina Garcia, and Colombian American Jaime Manrique are more representative in this sense; writing in English though fluent in Spanish, broaching controversial themes of gender and sexuality, they offer up glimpses of middle-class Latino life in the metropolis, with all the travails and fits of nostalgia, but consistently from the vantage point of those who need not worry about being taken for Blacks or ghetto-dwellers.

But the bifurcation of Latino writing and canon-making goes beyond the more explicit matter of the social provenance of the favored authors, or even the thematic and stylistic features of the works themselves. The difference, I would suggest, which goes to explain such privileges and critical predilections, lies in the differential positioning of the varied Latino groups in the prevailing structures of power and domination within the United States and internationally. Those whose collective identities in the United States were constituted by a long-standing history of conquest and colonization generate a literary expression which contrasts with that of comparatively recent arrivals from countries with less direct ties to U.S. imperial power. In particular, Chicano and Nuyorican writing stand out among

the emerging "Latino" literary configuration, sharing many of the bicultural themes with other works in that category but usually presenting a
markedly divergent angle on society. As in the case of other aspects of social experience, the variations within the literature now classified as "Latino" need to be dissected critically with these structural contrasts clearly in
view. Interestingly, the different placement of Puerto Ricans as compared
with other Hispanic groups in New York was recognized early on in the
community's history; already in 1928 an editorial in the weekly *Gráfico*
spoke of Puerto Ricans as "the most vulnerable group of those which comprise the large family of Ibero-Americans. Truly it seems a paradox," the article continues, "that being American citizens these should be the most de-
fenseless. The reality is sad, but true. People of Puerto Rican background
find themselves completely unprotected [desamparados] in this American
metropolis. While the citizens of other countries have their consulates and
diplomats to represent them, the children of Borinquen have no one."[20]

In terms of literature and culture, this sociologically grounded variation
within the pan-Latino concept refers to a differential relation to cultural capital, that is, to differing institutional infrastructures of production and consumption.[21] The newly arrived "Latino" writers, immigrating from countries relatively free of direct colonial subordination, find some degree of
accommodation within the support structures provided by their nation-
states of origin. Unlike their Nuyorican and Chicano counterparts, they are
viewed, however opportunistically, as "overseas" representatives of their
countries, and are thus eligible to turn to their varied embassies and cultural attachés for support, recognition, and exposure. Many of the readings
and gatherings, book publication parties, and other commemorative events
for New York writers of Dominican, Colombian, Mexican, and Honduran
extraction are routinely convened under the auspices of their respective
consulates or government-formed literary societies, which in cooperation
with publishing houses also facilitate publication and promotion of their diasporic writers and artists.[22] Of course, many of these writers write in Spanish and have literary training, and are thus easily considered integral to
their national literatures. But even English-language authors like the Dominicans Julia Alvarez and Junot Díaz, in addition to their access to major
U.S. publishing opportunities, gained rapid recognition in the Dominican
Republic and among Dominican writers, which included the translation
and publication of their work.[23] It is this cultural capital as an institutional
infrastructure that has meant for the makings of a "Latino" literary com-

munity in New York and, nationally, an umbrella of legitimation for the diverse but structurally akin writers of Latin American and Spanish background. For obvious political reasons, the situation is of course different for Cuban American writers, who have not had the same kind of governmental support by way of the mission and interest sections. But in the Cuban case too the cultural and literary projection of the diaspora has remained an intense diplomatic issue, and the privileges accorded the exile community have meant for an influential infrastructure to the benefit of the artistic and literary community in the United States.[24]

Cultural capital of this kind has been virtually absent for the Puerto Rican writers, especially those also lacking in educational and linguistic advantages. Selectively, some of them find a place among their fellow "Latinos" in the anthologies and literary assemblies, but as a group, movement, or tradition, Nuyorican writing and authors run askew of the prevailing model. Dismissed or ignored by the Puerto Rican government and literary establishment, what they have had by way of an infrastructure was built from the ground up, with no auspice or recognition coming from any official entities. Cultural institutions on the Island, such as the Instituto de Cultura Puertorriqueña and the Ateneo Puertorriqueño, have virtually never found occasion to include Nuyorican writers in their ambitious literary programs and publications. Indeed, it is this lack of mediation which is in part responsible for the seemingly unbridgeable divide between the two settings of Puerto Rican culture, a gulf that has led Nicholasa Mohr among other New York writers to speak of a "separation beyond language."[25] On the New York side, the Puerto Rican government's Office of the Migration has indeed served the interests of the migrant population in its nearly fifty years of activity since the late 1940s; but that entity was always considered part of the Department of Labor and devoted its energy entirely to issues of employment and social services. The closest it came to cultural policies was its facilitation with basic literacy and English-language skills, and the simplistic promotion of Puerto Rican cultural traditions. Its function became particularly anachronistic with the emergence of a new generation of New York Puerto Rican politics and culture in the 1960s, when community-based and nongovernmental organizations were formed to fill the representational void.[26]

This lack of a diplomatic sphere and cultural politics oriented toward the needs and concerns of the diaspora is directly attributable to the ongoing colonial status of the Puerto Rican government. Along with the overwhelmingly working-class composition of the postwar migration, with its attendant low level of cultural literacy, it is this absence of a public infrastructure of literary institutions that accounts for the sharp differentiation in the social position and prospects characteristic of today's Latino writing. New York Puerto Rican cultural workers have been made painfully aware of this vacuum and have responded by establishing makeshift, neighborhood spaces like the Nuyorican Poet's Café and the New Rican Village to accommodate the rising generation of bilingual and English-language writers. As a way to dramatize the quasi-diplomatic aspirations of such grassroots efforts at official institution-building, the example set by the New Rican Village has in recent years been directed toward the founding of the "Puerto Rican Embassy"; with his usual ironic irreverence, Nuyorican poet Pedro Pietri has teamed up with photographer Adal Maldonado in the issuing of Puerto Rican passports, complete with photos and to the accompaniment of Puerto Rican music and literary recitals. More explicitly, Lourdes Vázquez, a poet and fiction writer who has lived stretches of time in both Puerto Rico and New York, has written about the agonies of the colonial writer in the absence of a diplomatic apparatus to address the nation's literary life. Speaking with envious admiration of the successful consular promotion of writers from Colombia, the Dominican Republic, Nicaragua, and the English Caribbean, she comments repeatedly, "No es el caso nuestro" ("such is not our situation").[27] She recognizes that in the field of popular music New York's Puerto Rican culture has been able to transcend geographic and political divides ("Salsa has been our most complete ambassador"), but concludes by referring again to the frustrations of writers and other artists with no established structures to turn to, or contend with. We are "trying to understand," as she puts it, "how to lay claim to a citizenship in a nonindependent country. Here we are asking, where is the structure of government that nourishes us? Here we are wondering, where is the governmental agency to which we can pass the bill for such unrecognized individual effort, so many hours of creativity, discussion, and study."[28]

As the dramatis personae of *The Mambo Kings* illustrate, it is the Puerto Ricans who are "left behind" in the prevalent category of Latino literature. Not that they are totally or systematically excluded from the emerging canon, or that their literature is without parallels and commonalities with other writing under that heading. It is the particular social situation of that literary community when contrasted with that of other Latino nationalities, their differential access to literary and cultural capital as a result of direct colonial relations, that eludes the conceptualization of Latino writing as set forth by critics like Pérez Firmat and Stavans. For if the Latino hyphen as a sign of equilibrium stands for this interplay of cultural politics at an international level, Puerto Ricans in the United States live a life "off the hyphen." As is frequently noted, of all the ethnic groups it is the Puerto Ricans who pointedly refuse the hyphenation of their identity despite generations of life here and a rich history of interaction with U.S. culture at all levels. The term "Puerto Rican American" is rarely used by Puerto Ricans themselves, and when it is, as in the prestigious anthology of recent Latino literature *Iguana Dreams*, it stands as an immediate sign of unfamiliarity.[29] Rather than embracing the hyphen, or playing with it lovingly in the manner of Julia Alvarez, Puerto Ricans typically challenge that marker of collusion or compatibility and erase it as inappropriate to their social position and identity. In the case of colonial Latinos, another kind of punctuation and nomenclature is in order.

"LOWERCASE PEOPLE"

"Puerto Rican American," scowls Miguel, the protagonist of Abraham Rodriguez's novel *Spidertown*. "What a loada shit."[30] "It's not shit, Miguel," responds his girlfriend Cristalena. "It's people trying to find their own identities." But Miguel sticks to his point, distrusting any term that will make it appear either that he is American or that he comes from Puerto Rico. "I know my identity," he says. "I'm a spick. I like spick, okay? It tells me right away what I am. It don't confuse me into thinkin' I'm American. I'm a spick, okay? Thass how whites see you anyway" (267). *Spidertown* is set in the South Bronx of our own time, a return in the 1990s to the "mean streets" of inner-city Puerto Rican life first fictionalized by Piri Thomas in his 1967 autobiographical novel *Down These Mean Streets*. It is the story of young people, teenagers caught up in the engulfing, seemingly inescapable world of crack-dealing, gang warfare, and everyday violence; not once does the scene shift from the run-down streets and abandoned buildings, from the desperate, hopeless life of the ghetto. Time and again we are reminded that it is a world modeled after the American Dream, that it follows the rules of capitalist society. But at the same time, it is a bitter abortion of that dream, a "business" lacking in any real social power or recognition. And the people who inhabit it, the impoverished, uneducated children of the Puerto Rican migration, are condemned to an outcast status, invisible and finding no representation of any kind in the alien culture that surrounds them. "Born to rule the streets and make alliances and break them," it is said toward the end of the book. "Just like world powers and big corporations and successful businesses. It was all bigger than all of them. Miguel and Spider and all those shadows, they were tiny pins on a map, they hardly registered at all. Their kind came and went. They didn't write about them or direct plays or paint murals about their lives. They were all walking shit. Whether they lived in the South Bronx or Bed-Stuy or Harlem or Los Sures. It didn't matter. They didn't exist. They were all lowercase people" (288).

Standing at opposing extremes, *Spidertown* and *The Mambo Kings* illustrate the range of what is labeled as "Latino literature." Though written in the same years, in English, and by second-generation male authors, they portray diametrically contrasting realities and exemplify incompatible views of literature and its relation to society. While Hijuelos's prizewinner is built of nostalgia and the abiding power of cultural representation, *Spidertown* has no *I Love Lucy* show to harken back to, much less the dreamy reminiscences of a long-lost Cuban countryside. Abraham Rodriguez is mercilessly, programmatically, antinostalgic, the unabating presentness of the action contributing directly to the sense of entrapment and alienation of the social experience. In spite of the historical backdrop suggested by Hijuelos, though, both in *The Mambo Kings* and in his first novel *Our House in the Last World* (1985), it is the nonretrospective young Bronx author who seeks to offer a sense of social context and an explanation for the Latino lives captured in his book. The class and racial gulf between the two books could not be more obvious, Hijuelos maintaining a middle-class and "white" perspective and Rodriguez never leaving the world of the Latino bordering on destitution and intricately associated with blackness and the African American experience.

As for gender, the difference is equally striking. While both books center on male experience, *The Mambo Kings* leaves the relation of subordination unquestioned and intact, wallowing in a naturalized phallocentrism and relegating the many women characters to passive, dramatically ineffectual roles. In *Spidertown*, on the other hand, while examples of misogyny and homophobia abound, it is the young women who serve as catalysts of challenge and change and stand up to that stubbornly sexist environment by word and example. Miguel's girlfriend Cristalena, "a girl with a name like a poem," would seem a direct parallel to the "beautiful Maria of my soul" immortalized for her idealized purity in the Castillo brothers' hit ballad; but thankfully Cristalena is no goody-two-shoes, and wages a battle for independence of her own. Loving her, rather than reinforcing the Latin lover stereotype and leaving him his only domain of emotional power, leads Miguel to a bold and decisive rejection of that value system. In a love-making scene toward the end of *Spidertown* this serious life-change is made explicit: "In the world Miguel'd grown up in you start with backyards and rubble lots and then you conquer girls. You get your way with them and you learn that's the way, in life you are supposed to get your way. The woman is supposed to know where she's at, where she BELONGS. It was all in his blood. To be THE MAN. The woman just did what the man said. That was respect. Tradition. Yet Miguel was throwing it all away, the ghosts of a hundred million Latin machistas all hanging their heads and cursing him" (308).

As mentioned, it is its conservative, traditionalist treatment of women that Rodriguez finds most directly objectionable about the first Hispanic Pulitzer, and why he considers its author "full of shit." "It took Hispanic women like thirty years to get over that macho bullshit, and he brings it all back," he says of Hijuelos and his prizewinning book. His point is not that machismo is a thing of the past in Latino culture, but that it has been challenged by women, including women writers. Despite his iconoclasm and the sharply antihistoricist, here-and-now quality of his fictional settings, Rodriguez voices a sense of tradition here, an awareness that others have come before him in his literary project. Though he uses the term sparingly, he knows that he is a "Nuyorican" writer, recognizing that he is on a social turf staked out by Piri Thomas and relying in the lyrical sequences of his prose on a style reminiscent of the familiar cadences of poets like Pedro Pietri and Victor Hernández Cruz. He is also aware that since that outburst of literary expression by U.S. Puerto Ricans in the late 1960s, several women writers have emerged to present a different picture of the experience, such that the world of the Puerto Rican barrios can no longer be conceived of in literary terms without taking into account the contributions of Nicholasa Mohr, Judith Ortíz Kofer, Esmeralda Santiago, and others. This sense of a heritage, of belonging to a trajectory of literary representations of a historically forged community, differentiates the writing of long-resident Latino groups from that of more recent arrivals.

Even the Cuban experience in the United States, which does extend back to the past century and has given rise to a protracted literary representation, is different from the "Nuyorican" in this regard. For though Cuban American literature, with that of Mexican Americans and Puerto Ricans, counts as one of the three oldest among the Hispanic traditions, the tradition in this case is decidedly different from those two others because of the radical break occurring after the Cuban Revolution of 1959. For with the sharply altered social composition and ideological orientation of the exile population, Cuban Americans did not partake of the major political and cultural movements of the 1960s and 1970s which have been so formative of both Chicano and Nuyorican literary history. As a result, whereas a young contemporary writer like Abraham Rodriguez can harken back to the work of Piri Thomas and the Nuyorican poets, and even Island writers like Pedro Juan Soto, Julia de Burgos, and José Luis González, Cuban Americans like Hijuelos and Cristina Garcia have little by way of precedence in the literature produced by Cubans in the U.S. setting, the great, pathbreaking José Martí notwithstanding. The new "Latino" literature as it has been constructed in the 1990s, with all its assimilationist proclivities, now takes this relative newcomer experience, that of the "foreigner," as its prevalent model, while the longer-standing, resident Latino presence and literary background is more liable to be what is "left behind."

For it is not just differences in thematic concerns and stylistic features that distinguish these two variants of Latino literary expression. There is also, perhaps underlying the contrasts, the hyphen, that is, the differential sociological placement and grounding of the writing and social identity of its subjects. In *Spidertown* the main character Miguel is supposed to be writing a book about his mentor in the drug business, Spider; in fact, at several points his boss even commissions him to document his "amazin' life." But from early on Miguel dismisses the idea of becoming a writer as a "dead dream." "Miguel shouldn't have even blurted it out, because it was dumb. There weren't any Puerto Rican writers. Puerto Ricans didn't write books. Miguel had never even seen one" (62). But Spider doesn't relent, posing his question "how's the book coming?" throughout the heated action of the novel. By the end, Miguel does hand over his tapes of interviews with Spider, and perhaps the reader is to understand *Spidertown* itself as the fruit of Miguel's literary labors. Nevertheless, the incompatibility of literature as a profession and the social setting of the novel remain a constant, and echo something the author himself witnessed during his schooldays in the South Bronx. Rodriguez recalls frequently that when he mentioned he wanted to be a writer, his teacher told him that it was impossible because there was no such thing; Puerto Ricans don't know how to write. Forever the rebel, Rodriguez would not be dissuaded by these admonitions and went on to disprove them with a prolific career. But he has continued to recognize the improbability of literature coming from neighborhoods like his own, and from a people bereft of literary infrastructures and cultural capital like the Puerto Rican community in the United States.

The literature of "lowercase people" is a "lowercase" literature, a literature deriving from sources other than those identified with formal education and cultural literacy. Asked if he chose to write because he liked reading, Rodriguez answered, "No, it wasn't about books. It was about writing. My father, it's all his fault, really. He used to write poems, these beautiful, long, longing, yearning poems about Puerto Rico. . . . My first memory is hearing the typewriter. He used to rent these really big typewriters and type on them, and I remember that *clack, clack, clack.* When I was little, I used to sit on his lap and bang on it. Really, the whole writing thing is about typewriters; it's got nothing to do with literature at all."[31] Rather than philosophical ideas or artistic creativity, writing in this sense is a preeminently tactile, physical, oral experience; the sound of the typewriter, the touch of the keys, the perception of letters, words, sounds, images—such is the basis of the writer's craft among the formally uneducated. What the budding author inherited from his father was obviously not the flowery versifying in the Latin American modernist tradition ("he was into Neruda") but the artisan practice. The typewriter was for him what drums or a guitar might be for the aspiring musician: the physical tool of the trade, the object required to express himself. As a "lowercase literature," Nuyorican writing is illustrative of oral tradition and not an institutionalized, canon-forming literature conceived of as a profession.

Not that Abraham Rodriguez, the "lowercase," "amazin' spick" writer, didn't read books, of course; on the contrary. He has clearly become well-versed in the writings of other U.S. Puerto Rican authors, as well as those from the Island and by other Latinos. He has also read widely among other U.S. writers, especially African American literature. Black literature, in fact, and Black culture and opposition politics, hold a special place for him, standing in his view as a model and inspiration for Puerto Rican aspirations; at the end of *Spidertown*, it is his reading of Richard Wright's *Native Son* that helps push Miguel to his final resolve to quit the crack business and move on with his life. Sanchez, the almost unbelievably enlightened Puerto Rican cop who gave him a copy of *Native Son*, is clearly the raisonneur when he says to Miguel, "Sometimes I feel more Puerto Ricans should read it. We could learn so much from the black man" (322). But Rodriguez's literary education goes beyond these more directly accessible sources and extends to the canon of European fiction. Through *Spidertown* the philosophical problematics of Sartre are brought into play by Miguel's friend Amelia, a college student and crack addict, and there is continual reference to Miguel's own reading matter, notably Dickens and Tolstoy. Dostoevsky is an even more obvious influence on Rodriguez's portrayal of the eerie ghetto underground and the psychological desperation of his adolescent characters.

But his all-time favorite, beyond even Gorki and Kafka, is Balzac, and Rodriguez has been called "the Balzac of the Bronx."[32] He refers to Balzac as the "cool guy" when talking to school children on his local speaking engagements, and calls him "my most favoritist writer in the whole —— planet."[33] Surely it is the sheer ambition of the "Comédie Humaine" that captures Rodriguez's fantasy, who aims for a similarly totalistic portrait of contemporary inner-city life; as he sees it, his first book, *The Boy Without a Flag: Tales of the South Bronx* (1992), is but the first installment in a long-term project of "Scenes from Ghetto Life" meant to emulate Balzac's "Scenes from Provincial Life." What most impresses the young Puerto Rican writer, however, is not so much the details of nineteenth-century French society as such, but the rigorous realist method of which Balzac is the undisputed master. For what Rodriguez means by a "non-literary" kind of writing is one, like that of Balzac and the great realists, which confronts social reality directly, as everyday lived experience and institutions, rather than as a mediation of what is conveyed in books and other means of representation. *The Mambo Kings*, for instance, while not particularly bookish, relies for its social framing and narrative coherence on the refraction of Cuban-American life and Latin music by means of television and Desi Arnaz; without that representational device, any sustained interest in the book's character and plot would all but vanish. Nuyorican literature, on the other hand, and the writing of "lowercase people" in general, stands face-to-face with social experience, however harsh and however saturated with mass culture, with its characters, voices, and story lines all recognizable denizens of the "mean" but real streets.

Though he is part of a Nuyorican tradition in writing, and knows himself to be, Rodriguez's relation to that tradition is anything but smooth, and his disposition anything but happy. Indeed, the appeal of Balzac and his own appeal to classical realist fiction may be in part directed at what he sees as the evasiveness of the previous generation of Nuyorican writers and their irrelevance to contemporary Puerto Rican conditions. He delights in "pissing on" his out-of-touch elders, ranting that they are "stuck in another era":

"You'd think that I'm coming from a different place than these people. And while I respect literature, I don't see any use in stories about the blessed Diaspora forty years ago or of the first time I saw a snowflake. I think we should go beyond that now."[34] Piri Thomas, Pedro Pietri, Miguel Piñero, Nicholasa Mohr, Ed Vega, Judith Ortíz Kofer—the "older writers" had been formative for him, helping him belie the words of his teachers that there were no Puerto Rican writers. But when putting these writings to the test of present-day realities, and in view of the formidable political dilemma that underlies them, Rodriguez voices a dissatisfaction that he believes he shares with many of his contemporaries. "We've got young 14-year-old kids blasting each other to hell with automatic weapons, and the island has the same problem. I think these are bigger things, and we've got to find a way. . . . This is not all about politics. These are the dynamics of writing, but of course politics has to do something to it" (140–41).

With his bouts of youthful fury, which lashes out in many directions and not only toward his fellow "spick writers," Rodriguez is announcing his sense of belonging to a new literary generation. The 1980s and 1990s are new times, marked off socially from the previous, properly "Nuyorican" years by the ebbing of the political and cultural movement of the 1960s and 1970s and the conclusive dashing of all hopes for Puerto Rican equality and independence. The intervening period saw the transition from "el barrio" to "Spidertown," the definitive placement of the U.S. Puerto Rican population at the bottom of the socioeconomic and political hierarchy as a result of regional and transnational restructurings. The "mean streets" had gotten even meaner with the infusion of crack, and had found a distinctive mode of cultural expression in hip-hop. And of course Puerto Rico, the idyllic homeland and cultural womb for most of the earlier Nuyorican writers, appears now at a still greater remove; though the consequences of its colonial politics still bear down on today's U.S. Puerto Ricans, the evocation of the Island no longer carries the same symbolic weight or literary interest. Speaking about books that wallow in the past, Rodriguez says that "as a young person I was never interested in this kind of book. They had nothing to offer me because I didn't see anything I could really relate to inside of them. In terms of the voice, in terms of the language, in terms of the subject matter, nothing. It's like writing about the island. It's a myth to me. The island is a myth. I like reading about it, but it's a myth" (141).

The demographic outcomes of these same social changes indicate that even the term *Nuyorican* has become an anachronism. In the early 1970s, when New York Puerto Rican writing was coming into its own, most U.S. Puerto Ricans lived in New York City, and the city's Latino population was over 80 percent Puerto Rican.[35] Both proportions have changed dramatically since, such that by 1990 more than 50 percent of Puerto Ricans lived in U.S. settings other than New York City, and the Puerto Rican proportion of the city's Latino population, while still the largest, had declined to lower than 50 percent. Poet Tato Laviera was one of the first to acknowledge the inappropriateness of the usage because of diasporic dispersion around the country, and proposed, leaving room for poetic license, the alternative *AmeRícan*, "with an accent on the i."[36] In any case, even "post-Nuyorican" won't do because of its lingering geographic specificity, though the overused prefix "post-" may well be pertinent to the generational relation in this case.

Abraham Rodriguez is not alone in his generation, though he claimed until recently that he does not "know any young Puerto Ricans who write." In a way, of course, it is the women prose writers who initiated the generational shift, moving away from the male-centered version of the migration and growing up experience. But in Rodriguez's own chronological generation, there is Willie Perdomo, who takes up themes of race and identity in his poems like "Nigger-Rican Blues" and has published a book with Norton, *When a Nickel Costs a Dime*. Other young voices are also beginning to be heard, often in the context of hip-hop or performance art, and some of them are young women. María Fernández, for example, whose nickname is "Mariposa," is from the Bronx, a graduate of NYU, who has been reciting her poetry at cultural and political gatherings in and around New York City for several years. She agrees with Rodriguez about the need for something new in the writing, a feel more in tune with the times. One of her poems, in fact, proposes still another possible designation for the present literary generation. In "Ode to the DiaspoRican," Mariposa presents the intense bicultural dilemma, familiar from the poems of Sandra María Esteves, in a setting that is New York but could readily be in any other enclave of the scattered "diaspoRico." The poem reads in part: "Some people say that I'm not the real thing / Boricua, that is / cuz I wasn't born on the enchanted island / cuz I was born on the mainland /. . . what does it mean to live in between / What does it take to realize / that being boricua / is a state of mind / a state of heart / a state of soul . . . / *No nací en Puerto Rico / Puerto Rico nació en mi* . . . [I wasn't born in Puerto Rico / Puerto Rico was born in me]."[37]

The other demographic shift marking off "diaspoRican" writing from its Nuyorican antecedent is the Latinization of New York City, which brings us back to "Latino literature." The dramatic growth and diversification of "Latin New York" over the past decades, corresponding to developments throughout the country, has meant that Dominican, Colombian, Mexican, and many other Latino voices have joined those of the Puerto Ricans in presenting the migratory and diasporic experience. New and different versions of the story proliferate, many of them at extreme variance with those more characteristic of the Puerto Rican case in its contours and details. Predictably, the logic of social categorization generates a literary rubric to correspond to the demographic label, and "Latino literature" emerges as the new construct conditioning all literary production by Latinos of all national backgrounds. Suddenly the Puerto Rican writers have an umbrella, a point of access to mainstream multicultural literature that had so long eluded them. But along with the opportunities, for both recognition and potential creative sharing, there is for the Puerto Rican especially the pitfall of renewed marginalization and, on the other end, dilution of the collective experience.

And in 1990, as though to punctuate this precarious transition, *The Mambo Kings* wins the Pulitzer. As expected, the "older" Puerto Rican writers were disgruntled, and as expected, Abraham Rodriguez did not share their dejection. "They seem to be stuck in another era," he says of them. "The last time I was with those people, we were all sitting at this table, and they were all criticizing Oscar Hijuelos because he had just gotten a Pulitzer. It's just a waste of time. I don't see why writers do that. They should go home and write something. If they didn't sit around a table drinking, talking about other writers so much, arguing about Faulkner all day, maybe they'd get some work done."[38] If their work is indeed about "life off the hyphen," the need is strong in the present generation to dispel the anxieties over canons, prizes, and other marketing conveniences, and to concentrate more on bringing the "lowercase people" to literary life.

Puerto Rican Cultural Center, Chicago (c. 1995)

(Photo by Marixa Alicea, courtesy *Diálogo* magazine)

9

The Latino Imaginary

MEANINGS OF COMMUNITY AND IDENTITY

Is that Hispanic or Latino? What's in a name? A bewildered public puz-
zles over alternative signifiers, and even over who is being so designated,
and how. "What do we call them? What do they want to be called? What
do they call themselves?" Or, as the title of a thoughtful article on just this
problem of megalabels has it, "What's the Problem with 'Hispanic'? Just
Ask a 'Latino.'"[1]

The broadest identifying term, of course, long used as shorthand even
by many Latinos themselves, has been "Spanish," as in Spanish restaurant
or Spanish television, where the idea of a unifying language culture con-
spires with the suggestion of Iberian origins and characteristics. The ideological undertones of that label, which are of course retained in slight variation in both "Hispanic" and "Latino," go unquestioned, as does the reality
that many of those so designated do not even speak Spanish as a first language, or at all. The need for elastic and flexible usages stretches the field
of reference so far that Spaniards, and even Italians and French, sometimes find their place under that hopelessly porous umbrella. The signifying net is cast so wide that what would seem the defining experiences, migration and resettlement, become of secondary importance, and all of Latin
America is swept conveniently into the "Hispanic" bin. Or, to complicate
the picture beyond recognition, there is even the suggestion that "Latinos"
be used "to refer to those citizens from the Spanish-speaking world living
in the United States" and "Hispanics" to "those living elsewhere."[2]

With all the slippages and evident arbitrariness, though, what would
seem a terminological free-for-all actually does mark off limits and contexts, and pressing issues of power. "Where I come from, in New Mexico,

nobody uses Latino, most people never even heard the term. We're Mexicanos, Chicanos, Mexican-Americans, Raza, Hispanic, but never Latino. Anyone who comes around talking about Latino this or Latino that is obviously an outsider." Or, from a contrary perspective, it is "Hispanic" that raises the red flag: "Hispanic? For me, a Hispanic is basically a sellout, *un vendido*. Anyone who calls himself Hispanic, or refers to our community as Hispanic, just wants to be an American and forget about our roots."

Bits of conversation like these point up the range of contention over the choice of words to name a people, a culture, a community.[3] Behind the war of words, of course, there lurks the real battle, which has to do with attitudes, interpretations, and positions. In the dismissive indifference of many Americans there is often that undertone of annoyance which, when probed a little further, only turns out to be a cover for other, submerged emotions like ignorance, fear, and of course disdain. The gaps among Latinos or Hispanics themselves can be as polarized as they appear here, with one usage thoroughly discrediting the other. But usually the options are more flexible, operational, and mediated by a whole span of qualifying terms, tones, and situations. And over against those who use the words at all, there are many Mexican Americans, Puerto Ricans, Colombians, Cubans, or Dominicans who have no use for any such catchall phrases and would rather stick to distinct national designations.[4]

Yet this disparity over nomenclature, sharp as it is in the case of Latinos, should not be mistaken for a total lack of consensus or collective identity, nor as proof that any identification of the group or "community" is no more than a label imposed from outside, and above. Regardless of what anyone chooses to name it, the Latino or Hispanic community exists because for much of the history of the hemisphere, and multiplying exponentially the closer we approach the present, people have moved from Latin America to the United States, while portions of Latin America have been incorporated into what has become the United States. Along with their increase in numbers there has also been a deepening of their impact, real and potential, on the doings, and the destiny, of this country.

It is becoming clear that any discussion of an "American community" must be inclusive of Latinos and cognizant of the existence of a "Latino community" intrinsic to historical discourses about U.S. culture. The real challenge, though, is that the Latino presence makes it necessary to recognize that the very meaning of the word, the concept of *community* itself, is relative according to the perspective or position of the group in question:

there is both a "Latino community" and a "community" in the Latino sense of the word.

Comunidad: the Spanish word, even more clearly than the English, calls to mind two of the key terms—*común* and *unidad*—in the conceptualization of this notoriously elusive idea. What do we have in "common," and what "unites" us, what are our commonalities and what makes for our unity? It is important to note that though the two terms point in the same semantic direction they are not synonymous, and their apparent coupling in the same word, *comunidad*, is not a redundancy. For while *común* refers to sharing—that is, those aspects in the cultures of the various constitutive groups that overlap—the sense of *unidad* is that which bonds the groups above and beyond the diverse particular commonalities. The point of this admittedly rather willful deconstruction is, once again, that the Latino "experience," the group's demonstrable reality and existence, includes but is not coterminous with its self-consciousness: *común* stands for the community *in* itself, while *unidad* refers to the community *for* itself, the way that it thinks, conceives of, imagines itself.

The "Latino community" is an "imagined community"—to summon Benedict Anderson's well-worn though useful phrase—a compelling present-day example of a social group being etched and composed out of a larger, impinging geopolitical landscape.[5] The role of the social imagination and the imaginary in the self-conception of nationally, ethnically, and "racially" kindred groups is of course central, but must always be assessed with a view toward *how* they are being imagined (i.e., from "within" or "without") and to what ends and outcomes. Distinguishing between interior and exterior perspectives is thus a necessary step, and given that in the case of Latinos the outside representation is the dominant one, any instance of cultural expression by Latinos themselves may serve as a healthy corrective to the ceaseless barrage of stereotypes that go to define what is "Latino" in the public mind.

But the marking off of "us" and "them," though the foundational exercise in "imagining" communities, has its own limits, as it becomes evident that there is from both angles as much blurring involved as clear and meaningful bounding. Vexing questions like who's Latino and who isn't, and what kind of Latina(o)(s) we are talking about, quickly press in on any too facile dichotomy. Beyond the issue of names and labels, and even who is using them, there are differing levels or modes of meaning simultaneously at work in the very act of apprehending and conceptualizing the "community" and "identity" in question. "Latino" or "Hispanic" not only mean different things to different people; they also "mean" in different ways and refer to different dimensions of collective social experience.

I would suggest that by distinguishing between a *demographic*, an *analytic*, and an *imaginary* approach to Latino unity and diversity it is possible effectively to complicate and deepen our understanding of cultural expression, identity, and politics without becoming paralyzed by the sheer complexity and contradictoriness of it all. Whether Latinos or Hispanics are thought of as an enumerated aggregate of people, an analytically differentiated set of constituent groups, or a historically imagined cultural "community" or "ethnoscape," is at the core of ongoing debates and confusions.[6] Not that these diverse conceptualizations are mutually exclusive, nor are they to be considered in any mechanically sequential or hierarchical way. On the contrary, as I seek to describe them it will be obvious that all three are necessary, and that they are complementary. That is, they are really different methodological and epistemological emphases rather than discrete forms of explanation. But scrutinizing them in hypothetical discreteness not only helps understand their interrelation but may also enhance our analysis and appreciation of the voices and images of Latino art.[7]

The demographic conception of Latinos, or of a "Latino community," refers to an aggregate of people whose existence is established on the basis of numerical presence: count them, therefore they are. Here Latinos—or more commonly at this level, Hispanics—comprise not so much a community as a "population," a quantified slice of the social whole. As limited as such a means of identification may seem, it is nevertheless the dominant one, serving as it does both government bureaucracies and corporate researchers in setting public taste and policy. This definition of the Hispanic community by official measurement is thus inherently instrumental, since the immediate goal is really to identify, not so much social groups or lines of cultural unity and diversity, but voting blocs and consumer markets. From this angle, Latinos appear as a homogeneous, passive mass, a "target" public, with any concern for internal differentiation or possible social agency itself geared toward those same pragmatic goals of electoral or commercial utility.[8]

But it is not only campaign managers and admen for whom Latinos are, first of all, numbers. The labels and tallies they arrive at for their convenience—be it Hispanic or Latino, at whatever percentile—are made visible, credible, "real," by means of a whole sensorium of images, sounds, and flavors. The demographic label thus aims not only to buy the Hispanic package but to sell it; it targets not only potential customers but merchandise, or even movers of merchandise. Whatever the particular purpose, though, the means and result are usually the same—stereotyped images offering up distorted, usually offensive, and in any case, superficial portrayals of Latino people.[9] And these are the only images of Latinos that many people in the United States, and around the world, are ever exposed to, which makes it difficult for the public to gauge their accuracy. It is important to recognize these images as products not just of opportunist politicians or greedy marketeers but also of the demographic mentality itself. Numbers call forth labels, which in turn engender generic, homogenized representations— stereotypes. According to the same logic, holding economic and political power relies on the work of both the census-taker and the cameraman.

The most loudly proclaimed finding of this aggregative endeavor, by now a demographic truism of our times, is that Hispanics are the nation's "fastest-growing minority," on course to become the "largest" minority at some (variously defined) point early in the coming century. Whether greeted by alarmist jitters or triumphalist joy, this momentous news item rests on an abiding confidence in the validity of the count, and an unquestioned consensus that like social units are being summed and demarcated from unlike, incompatible ones. The often unspoken allusion, of course, is to African Americans, who are thus cast as the main rival in the numbers race and the main instance, among "minorities," of the non-Hispanic other. Asian Americans, too, are in the running, with all lines of historical interaction and congruency again erased from the calculation. In both cases, it is clear how tools of advertent inclusion and conjunction may at the same time serve as wedges between and among groups whose social placement and experience in the United States could just as well, given a different political agenda, point to commonalities as to differences. The tactics of divide and conquer are still prominent in the arsenal of power, and nowhere more so in the contemporary equation than in the talk of Hispanics as undifferentiated numeraries.

The process of adding up is accompanied by the need to break down, to identify not the sum total but the constituent parts. The analytical approach—the business, above all, of positivist social science—is bent on de-aggregation; it presumes to move closer to Latino "reality" by recognizing and tabulating the evident diversity of Latino groups and experiences. Such varying factors as country of origin, time in the United States (generation), region or place of settlement, occupation and socioeconomic status, educational background, and the like, move into focus as the only meaningful units or vantages of analysis, with any cohesion among Latinos referred to only in the plural: typically, there are only Latino "populations," groups, or at best "communities."

This analytical account of Latino multiplicity is indeed often helpful in counteracting stereotypes and monolithic categories, and the elaborate discussion of "modes of incorporation" certainly allows for a sense of the dynamic relation among a too hastily posited aggregate of structurally differentiated social experiences.[10] But resting as it overwhelmingly does on socially constructed statistical evidence and an objectification of collective historical actors, it is still close kin to the demographic approach. Even the census evidences an increasing official need to break the composite down, with "Hispanics" now grouped into Mexican, Puerto Rican, Cuban-origin, Central and South American origin, and "Other Hispanic," subcategories which then serve as the basis for much quantitative research. Commercially geared demographics are also far along in their analytical enterprise, having persuasively charted both a "pan-Hispanic" as well as regionally differentiated Los Angeles, Miami, and New York centered markets, along with countless other target-specific variables.

To this extent, and in many social scientific studies, the pluralizing "analysis" of Latino reality is still dealing with a community "in itself," constructed in terms of relatively inert categories with their appropriate labels and generic representations. The focus on "labor market experience" as the "key factor in the structuring of [Hispanic] ethnicity," for example, while an invaluable starting point for differentiating social positions among the groups and subgroups in question, leaves unaddressed what would seem the crucial issue of "the complexities of the interaction between social and ethnic identities," that is, the "interdependency between socioeconomic placement and cultural (self-) identification."[11]

Ultimately, the limitation of analytical methodologies of this kind is not the act of differentiation itself, but a failure to differentiate among differences, and among kinds and levels of difference. For example, the vast research on Latinos as part of immigration studies, perhaps the most prevalent paradigm for treating Latino social experience, tends to stumble in the face of the glaring fact that the majority of Latinos, comprising the largest national groups within the composite, are not even "immigrants" in any quantifiable or recognized sense: because of their citizenship status, Puerto

Ricans are not counted among the nation's immigrant populations, and a large share of the Mexican Americans are here not because they crossed the border, but because "the border crossed them." Characteristically, this most severe and telling divide among the Latino pan-ethnicity, the difference between immigrant and "resident minority" Latinos having much to do with issues of colonial status and class, tends to elude even the most thorough and cautious scrutiny of Latino realities, which as a result arrive at misleading conclusions. Even historically informed and critically "balanced" accounts of Latino immigration and communities, such as those of Roberto Suro and Rubén G. Rumbaut among others, lose interpretive cogency because of this overly "objectivist" method and inattention to such structurally larger but less readily quantifable dimensions of contrastive analysis, and lead to continual equivocation and inconsistency—like that of Rumbaut—as to the validity of any unifying concept at all, or, in the case of Suro's *Strangers Among Us* (1998), to an inadequately critical relation to "culture of poverty" and "underclass" theory in speaking of "Puerto Rican-like poverty," a central message of his book being that "the entire nation will suffer if the the Puerto Rican fate is repeated" by "today's Latino newcomers."[12]

Yet Latinos are also social agents and not just passive objects in this analyzing process, nor do they tend to sidestep the task of "telling Hispanics apart." Consciously and intuitively, personally and collectively, Puerto Ricans, Mexicans, Cubans, Dominicans, and each of the other groups most often project their own respective national backgrounds as a first and primary axis of identity and on that basis, fully mindful of differences and distances, negotiate their relation to some more embracing "Latino" or "Hispanic" composite. Here the force of analysis, rather than an extension of demographic aggregation and labeling, stands in direct opposition to it, an instinctive reaction against instrumental measuring and its pernicious consequences. Of course, there are interests involved here too, but in this case they are the interests of the "object" of analysis itself, the Latino peoples and communities.

From a Latino perspective understood in this way, analysis is guided above all by lived experience and historical memory, factors that tend to be relegated by prevailing sociological approaches as either inaccessible or inconsequential. Rather than as slices or cross-sections, the various groups and their association may be seen in dynamic, relational terms, with traditions and continuities weighing off subtly against changes and reconfigurations. At this level of conceptualization, differences are drawn among and within the groups not so as to divide or categorize for the sake of more efficient manipulation, but to assure that social identities, actions, and alliances are adequately grounded in the specific historical experiences and cultural practices that people recognize as their own, with appropriate attention to the sometimes sharp class and racial cleavages that always crosscut any too hasty presumption of equivalence. The logic is that solidarity can only be posited when the lines of social differentiation are fully in view, but the goal, nevertheless, is solidarity.

It is this critical, historically based approach to diverse and changing Latino realities that underlies and sustains what I refer to as the "Latino imaginary," another sense or conceptual space of pan-group aggregation that is too often and too easily confused with the official, demographic version. Not that calculation is itself foreign to an "imagined" Latino community; in fact it is at this epistemological level that the very act and authority of counting and measuring become issues of vital social contestation. The "imaginary" in this sense does not signify the "not real," some make-believe realm oblivious to the facts, but a projection beyond the "real" as the immediately present and rationally discernible. It is the "community" represented "for itself," a unity fashioned creatively on the basis of shared memory and desire, congruent histories of misery and struggle, and intertwining utopias.

The Latino historical imaginary refers, first of all, to home countries in Latin America, the landscapes, life-ways, and social struggles familiar, if not personally, at least to one's family and people, and in any case indispensable to Latinos in situating themselves in U.S. society. Mexico, Puerto Rico, and Cuba are very different points of imaginative reference, to be sure, and again, it is always through their particular national optics that Latinos tend to envision some generic Latin American or Latino "We." But the features of José Martí's "nuestra América" do stand out in the Latino historical unconscious in that long narrative of Spanish and North American colonial conquest, the enslavement and subjugation of indigenous and African peoples, the troubled consolidation of nations under the thumb of international power, and the constant migratory movement of peoples, cultures, and things which has been attendant to all aspects of the Latino saga. For Latinos in the United States, the passage to, and from, "el Norte" assumes such prominence in the social imaginary that migration is often confounded with life itself, and any fixity of the referential homeland gives way to an image of departure and arrival, the abandoned and the reencountered.

This nomadic, migratory dimension of the Latino imaginary is anchored in the historical reasons for coming here, and in the placement assigned most Latinos in U.S. society. Unlike earlier waves of European immigrants, Latinos typically move to this country as a direct result of the economic and political relationship of their homelands, and home region, to the United States. However much Cuba, Mexico, and Puerto Rico may vary in status and social arrangement—and if we add the Dominican Republic and Colombia the range could hardly be wider in present-day geopolitics—huge portions of their respective populations have come to live in the United States because of the gravitational pull of metropolitan power and dependency at work in each and all of their histories. Since World War II, its economy on a course of shrinkage and transition rather than unbridled expansion, the United States has been tapping its colonial reserves to fill in its lower ranks, and its Latin American and Caribbean neighbors have proven to be the closest and most abundant sources at hand.

Colonial relations of hemispheric inequality underlie not only the historical logic of Latino migration but also the position and conditions of Latinos here in this society. Differential treatment is of course rampant, as has been dramatically evident in recent years in the contrasting fates of Cubans and Haitians arriving on the same rafts from their beleaguered home islands. Yet today even many Cuban Americans, recent arrivals and long-standing citizens alike, are finding the red carpets and gold-paved streets illusory at best, and are coming to resent being cited as the exception to the rule of Latino disadvantage. For the Latino imaginary, even when the relatively "privileged" Cuban Americans are reckoned in, rests on the recognition of ongoing oppression and discrimination, racism and exploitation, closed doors and patrolled borders. Whether sanguine or enraged, this recognition structures the negotiated relations among Latinos, between Latinos and the dominant culture, and with other groups such as African Americans and Native Americans.

Memory fuels desire: the past as imagined from a Latino perspective awakens an anticipatory sense of what is, or might be, in store. The alarmist hysteria over the prospect of "America's fastest-growing minority" overrunning the society is directed not only at Latino people themselves but at the ground shift in power relations implied in that new calculus. For the desire that these demographic trends awaken in Latinos is directed first of all toward recognition and justice in this society, but wider, hemispheric changes always figure somewhere on the agenda. The Latino imaginary infuses the clamor for civil rights with a claim to sovereignty on an international scale; retribution involves reversing the history of conquest and subordination, including its inherent migratory imperative. A full century after its initial pronouncement, Martí's profile of "nuestra América" still looms like a grid over the map of the entire continent, with the northern co-optation of the name America demanding special scrutiny and revision.

But Latino memory and desire, though standing as a challenge to prevailing structures of power, are not just reactive. The imaginary articulates more than a reflexive response to negative conditions and unfavorably weighted relations which, though oppositional, is as a response still ultimately mimetic and confined to extrinsically set terms. It is important to recognize that the Latino imaginary, like that of other oppressed groups, harbors the elements of an alternative ethos, an ensemble of cultural values and practices created in its own right and to its own ends. Latinos listen to their own kinds of music, eat their own kinds of food, dream their dreams and snap their photos not just to express their difference from, or opposition to, the way the "gringos" do it. These choices and preferences, though arrived at under circumstances of dependency and imposition, also attest to a deep sense of autonomy and self-referentiality. Latino identity is imagined not as the negation of the non-Latino, but as the affirmation of cultural and social realities, myths and possibilities, as they are inscribed in their own human trajectory.

The conditions for the emergence of a Latino cultural ethos were set around midcentury, as it began to become clear that these "new immigrants" filing in from the southern backyard make for a different kind of social presence than that constituted by European arrivals of earlier years. Of course, the histories of each of the major U.S. Latino groups extend much further back than that: Cubans and Puerto Ricans to the mid- to later nineteenth century, when colonies of artisans and political exiles formed in New York and Florida, while today's "Chicanos" were "here" all along, for centuries before the fateful year 1848 when the northern third of their nation was rudely moved in on and annexed by the bearers of Manifest Destiny. In fact, in the long historical view, the literary and cultural presence of Spanish-speaking people in the territory now called the United States actually precedes that of the English. And if we add to that the Indian American and Afro-American dimensions of "nuestra América," a full-scale revision, or inversion, of the national history results, with the supposed "core," Anglo-Saxon culture appearing as the real intruder, the original illegal alien.

It is a serious fallacy, therefore, to think of Latinos in the United States as "recent arrivals," as is often the tendency in their treatment in scholarly research on immigration.[13] But despite their long-standing, constitutive role in North American history, sheer demographic growth and diversification point to a markedly new structural positioning and cultural dynamic for Latinos in the second half of the twentieth century. Now more than ever, in the present, "postcolonial" era, many Latinos are here as colonial migrants, whose very locations and movements are defined by the status of their "home" countries within the system of transnational economic power. Rather than an ethnic, minority, or immigrant group, those trusty old concepts of cultural pluralism, Latinos may now be more accurately described as a diasporic community or, more suggestively in view of the intensified transnational linkages, as an "ethnoscape" or "world tribe." But a still more satisfactory neologism to characterize the social and cultural space occupied by Latinos is that of the "delocalized transnation," of whom it is also said that they "become doubly loyal to their nations of origin and thus ambivalent about their loyalties to America."[14] Precisely because of the persisting hierarchies of transnational power, if convergences among today's Latinos involve the formation of a "Hispanic nation," it promises to be decidedly less an "American" nation, less a "step toward joining America," than commentators like Geoffrey Fox might propose.[15]

The social consciousness and cultural expression of this new geopolitical reality burst forth in the late 1960s and early 1970s, surely the watershed years in the construction of a new language of Latino identity. Inspired by the Civil Rights movement, the opposition to the war against Vietnam, and the Cuban Revolution, countless movements, causes, and organizations rallied thousands of Chicanos and Puerto Ricans to the cries of "¡Viva la Raza!" and "¡Despierta Boricua!" The political horizon of the Latino imaginary was set in those spirited movements and found vibrant artistic expression in such diverse forms as wall murals, bilingual poetry and street theater, and hybrid music and dance styles like boogaloo, Chicano rock, Latin soul, and salsa. *Talleres* (workshops) and *conjuntos* (musical groups), readings and *actos* (dramatic sketches) proliferated, lending voice and vision to the fervent political struggles of Latino and Latin American peoples and often attesting to close cultural affinities and political solidarities with other, non-Latino groups, notably African Americans and American Indians.

By our time, in the 1990s, that heyday is long past, hardly even a living memory for many young Latinos; all too frequently in the burgeoning scholarly and journalistic literature on Latinos of recent years, the importance of that foundational period in the story of Latino identity-formation is minimized or erased. But the Brown Berets and the Young Lords Party, the Chicano Moratorium and the Lincoln Hospital takeover, the causes of the farmworkers and Puerto Rican independence, along with many other manifestations of cultural and political activism, are still an inspiration and a model of militancy and righteous defiance for the present generation of Latinos of all nationalities as they sharpen their social awareness. For although the immediacy, intensity, and cultural effervescence has no doubt waned in the intervening decades, Latinos in the United States have just as assuredly continued to grow as a social movement to be reckoned with, nationally and internationally, in the years ahead. This is true demographically in the striking (for some startling) multiplication in their numbers, and analytically in the equally sharp diversification of their places of origin and settlement. As contrasted with earlier stages, the Latino concept is today a far more differentiated site of intersecting social identities, especially along sexual, racial, and class lines.

But the persistence and expansion of the Latino social movements are most prominent as a cultural imaginary, a still emergent space or "community" of memory and desire. In the present generation, Latino youth from many backgrounds have played a formative role in the creation of hip-hop and its inflection toward Latino expression and experience; though not always explicitly political in intention, the Latino contribution to contemporary popular music, dance, performance, and visual imaging has accompanied important signs of social organization and self-identification among young Latinos in many parts of the country. The emergence of "Latino literature," though in important ways a marketing and canonizing category having the effect of concealing distinctions necessary for purposes of literary history and criticism, has also involved expanded horizons and greater intercultural exchange than had been true in the previous, Nuyorican and Chicano generation. In the case of the "casitas" in the New York barrios—another richly suggestive and often-cited example from recent Latino experience—entire neighborhoods across generational and many other lines are drawn together by way of sharing in the enactment of collective cultural memory.[16] Present-day considerations and representations of Latino life which would do justice to that complex reality find it necessary to incorporate such instances of cultural innovation and "invented traditions" by way of complementing their reliance on social scientific insights.[17]

Hispanic? Latino? Settling on a name never comes easy, and when it comes to an all-embracing term for Mexicans, Puerto Ricans, Cubans, Dominicans, Colombians, Salvadorans, Panamanians, and an array of other Latin American and Caribbean peoples in the United States, consensus does not seem to be near at hand. But the search for a name, more than an act of classification, is actually a process of historical imagination and a struggle over social meaning at diverse levels of interpretation. Rigorous demographic and social science analysis is no doubt essential to the task of circumscribing that process, and especially for identifying structural variations in the placement of the different national groups relative to hierarchies of power and attendant histories of racialization. But only a fully interdisciplinary approach, guided by an attention to cultural expression and identity claims and transcending the bounds set by positivist analysis, allows for an integral understanding of Latino experience. In that sense the search for Latino identity and community, the ongoing articulation of a pan-ethnic and transnational imaginary, is also a search for a new map, a new ethos, a new *América*.

CUNY student protest (October 1995)

IO

⁂

Latino Studies

NEW CONTEXTS, NEW CONCEPTS

Latino Studies has been in the news of late. The most visible student protests of the mid-1990s on university campuses throughout the country have been directed at securing commitments from university administrations to establish programs in Latino Studies as well as in Asian American Studies. The office takeovers, hunger strikes, and angry teach-ins represent a clamor for new programs, faculty, courses, and resources in these neglected areas of social knowledge. And it's making the news not because of any alarming tactics or massive participation, but because the demands are being lodged at the loftiest halls of postsecondary education in the country, the Ivy League schools. After a twenty-five-year history of such programs at public urban universities like the City University of New York (CUNY) and San Francisco State, the call for Latino Studies and Asian American Studies has been raised and can no longer be ignored—at Columbia, Princeton, Cornell, Brown, the University of Pennsylvania, and most of the other Ivies.

There is of course always another face to such news, a more somber mobilization generally obscured from public view. While Latino and Asian students at the elite institutions were busy facing down deans and fasting in their tents, the iron hand of fiscal constraints and shifting ideological priorities was (and still is) at work slashing, reducing, and consolidating those very programs and services at often nearby public colleges and universities. For example, in the spring of 1996 the president of CUNY's City College announced that the departments of Africana, Latin American and Hispanic Caribbean, Asian American, and Jewish Studies were being downgraded into programs, under the umbrella of Ethnic Studies. Though CCNY president Yolanda Moses claimed that she only intended to "strengthen" instruction in those fields, the signal is clear from City College—a mere twenty Harlem blocks from the hunger tents at Columbia—that all such programs focusing on the experience of oppressed and historically excluded groups are under the gun as likely candidates for "consolidation." After all, President Moses was herself acting under strong fiscal and political pressures within CUNY, and her decisions were very much in tune with the tenor of the times set by Republican state and city administrations.[1]

The real news, then, is that Latino Studies, and the nascent (or renascent) movements to institutionalize the study of African American, Asian American, and other group experiences, are caught in a crossfire. As interest in Latino Studies grows at Harvard, Black and Puerto Rican Studies are threatened at Hunter. The conjuncture is actually one of clashing priorities, a collision between the expressed educational needs of an increasingly non-white student population and the conservative inclinations of many social and educational power brokers. What would appear a threshold is at the same time a closing door; all attempts at curricular innovation are met with equally avid moves at intellectual retrenchment and wagon-circling. This eminently contradictory cultural climate sets the immediate context for the struggle over Latino Studies.

NEW CONTEXTS

An alert reading of prevailing and countervailing winds in the academy is a necessary starting point for an assessment of Latino Studies and parallel movements for educational change. The calls for inclusion, focus, and self-determination, and the reluctance with which they are met by entrenched faculty and wary administrators, reflect larger social contentions in which the issues at stake are not courses and professors but food, shelter, and citizenship. Like Asian American Studies, Latino Studies has its historical raison-d'être in the unresolved historical struggles over immigration, racism, and colonialism. The proliferation of students of color, and the contestatory nature of their presence in higher education, attests to the salience of these issues to the attendant curricular challenges. The attacks on minority admissions, as manifested by Proposition 209 in California, are at the political crux over any claim for educational inclusion. As such, Latino Studies needs to be understood as a social movement, as an extension within the academy of the movements against racism and on behalf of immigrant rights afoot in the wider society. Demographic, economic, and political changes, and the resolute efforts to stem their tide, thus undergird the widespread appeals for changes in educational institutions and their offerings. Only in such terms does the emergence of Latino Studies harbor the legitimation enjoyed by the empowered gatekeepers of academic discourse.

Equally important is the need for historical memory. Today's Latino students, and much of the faculty, were very young or not yet born when coalitions of Black, Chicano, Puerto Rican, Asian, and Native American students first claimed their intellectual spaces at the university in the late 1960s and early 1970s. There is an awareness, of course, that all this happened before, and that many of the present demands closely echo those which inaugurated the varied ethnic studies programs still in place, however precariously, in the 1990s. But that sense of continuity, and an understanding of the disjunctures, has been blurred with the passing of an entire generation and the dramatic geopolitical changes of the intervening years.

One of the most obvious differences between previous and more recent university movements is that the earlier initiatives did not go by the name of "Latino" Studies. By and large they were called "Chicano Studies" or "Puerto Rican Studies," the university movements corresponding directly to the vocal, spirited, and politically grounded struggles of the Chicano and Puerto Rican communities for justice and liberation. There were exceptions, such as "Raza Studies" at San Francisco State, where the Latino student constituency was largely non-Chicano, or "Chicano-Boricua Studies" at Wayne State, where comparable numbers of students from both groups joined forces. However, for the most part, the forebears of the present-day Latino Studies efforts tended to be focused on specific national groups, and the "communities" to which they were invariably accountable were nearer at hand, both geographically and culturally.

Much of this difference in nomenclature, and in relative distance from the communities, may be attributed to the ebb and flow of historical movements for change. The previous generation of Latino students and faculty activism coincided with a time of radical challenges to persistent colonial oppression on a global, national, and local scale. Militant opposition to the Vietnam War, support for the Cuban Revolution, and the Black and Brown Power movements informed the rhetoric and strategic vision of Chicano and Puerto Rican Studies at their inception. That charged revolutionary aura does not surround the Latino Studies agenda in our time, though further ebbs and flows may eventually reconnect the unversity-based struggle to such systemic types of social confrontation.

The point of this historical view of Latino Studies is neither to romanti-
cize nor to reject the past, but to help save us from reinventing the wheel.
Drawing lessons from the past must not blind us to the new insights and
approaches, or to the possibility that conditions today may in some ways be
even more propitious for the establishment of Latino Studies than they
were a generation ago.

The main shift marking off the present context of Latino Studies from its
previous manifestation twenty-five years ago is perhaps best summed up in
the words *global* and *globalization*, with all due caution of what has aptly
been called "globaloney."[2] The economic restructuring of world capitalism
that took off in the mid-1970s, along with the further revolutionizing of tele-
communications, have made for radically new levels of interaction and in-
terconnectedness among populations at a regional level. The growing mass
migrations generated by these changes are also affected by them, and in
their circular and transnational character differ markedly from the migratory experiences of the early 1970s.

The diversification and geographic dispersal of the Latino population is
the most visible evidence of these changes in the present-day Latino Studies
context. In addition to the largest groups, Mexican Americans and Puerto
Ricans, there are now sizable immigrant communities in the United States
from most Latin American countries. As many of these diasporas, notably
the Mexican and the Puerto Rican, have fanned out across the country, the
demographic landscape, as well as the political and cultural setting, has
been further altered for U.S. Latinos.

This "globalizing" of the Latino presence is, of course, clearly evident at
U.S. colleges and universities. On most campuses the Latino student body
is diverse, often a mix between one large group—Mexican American, Puerto Rican, Cuban, or Dominican—and Latinos from a variety of other backgrounds. In some areas where there is a preponderance of one national
group, it remains necessary, and feasible, to mount and sustain programs
focusing on that group—such as departments, programs, and research centers in Mexican American, Puerto Rican, or Cuban Studies. But at most
sites—including those in which students are calling for programs—Latino
Studies makes sense, not only bureaucratically but also because of the increasingly transnational nature of the student population and of their communities, as well as the geopolitical relations in which they find themselves.

For it is not only the pan-ethnic demography that explains—and perhaps justifies—the shift from a Chicano or Puerto Rican to a Latino Stu-

dies framework. The global reach which so willfully moves people to and from determined places does so by adjusting and altering the historical relations among societies and their fragments relocated by impelled migratory movement. The student constituency and subject matter of Latino Studies has not only become more multigroup in the sense of numerical diversity; rather, because of global and hemispheric restructuring, exemplified in the past decade by such moves as NAFTA (the North American Free Trade Agreement) and the Caribbean Basin Initiative, the Latino communities in the United States are far more intricately tied to economic and political realities in their countries and regions of origin than ever before. Pan-Latino necessarily implies "trans-Latino," a more rigorously transnational unit of Latino Studies analysis than even the staunch "Third World" and anti-imperialist perspective of Latino Studies in its foundation.

NEW CONCEPTS

This sociohistorical context thus generates new concepts and conceptual approaches for what remains essentially the same object/subject of study: the experience of Latin American and Caribbean peoples in the United States. With all the caveats, and fully recognizing that the very terms *Latino* and *Hispanic* are first of all imposed labels, ideological hoodwinks aimed at tightening hegemony and capturing markets, the "Latino" concept is still useful, if not indispensable, for charting out an area of contemporary intellectual inquiry and political advocacy.[3] It builds on and complements the perspectives, curricular orientations, and programmatic structures of established Chicano and Puerto Rican Studies programs. The concept of "Latino Studies" allows for some space to mediate issues of inclusion and solidarity sometimes strained in nationality-specific situations; for example, what to do about Central Americans, Dominicans, Colombians, and "other" Latinos who do not feel they fit into, say, a Chicano-exclusive notion of "La Raza." Such strains persist, of course, and it is still often difficult in many settings to get Puerto Ricans, Chicanos, and Ecuadorians, for instance, to come to the same "Latino" meetings, or to the same "Latino" dances.

In addition to the "global" economic and political shifts and their impact, the period since the first wave of Latino Studies has also witnessed significant new developments in social theory and methodology, or at least new emphases in thinking about issues of race, ethnicity, colonial status, nationality, gender, sexuality, and class. The altered historical field has made for a changed discursive field, much of it occupied by questions of cultural and group identity. If the early 1970s articulation of Latino Studies was guided by a rallying cry of cultural nationalism—boisterous and contestatory but also often parochial and unreflexive—a current understanding of Latino experience is necessarily informed by insights and approaches developed by feminist, postcolonial, and race theory, as well as lesbian and gay studies. The presumed seamlessness and discreteness of group identities characteristic of earlier Latino perspectives have given way to more complex, interactive, and transgressive notions of hybrid and multiple social points of view.

Theorizing about gender and sexuality has done the most to dissolve the sexist and heterosexist conception of Latino group unity and inclusion, and to complicate the meanings of Latino claims and affirmation. Latina, Chicana, and Puertorriqueña areas of political activism and intellectual work have involved changes in prevailing ideas of Latino history and culture, and have helped bring into the foreground testimonial and ethnographic methods of social research. Revamping the canonical (i.e., straight male) notion of "Latino identity" with a view toward contemporary theories of sexuality leads not only to new political stances and possibilities but, beyond that, to new kinds of knowledge about cultural history, and even a new, more variegated relation to theoretical practice. A striking account of this interface of Latino and sexual identities and its intellectual consequences was voiced cogently by Oscar Montero, a Cuban American professor from CUNY, at the 1994 conference of the East of California Network of the Association of Asian American Studies, held in New York City. "It goes without saying," Montero states, "that 'Latino' and 'homosexual' signal different histories and different stories, unevenly deployed. Bringing the two together creates a lopsided image, but perhaps a useful one. The experiences of the body justify the mask, and this mask wants to question the received metaphors for defining identity: Latino by birth, queer by choice. Latino by choice, queer by birth. What matters is that having taken a stance, linking with this mask the two identities, a reader, a critic, a student, can turn to the salient works of his or her tradition and read them anew, availing herself of whatever theories might do the job."[4]

The contemporary Latino construct, and the intellectual project of Latino Studies, is laced with this open, multidimensional disposition toward theory and must also incorporate critical understandings of processes of "racialization" and "translocality." In addition to differentiation along lines of gender and sexuality, the specific identity positions of "black Latinos" and of mixed Latino backgrounds—Puerto Rican and Dominican, Mexican and Salvadoran—have drawn increasing attention and have done much to sunder the more or less monolithic and essentialist tenets of inherited conceptualizations. Angie Chabram, the noted Chicana feminist and cultural studies theorist, has staked out new grounds for a critique of traditional Chicano (and even Chicana) perspectives by reading the newfound significance of her other, "repressed" Puerto Rican half. In her essay " 'Chicana! Rican? No, Chicana-Riqueña!' Refashioning the Transnational Connection," Chabram writes forcefully of the residual identity traces left by her absent Puerto Rican father, as filtered through her rooted Chicana mother, and their jarring repercussions on her Chicanismo.

> It does not cease to amaze me that it was *she* who nurtured a sense of
> Puerto Ricanness in me—she who had all the right to be a nationalist
> following the purist dictates associated with this politics, for she was a
> Chicana, she was not mixed in my way with the Riqueña. In retrospect,
> it occurs to me that what she presented me with throughout one of the
> trajectories of our lives as mother and daughter was a pedagogy of
> Chicanas/os, a mode of knowing Puerto Rico from inside of Chicana/o,
> a way of speaking across fractured ethnicities, a way of initiating a
> dialogue among and between different ethnic groups.[5]

Chabram draws from these lessons a way of "countering our presumed singularity with our historically verifiable pluralities, the ones that are intersected, and . . . engage positions from diverse fields of contestation"; she builds on her personal experience to summon "a strategic location from which to refashion a transnational connection to ourselves and one another, and to contribute to a widening of imagined communities and spheres of contestation."[6]

Opinions will vary as to the utility and relevance of an explicitly "postmodern" frame and vocabulary for these new lines of theoretical inquiry, and particular reluctance is surely due any too hasty applications of "postcolonial" models to situations, like those of Chicanos and Puerto Ricans, which would still seem to be emphatically colonial in both historical trajectory and present condition.[7] The term *multicultural* itself is another coinage of the last decades that Latino Studies should treat with caution, since in its most prevalent usage it echoes clearly the grave inadequacies of its ideological predecessor, cultural pluralism. Yet while Marxist and other anti-imperialist intellectual and political traditions remain pertinent to a liberatory analysis of Latino reality, these new insights from multicultural and postcolonial theory are by now invaluable for purposes of spanning the full range of Latino perspectives under the complex transnational conditions of our time. Whatever we may think of the vocabulary, reflections on questions of "hybridity," "liminality," "transgressivity," and the like, and the new intellectual horizons they signal, are clearly germane to any contemporary work in Latino Studies. They complement, and add philosophical range to, what has been the guiding metaphor of Latino Studies: "la frontera," the border.

It is the idea of the nation, and of national culture and identity, that has entailed the recent rethinking perhaps most pertinent to a new discursive field for Latino Studies. Both Chicano and Puerto Rican Studies have relied, for their foundational narratives, on the national concept, whether that term referred to historical home countries or newly formed internal colonies in U.S. barrios. Latino social experience was conditioned and defined by the hierarchized interaction of nations, and cultural identities were first and above all national identities. The boundedness and relative uniformity of their original territories went largely unquestioned, particularly in demarcating each Latino group from an "American" nationality, mainstream or otherwise. The guiding theoretical premises were adopted directly from thinkers like Frantz Fanon, Amilcar Cabral, and of course Lenin, with Black nationalism, Pedro Albizu Campos, and even José Vasconcelos and Octavio Paz being more immediate intellectual sources.

Nationality is still no doubt the main binding principle and sensibility for each of the Latino groups, as evidenced at the annual Puerto Rican Day Parade, Cinco de Mayo, and other celebrations. Indeed, it is important to insist upon this persistence of specifically "national" affiliation in countering the tendency of U.S. social science and public policy to reduce Latinos to an "ethnic" group experience, with its implicit analogy to the prototypical story of immigrant incorporation. Yet despite the non-assimilationist thrust of most Latino discourse, the idea of the nation as the ontological locus of difference and opposition to the hegemonic Anglo "Other" has been seriously revised from many theoretical angles and Latina/o subject positions.

Here again, the varied feminist and queer critiques have been most incisive in their exposure of the "brotherhoods" of nations and their foundational narratives. For contemporary Latino Studies this undermining of the nation as hetero-masculinist mask extends to the diasporic communities spun off of the "home" nations in the course of global and regional reconfigurations. The nation also continues to be dissected and deconstructed along lines of race and class, dimensions that were already strongly etched in the earlier stage of Latino Studies. Yet even the strident Third World, anti-imperialist stance of the early 1970s did contain some serious gaps, which subsequent theoretical work, especially on race, does much to fill. Updating the class critique of the nation is less visible within Latino Studies since the Marxist analyses of around 1980 (such as the Center for Puerto Rican Studies' *Labor Migration Under Capitalism* and Mario Barrera's *Race and Class in the Southwest*), though some fruitful lines of thinking have emerged from an application of "subaltern studies."[8] It is as though, with the abruptly changing economic geography of the past decade, historical reality has lunged far ahead of the reach of social theory: no new sociological terminology has surfaced that can account for the class relations resulting from the radical changes in the socialist world and the intricate transnational alignments and restructurings of present-day capitalism.

None of these critical assaults on the nation, nor even a broadside of all combined, has spelled the final demise of the concept, which continues to be central as a social category to the intellectual agenda of Latino Studies, and to the struggle of Latino national groups in the United States. But these critiques have generated a radical rethinking of the meaning of nationality, and a recognition that the concept of nation is reliable as a political principle and rallying point only in its interaction with these other forms of social differentiation and liberatory movements.

The reinterpretation of the nation which informs today's Latino Studies hovers around the idea of "imagined communities" as formulated by Benedict Anderson in his frequently cited book of that title. The nation as a fixed and primordial territory of inclusion/exclusion becomes a malleable, fluid, permeable construct, a group given form by shared imaginaries. The idea of "imagined communities" lends itself well to the conceptual terminology of Latino Studies today because it helps to describe the "national" experience of Latino diasporas in all its ambiguity. The sense of belonging and not belonging to the nation—driven home to Nuyoricans and Chicanos when they "return" to their "native" lands—confirms that nationality can not only be imagined but actually created as a social reality by the force of the imagination. The paradox of being "nationals" in a thoroughly "transnationalized" economic geography—Latinos as "transnations" or translocal nationalities—is captured well with a loose, dynamic, and relational concept like "imagined communities." Such a concept is certainly more adequate than the essentialist and mechanical categories of the "national question" that had informed much of Latino Studies in its earlier stage.

Some theorists used to refer to this problematic of nationality and nationhood, true to Marxist-Leninist vocabulary, as the "national-colonial question." Indeed the renovation of the concept of nation and national culture begs the question of colonialism itself and, for Latino Studies, the pertinence of "postcolonial" theory. When Latino Studies programs were founded, nobody spoke of a "postcolonial" condition or era; on the contrary, colonialism and anticolonial struggle were precisely the terms around which that and simultaneous movements were defined. In the United States, at least, the postcolonial discourse is definitely a child of the intervening years, gaining ground in theoretical debates only in the past decade or so. Imperialism—which became a buzzword during that same period—is surely one of the subtexts. But the pressing question from the perspective of Latino Studies is whether Puerto Rico and the Southwest at some point ceased occupying a colonial position, and if so, when and how. More particularly, can the experience of diasporic migrants from former colonial nations serve as a model, or analogue, for that of transnational communities like those of U.S. Latinos? The insights of theorists like Homi Bhabha and Gayatri Spivak are no doubt of great explanatory value, as is the critique of Anderson's "imagined communities" by Partha Chatterjee and others.[9] However, for the purpose of identifying the conditions faced by Puerto Rican, Mexican American, Dominican, and other Latino peoples in the United States, and the economic and political domination of their home countries, the term *postcolonial* seems to be jumping the gun at best. Even those most bent on minimizing the collision and incompatibility between Latino and U.S. nationalities cannot fail to detect the signs of some kind of systemic social subordination, call it colonial or otherwise, and independent of any proposed remedy.

PROSPECTS AND PREMISES

While the activist relationship of Latino Studies programs to their social contexts and communities is weaker than in its founding years, the theoretical field of Latino Studies is now wider and more complex. The implementation of this rich intellectual agenda is also more complex, and certainly as challenging as in the years when Latino and other ethnic studies programs were first set in place. Current ideological and fiscal obstacles are the most obvious challenges in this regard and must be faced without the momentum of the Civil Rights movement to build on. But even more pragmatic questions of institutional location and leverage present problems that were not faced when building ethnic studies was still a matter of filling a vacuum.

By our time there are already ethnic and minority studies programs long in place on many campuses, including of course Chicano, Puerto Rican, and, more recently, Cuban, and Dominican Studies. There are professional associations, academic research centers and networks, policy institutes, journals scholarly and otherwise, and a proliferation of Websites all devoted to ethnic and minority studies. Within the academy there are also emergent disciplines and areas (such as ethnic, cultural, and multicultural studies) and groundswells of change in already established interdisciplines and area studies (communications, comparative literature, and American, Latin American, and Caribbean Studies), all of which run parallel with or border closely on Latino Studies. It is also important to constantly rethink the relation of a reemergent area like Latino Studies to the traditional disciplines, where some of the best work about Latinos is being produced, and most of which are also in flux or in a state of crisis.

What the best "fit" for Latino Studies may be in the present and shifting structure of the U.S. academy is clearly an enigma, especially as none of these umbrellas or potential federations is guaranteed to feel like home in a suspicious, reluctant, and sometimes dog-eat-dog institutional environment. Like Latino Studies itself, all of these abstractions from the specific historical experiences of the composite groups tend to dilute and distort those experiences, and to set up new exclusions and reductions. Furthermore, each of these transdisciplinary rubrics has its own trajectory and baggage that is often at odds with guiding tenets of Latino Studies. Think of Latin American Area Studies, for instance, or even American Studies, which in their founding intentions were so consonant with the interests of U.S. and Anglo hegemony.[10] Special caution should be observed in dealing with concoctions that sometimes go under the name of "Hispanic Studies," but that are often no more than opportunistic creations of Spanish Departments desperate to shore up their ever-waning student ap-

peal, while retaining their doggedly Hispanophile ideological conserva-
tism. It would seem that nothing short of an autonomous, freestanding
university Department of Latino Studies could promise a location condu-
cive to the confidence needed to carry forward an adequate instructional
and research project.

While departmental status may stand as a goal or desideratum for Latino Studies, a pragmatic and flexible approach is probably advisable under
the present political conditions. Whether and how Latino Studies may be
folded or built into some larger configuration would seem to be a case-by-
case kind of decision, depending on the relative strength and compatibility
of existing programs and alliances. Ethnic Studies, for example, might be
right, provided there is a strong accent on questions of race and social oppression, and insofar as it is moving from a focus on strictly domestic issues of group difference and rights into the international arena. Some affiliation within American Studies could also work, as scholars and students
in that area deepen their critical analysis of the field's reactionary and chau-
vinist origins and expand its horizons toward something like "Americas
Studies" or "New American Studies." With certain intellectual and political
provisos, Latino Studies could also find a hospitable and productive place
in relation to Latin American or Cultural Studies. An issue of central importance, though (and one often obscured in this quest for a larger floor
plan), is the relation of Latino Studies to African American Studies, on the
one hand, and to Women's Studies on the other. The circumscription of the
"Latino" concept in terms of ethnicity, geography, and language culture
tends to cordon off Latino Studies from full engagement of issues of gender, sexuality, and "racial" identity.

If certain key theoretical principles of methodology and research practice are clear, the main immediate goal at some institutions may be getting
a foot in the door, in others standing firm in defense of the spaces that have
already been created, however flawed. For in the longer view, the objective
is not limited to securing those spaces and opportunities, but extends to
advancing new knowledge and new ways of understanding what knowledge is for and about. Latino Studies will become ghettoized and easy prey
for closure or consolidation if it is divorced from this wider intellectual and
social project, both at the university and in the larger community.

In this respect, and with all the contextual and conceptual changes, contemporary Latino Studies has much to learn from, and reaffirm in, its own
history. In their founding meetings and declarations, Chicano Studies and

Puerto Rican Studies set forth certain principles of research and educational practice which continue to underlie the Latino Studies project
today.[11] To extrapolate from the many goals and methods proclaimed, these
founding plans called for knowledge production which was to be interdisciplinary in its methodological range, collective in its practice, and tied to
the community. The primary methodological aim of bridging the divide between the humanities and the social sciences remains the order of the day,
with areas like ethnic and cultural studies and communications moving
the discourse from "inter" in the direction of "trans-," "post-," and even
"anti-disciplinary." Collective research practice is still an obvious necessity,
if only for the volume and scope of this supposedly narrow and particular-
ist object of study. We are now more aware that collective work means
more than coauthorship or tight-knit study groups; rather, coordinations
and collaborations at many levels, from anthology readers and conference
panels to on-line cothinking, are indispensable to cover the ground and live
up to the many challenges posed by recent theorizing. For one instance,
the close attention to multiple histories in the analysis of sociocultural experience reinforces the need for the coordination of diverse research and
teaching perspectives.

As for the ties of Latino Studies to "community," that tenet would seem
to hold more strongly than ever, because of the relative distance of much
academic work—Latino and other—from the extramural "Other," but also
because there is an immense ideological stake in keeping Latino higher education and Latino communities apart, and even at odds. The notion of
"community," of course, has also been subjected to critical deconstruction
and demystification. Though the concept of "imagined communities" is
useful in displacing nation in its traditional sense, the very vagueness and
mantralike resonance of "community" can render it as meaningless as the
oft-stated sanctities of the "national family."

Still, an affiliation, reference, and accountability to Latino people and social realities remains a sine qua non of Latino Studies, as it does for any
emergent area focusing on an oppressed group in our society. It is not a
matter of studying the community/communities as something outside of
and separate from ourselves. Socially, many of us are part of and from
these communities, and it is in this sense of intellectual work that the political is also personal. With all due caution with regard to fallacies of authenticity and a politics of "experience," Latino Studies does affirm the
need for (for lack of a better word) "indigenous" perspectives on the reali-

ty "under study," perspectives that are generally ignored, or colonized, in much academic and journalistic coverage of Latino life.

For all its sensitivity to differences within the "Latino community," and its critical rejection of imposed group labels, Latino Studies also needs to reflect continually on the real or constitutive unities within and among the Latino population as a whole. The history of Latinos is already in mid-narrative, and even if we don't propose to "imagine" the Hispanic community as a "nation" in formation—a recent book on the subject is actually entitled *Hispanic Nation*[12]—some form of pan-group amalgam is always at least potentially on the horizon. Though it is important to view *lo Latino* ("Latinoness") from the optic of the particular national groups, the social and cultural perspective of each group also harbors and evokes some relation to a "Latino" ethnoscape of transnational dimensions.[13]

But even to consider such prospects, to trace historical congruences and study practical interactions, requires not only new curricula but also new attitudes about mounting curricular strategies adequate to the task. It also requires a space very different from that provided by many universities in the present climate. Oscar Montero, cited earlier, summons this broader discursive and institutional agenda in his closing remarks. "New curricula cannot succeed," he says, "by mere inclusion of emergent discourses, after the fashion of eighteenth-century encyclopedists. It must incorporate a point of view, or a series of points of view, a different dialectic, and in the long haul, perhaps a different kind of university."[14]

Puerto Rico plebiscite, 1998: "None of the Above"

(Photo by Ana Martinez; courtesy of Reuters and Archive Photos)

Postscript

"NONE OF THE ABOVE"

A governmental crisis, a general strike, a devastating hurricane, a national plebiscite—1998 was an eventful year for Puerto Ricans, one filled with the kind of symbolic drama expected on the centenary of the fateful invasion by U.S. military forces that makes "el '98," 1898, the turning point in the country's long colonial past. On July 25, the day of the landing, thousands joined the pilgrimage to the southern coastal town of Guánica, where the troops under General Miles first disembarked. They came to commemorate the event, some in celebration and others in angry condemnation, while still others gathered at the historical Morro Castle in San Juan to herald forty years of commonwealth status. Age-old divisions and ambivalences in Puerto Rican public life were thus reenacted in a show of the ongoing contestation over historical memory.[1]

But with all the debates and fanfare, the scholarly conferences, news specials, and official proclamations, there were other events, largely unrelated to the commemorative calendar, that marked off the significance of the anxiously awaited centennial year. First, the Island's governor, Pedro Rosello of the statehood party, drew the wrath of the country's press and news media by trying to stifle dissent and critical coverage through his control over advertising monies, which brought him under the denunciatory scrutiny of international editors and journalists. The governor's arrogant faceoff with the widely respected news writers from many Latin American countries exposed the tenuousness of Puerto Rico's democratic facade and the ominous implications of its path toward neoliberal privatization.

On the heels of that troubling confrontation, with the approach of summer, came the strike by the country's telephone workers, a stoppage in protest against the imminent sale of the publicly owned telephone company to private corporations. While beginning as an action by organized labor over conditions and contract terms, the movement quickly expanded to involve all of those, including many supporters of the governor and of statehood, who objected to the betrayal of public trust in disposing of an enterprise which the people felt was their own. "La Telefónica," amiably referred as "Fortunata," the cash cow, was the source of ample public revenue and was considered by many a symbol of the country itself. The protest, which made for a rare show of unity across the otherwise fractious political spectrum and drew the attention of antiprivatization sentiment throughout Latin America, resounded to the cry of "La patria no se vende" ("our country is not for sale") as the annexationist government suffered another blow to its shaky legitimacy.[2]

Then, as though to accentuate the turmoil, came Hurricane Georges, the worst natural disaster to hit the Island in recent memory. Scores of families were left homeless, thousands were without water and electrical service for months to follow, and relief efforts were tragically bungled and slow in coming. Favorable comparisons with the fate of the Dominican Republic and other Caribbean islands, and even with the catastrophe in Central America, did little to persuade the public of the blessings of U.S. federal aid and served as a cruel reminder to many of the ongoing dependency and subservience of their country in U.S. national affairs. Residents on the southwest part of the Island, where the wrath of Georges took its greatest toll, witnessed the landing of federal relief forces in the bay of Boquerón and more than a few were made to think, resentfully, of the historic events in the nearby town of Guánica one hundred years ago.

Finally, as the centennial year reached an end, there was the plebiscite. What would "el '98" be, after all, without a poll of the population as to the preferred status and future of their country? As political leaders of all stripes succeeded in assuring the exclusion of Puerto Rico's huge diaspora from any role in the vote, the governing party was intent on securing a decisive consensus for statehood to present to the U.S. president and Congress. Unilaterally devising a ballot that would divide the commonwealth option and further marginalize the independence vote, the statehooders included the famous "fifth column"—after "Commonwealth As Is," "Revised Commonwealth," "Statehood," and "Independence"—under the heading "None of the Above." But the devious tactic of framing the country's political alternatives as a multiple-choice question backfired, as a 50.2 percent majority of the voting population joined the fifth column and entered "None of the

Above." Unrelenting, the governing party immediately celebrated victory with 46.5 percent of the vote, claiming that "none of the above" did not constitute a status option. Leaders of the "Populares" (Popular Democratic Party), representing the commonwealth options, launched a legal objection to the officially declared outcome and held their own victory party based on the interpretation that "none of the above" was a coordinated protest against statehood and in their own favor. And the "independentistas," noting the defiance implicit in the favored option, took the outcome as demonstration of the generalized public distaste among Puerto Ricans for the corrupt machinations of colonialist politics as such.[3]

Whatever the specific intentions of "fifth column" voters, the phrase "none of the above" ("ninguna de las anteriores") may well stand as a tidy summation of the prevailing temperament among Puerto Ricans in their symbolic year of 1998. It punctuates that commemorative period with the sense of indecision, but also signals the widespread dissatisfaction and frustration, after one hundred years of U.S. control. It is testimony, as well, to the irony and indirection with which the people confront the official public sphere in their country: the practice of "diversion," the tactic of playful obliqueness, is capsulized in that resignified cliché, "none of the above." That slogan, along with the symbolical weight given the two most prominent events of the year, the "Telefónica" strike and Hurricane Georges, illustrate well the signs of what I term the "lite colonial" situation of contemporary Puerto Rico, where hegemony is maintained, and challenged, largely in the cultural field, as a struggle over meanings and images. The game is serious, and precarious, what with the traces of political despotism, the nagging poverty and unemployment, and the rampant social violence as stark reminders of what colonialism is all about. But there is something of the game to it, after all, when the prospects of positive social change are nowhere on the historical horizon at the threshold of a new "American century."

For Puerto Ricans in the United States, meanwhile, the half of the total population making up the diaspora, "none of the above" is equally appropriate, and perhaps even euphemistically so, to convey what life has been like in the celebrated '98. While attention is turned to the handful of entertainment and sports celebrities, and official reports tell glowingly of the emerging middle class, the overwhelming majority of Puerto Ricans remain at the bottom of the socioeconomic ladder, even among their fellow "Latinos" with whom they are increasingly grouped. They are also the victims of constant degradation in the public eye, and 1998 was particularly harsh in that regard. Though the Puerto Rican Day Parade in June was the largest ever, and remains the largest national day parade in New York City, that boisterous show of pride was smeared from the beginning of the year to the end.

First it was *Capeman*, the Broadway fiasco orchestrated by Paul Simon in what was intended as a goodwill gesture toward Puerto Ricans. Of course it did provide jobs for many Puerto Rican actors, musicians, and theater workers, and it was indeed heralded by some as a positive, pro-Puerto Rican event—one well-known political commentator went so far as to proclaim "Puerto Rican Nationalism Hits Broadway."[4] But artistically *Capeman* was a flop, lacking in all narrative energy and flawed as well in its allusions to Puerto Rican music; while politically, in its romanticized treatment of a legendary gang leader and repentant murderer, it only goes down as a reminder of the days of *West Side Story* and its supposed benevolent typecasting.

Then followed the infamous *Seinfeld* episode, which showed Kramer, detained in traffic by the Puerto Rican Day parade, heedlessly stamping on the Puerto Rican flag. When the public protested, Seinfeld claimed that he had been misunderstood, explaining that the flag was burning and that Kramer had only jumped out of the car to help put out the fire. But from the response it was clear that he had touched a tender nerve, and that no disclaimers, nor his gratuitous presenting of the Puerto Rican flag to actress Jennifer López at the 1999 Grammy award ceremonies, would dispel the indignation felt by Puerto Ricans and much of the general public.[5]

As if that were not enough of a barrage, the year could not end without still another offense against Puerto Ricans in the U.S media. On November 30, 1998, a few weeks before the plebiscite, an article appeared in the *Boston Herald* entitled "No Statehood for Caribbean Dogpatch."[6] Signed by columnist Don Feder, the article set forth many of the conservative arguments against statehood for Puerto Rico, arguing for the "right" of Americans "not to be saddled with an impoverished, crime-ridden island of non-English speakers as our 51st state." Feder cites the "English First" crusade in warning that to incorporate Puerto Rico would put "America well on its way to becoming a bilingual nation," mentioning that support for statehood is not even evident among other Hispanics; as he puts it, "as if Mexicans in California and Cubans in Florida really give a hill of frijoles for Puerto Rican statehood."

Feder also makes it clear that his "Caribbean dogpatch" refers not only to the Island but to Puerto Ricans in the United States when he says that "with Puerto Rican statehood, to the problem of unassimilable immigrants we would add an unassimilable state." From such scurrilous language it becomes evident that, like statehood, the "assimilation" of U.S. Puerto Ricans is not for Puerto Ricans to decide, and that the inflammatory "Puerto Rican problem" spans the divide between the national homeland and the diaspora communities. The local "dogpatch," of course, encompasses the impoverished inner-city neighborhoods where most Puerto Ricans live, the slums and ghettos of the South Bronx, Williamsburg, Hartford, Philadelphia, Chicago, and scores of other enclaves of abandonment and neglect. It's the "mean streets" of Piri Thomas, the "Spidertown" of young novelist Abraham Rodriguez. But how different the settings of Puerto Rican diasporic life appear in these fictional works, where the crushing, dehumanizing conditions are presented in dynamic social and psychological context, and not for the purpose of reinforcing stereotypes and pathologies. How necessary it is to approach this situation from within, from the perspective of the community in question, and in the new, youthful terms exemplified by Rodriguez and others of the present generation. It becomes clear why in 1998 Spidertown, too, votes "none of the above."

The centenary year was also a watershed period for the sites of popular cultural expression explored here. The struggle to "save" the casita "Rincón Criollo," for example, reached a new level of intensity as city developers proceeded with their plans to convert the neighboring Melrose area of the South Bronx into a model redevelopment project, with the corner of Brook Avenue and 158th Street earmarked for more of the townhouses which now surround that historic spot as part of the ambitious Melrose Commons development. In deference to the cultural significance of the casita, planners agreed to set aside a lot one block to the south, with the idea of moving "Rincón Criollo" and reassembling it behind a planned community "museum." Despite the promise of recognition and stability, however, casita members reject this plan from above, out of fear that a great deal more would be lost than gained in the transition. As the conflict came to a head in late summer 1998, José Manuel Soto ("Chema"), José Rivera, and other long-standing leaders sent out still another call for "Salvación Casita," and another of the memorable rescue parties attracted hundreds of neighbors and friends of the casita. Because of the growing public attention to this remarkable cultural institution, the activity this time drew two TV crews as well as special guests Yomo Toro, the renowned Puerto Rican *cuatro* player, and Tito Puente, both of whom played along with the familiar *pleneros* who form part of the scene. The message: "We're not moving anywhere!" As Chema commented, "What are we supposed to do, take our peach and apple trees out by the roots? Over there, the ground is full of rocks. It took us more than 20 years to do this. Before we see trees like this over there, we'll be dead."[7]

The music of the casita culture, bomba and plena, is also holding its ground in the symbolic 1998 period. Two new groups, both spawned of the long-standing Los Pleneros de la 21, have made their appearance in these years, both of them combining traditional styles with contemporary musical developments. The Rivera brothers, José and Ramón ("Papo Chín"), founded a new ensemble, Amigos de la Plena, which uses the bomba and plena rhythms as a base for blending with salsa, merengue, and rap as well as with *seis, aguinaldo,* and other forms of peasant music from the Island. Television appearances on Spanish-language stations along with ongoing performances at the casita and other community settings have given them rapid visibility in the New York and other Puerto Rican neighborhood contexts. Another new group, which surfaced in 1998, calls itself Viento de Agua, and its skillful fusions of sounds from jazz, salsa, rock, and *nueva canción* with the familiar plena and bomba stylistic features has made their CD, *De Puerto Rico al Mundo,* a significant hit both in the United States and in Puerto Rico.

It was also a landmark year for Latin boogaloo, that throwback style of the pre-salsa era sometimes referred to as the "first Nuyorican music." Though no "revival" of the style by its originators of the 1960s seems to be in store, strong reminiscences among a broad public were registered with the immense success of popular *salsero* Tito Nieves's album *I Like It Like That,* which topped the Latin charts for the year. Aside from the title song, a remake of the Pete Rodríguez band's classic boogaloo number of thirty years earlier, Nieves's version of "Bang Bang" also struck a chord and made it clear that, though boogaloo was handily eclipsed by the Fania brand of "salsa," the airs of that Puerto Rican-flavored rhythm and blues linger on in the sensibility of many Puerto Rican New Yorkers, and many others as well. Historical interest also heightened, such that a major discussion and performance event entitled "I Like It Like That: Remembering the Boogaloo Era" was scheduled for the Public Theater, featuring the recollections of such musicians as Jimmy Sabater, Hector Rivera, Frankie Lebrón, and Joe Bataan.

On the rap scene, 1998 saw Big Pun go platinum and Nuyorican rappers finally gain their due recognition in the mass culture. Following in the path of his friend and mentor Fat Joe (Joseph Cartagena), Big Punisher

(Christopher Rios) broke onto the scene with his chart-topping CD *Capital Punishment* on RCA, with his track "Still Not a Player" featuring Fat Joe capturing nationwide hip-hop audiences with its powerful, suggestively bilingual rhymes. The way to this supreme popularity had been paved by the movement to get back to "old school" rap, the days when with African Americans Puerto Ricans played an instrumental role in the forging of the style in the first place. Identified with other well-known performers like Frankie Cutlass, the Beatnuts, Tony Touch, and Hurricane Gee (Gloria Rodriguez), this tendency in late-nineties hip-hop predilections is not merely nostalgic or revivalist in purpose; in fact, rather than acting on the retrospective notion of "old school," some performers and commentators, reacting to the thoroughgoing commercialization and dilution of the genre, prefer to speak in terms of a continuity of "true school" rap. Though part of this renewed presence and recognition of Nuyorican themes and artists results from the continued attraction and growing selling power of things "Latin," as is clear from the use of Spanish words and phrases by big-time favorites like the Fugees and Puff Daddy, the specifically Nuyorican dimension includes a strong sense of unity and interaction between Puerto Rican and Black cultures.[8]

It happens that 1998 also saw the publication of a lengthy conversation with three contemporary writers from Martinique, and again some interesting parallels and insights can be drawn as to the issues of contemporary colonialism.[9] Acknowledging the influence of Edouard Glissant's theoretical perspectives, Patrick Chamoiseau, Raphäel Confiant, and Jean Bernabé call themselves "créolistes" and are seeking new ways of understanding the cultural and political aspects of colonial relations in today's world. Chamoiseau, author of the widely admired novel *Texaco*, offers a three-stage typology of colonial history, starting with the "brutal, violent" stage, followed by the neocolonial stage of "domination from a distance," and then a present-day stage which would surely resonate in thinking of the "lite colonial" condition of Puerto Rico. He calls it the "third stage, furtive domination, which works through the great communicative circuits that link up the world today." When he came to understand this new situation, Chamoiseau explains that he had to transform himself "from a word scratcher into a warrior . . . who can recognize that the battle against oppression and domination has moved into the realm of the imaginary. We're planed down, crushed, deadened by the dominant imaginary, without even realizing that we're being subjugated and transformed. The domain of the imaginary is an absolutely fundamental theater for resistance" (140).

In staking out their new position, the "créolistes" are openly critical of their forebear, the monumental Martinican poet and statesman Aimé Césaire, in part for what they see as the essentialism of his Négritude movement, and in part for the annexation of Martinique as a department of France which he oversaw. In his book on Césaire, Confiant comments that he would like Martinique to have a status vis-à-vis France like that of Puerto Rico to the United States. Aware of the disastrous social problems facing Puerto Rico, he explains that for him "becoming an associated state— like Puerto Rico—is an indispensable phase in the reconstruction of our economy" (which is in a shambles as a result of departmentalization), and toward national sovereignty. As the status of autonomy does not exist in the French constitution, "the only thing we can call for is the status of associated statehood, a separation like Puerto Rico's" (158–59). Though their position is clearly an anticolonialist one aimed at self-determination, the "créolistes" are cautious about the idea of independence. Citing Jean-Marie Tjibaou, the assassinated Kanak leader, Confiant comments that "in this day and age, independence is the possibility to choose your interdependencies," and Chamoiseau explains in terms that are of interest to contemporary thinking about national liberation: "I don't think anyone can declare themselves independent in this day and age. We're all dependent on each other. You can't simply raise the flag, dance around the pole, and imagine you're free. Concepts like liberty, sovereignty, and responsibility can only be articulated once you've taken the ongoing process of globalization into consideration" (160).

Raphäel Confiant envisions a way out of this modern-day quagmire of annexation, where even the prospect of Puerto Rico's political limbo has its attraction. "I *do* talk of independence," he states, "but independence within a Caribbean Federation." In the face of the splintering process that has plagued the region throughout its history, and the "retractile tendencies" toward essential and pure identities, Confiant sets forth his vision of independence within an "interdependent" Caribbean, and again the cultural front is central to the change. "If we manage to modify the collective Antillean imaginary," he concludes, "there'll be writers here in French, in Creole, in English, in Spanish, in any language that entices them. No one can foresee what will happen in the *totalité-monde*" (160).

Notes

INTRODUCTION

1. Meagan Morris, *Too Soon Too Late: History in Popular Culture* (Bloomington: Indiana University Press, 1998), 24.
2. See Johannes Fabian, *Moments of Freedom: Anthropology and Popular Culture* (Charlottesville: University Press of Virginia, 1998), 133 passim.
3. See Argeliers León, *Del canto y el tiempo* (Havana: Letras Cubanas, 1974), and Angel G. Quintero Rivera, *!Salsa, sabor y control!: Scociología de la música tropical* (Mexico City: Siglo XXI, 1998), 32–86.

1. "PUEBLO PUEBLO": POPULAR CULTURE IN TIME

1. Peter Stallybrass and Allon White, *The Politics and Poetics of Transgression* (Ithaca: Cornell Univesity Press, 1986), 3. This process of "symbolic inversion," developed by Stallybrass and White, is actually taken from Barbara Babcock, *The Reversible World: Symbolic Inversion in Art and Society* (Ithaca: Cornell University Press, 1978), 3. The concept of "moments of freedom" forms the title of the book by Johannes Fabian, *Moments of Freedom: Anthropology and Popular Culture* (Charlottesville: University Press of Virginia, 1998).
2. See Stuart Hall, "Notes on Deconstructing 'the Popular'," in Raphael Samuel, ed., *People's History and Socialist Theory* (London: Routledge, 1981), 227–40. See also note 22, this chapter.
3. Such, for example, is the perspective of John Fiske in his frequently cited primer *Understanding Popular Culture* (London: Routledge, 1989), as well as that of the thoughtful critical response by John Frow, *Cultural Studies and Cultural Value* (Oxford: Oxford University Press, 1995). For an extended discussion of this theoretical shift, see my "Reinstating Popular Culture: Responses to Christopher Lasch," *Social Text* 12 (1985): 113–23.
4. See John Frow, *Cultural Studies and Cultural Value*, esp. 75–79, where frequent reference is made to the relevant writings of Hall and others.

5. See García Canclini, *Culturas híbridas: estrategias para entrar y salir de la modernidad* (Mexico City: Grijalbo, 1989), and *Consumidores y ciudadanos: conflictos multicultur-ales de la globalización* (Mexico City: Grijalbo, 1995).

6. See García Canclini, *Consumidores y ciudadanos*, 27–30.

7. See Arjun Appadurai and Carol A. Breckenridge, "Why Public Culture?" *Public Culture Bulletin* 1.1 (Fall 1988): 5–9.

8. See Arjun Appadurai, *Modernity at Large: Cultural Dimensions of Globalization* (Minneapolis: University of Minnesota Press, 1996), 12 passim.

9. Fabian, *Moments of Freedom*, 133.

10. Ibid., 133–34.

11. Edgardo Rodríguez Juliá, *El entierro de Cortijo* (Río Piedras, P.R.: Ediciones Huracán, 1983), 12 (". . . ya se perfila que esta crónica será el encuentro de muchas cruces históricas").

12. Ibid., 18. ("¿Cómo definir este pueblo? Definirlo es fácil, pero ¡qué difícil es describirlo! Es pueblo pueblo, mi pueblo puertorriqueño en toda su diversidad más contradictoria.")

13. Jesús Martín Barbero, *De los medios a las mediaciones* (Barcelona: Grijalbo, 1987).

14. On the role of the "imagination" in the study of contemporary popular culture, see especially Appadurai, *Modernity at Large*, 3ff.

15. Rodríguez Juliá, *El entierro de Cortijo*, 18 ("las perlitas de su grasoso sudor me recuerdan aquellas abnegadas planchadoras y cocineras que pasaban los sábados por la calle de mi infancia, allá dirigiéndose al proletario culto evangélico").

16. Stuart Hall, "What Is This 'Black' in Black Popular Culture?" in Gina Dent, ed., *Black Popular Culture* (Seattle: Bay Press, 1992), 21–33.

17. Hall, "What Is This 'Black' . . . ," 26.

18. Ibid., 27.

19. Ibid., 22.

20. See Renato Ortiz, *Mundializaçáo e Cultura* (São Paulo: Braziliense, 1994), 105–45.

21. Hall, "What Is This 'Black' . . . ," 26.

22. See Peter Burke, *Popular Culture in Early Modern Europe* (New York: New York University Press, 1978), esp. 3–22. See also William A. Wilson, "Herder, Folklore, and Romantic Nationalism," *Journal of Popular Culture* 6:4 (Spring 1973): 819–35; and Renato Ortiz, *Románticos e Folcloristas: Cultura Popular* (São Paulo: Editora Olho d'Agua, n.d.). On the history of the concept, see Morag Schiach, *Discourse on Popular Culture: Class, Gender, and History in Cultural Analysis, 1730 to the Present* (Stanford, Calif.: Stanford University Press, 1989)

23. George Yúdice has pointed out the need to differentiate further between the "national" and the regional or local dimensions. Speaking of the situation of popular culture in Latin America, Yúdice states: "Historically, national cultures have entailed the priorization of some local cultures above others, and at least since the early 20th century, through mass culture, especially radio. . . . I would argue that those forms of culture identified with the national in Latin America tend to have gotten that valence

through mass culture, since the twenties. And a controlled mass culture has prioritized one local culture as the national culture" (letter to author, March 7, 1999).

24. See García Canclini, *Culturas híbridas.*

25. See García Canclini et al., *Tijuana, la casa de toda la gente* (Iztapalapa [Mexico]: INAH-ENAH, 1989).

26. Hall, "What Is This 'Black . . . ,'" 32.

27. For the following, see Peter Applebome, "The Medici Behind Disney's High Art," *New York Times,* October 4, 1998, sec. 2, pp. 1, 38.

28. Stallybrass and White, *The Politics and Poetics of Transgression,* 5.

29. Hall, "What Is This 'Black' . . . ,'" 24.

2. THE LITE COLONIAL: DIVERSIONS OF PUERTO RICAN DISCOURSE

1. The Madonna incident was discussed in all the Island's newspapers in the days following the event, from late October through early November 1993. See especially Luis R. Dávila Colón, "En-madonnados," *El Nuevo Día* (San Juan), October 29, 1993, 69; and Mateo Mateo, "La caída del ídolo," *El Nuevo Día,* November 12, 1993, 57. For an extended critical discussion, see Carlos Pabón, "De Albizu a Madonna: para armar y desarmar la nacionalidad," *Bordes* 1 (1995): 22–40; and Madeline Román, "El Girlie Show: Madonna, las polémicas nacionales y los pánicos morales," *Bordes* 1 (1995): 41–53.

2. See Dávila Colón, "En-madonnados," 69.

3. These remarks and their implications are discussed in Pabón, "De Albizu a Madonna," 33. It is interesting that though Pabón offers a sharp critical analysis of the whole affair in its ideological context, he cites the usage "cocolo" by Dávila Colón without a mention of its racist overtones. Indeed, Dávila Colón makes it even clearer by referring to his informant in the street as "the cocolo que se coló," roughly "the black dude who sneaked in."

4. See Luis Dávila Colón, "Perspectiva," *El Nuevo Día,* January 18, 1997; Manuel de J. González, "Nacionalismo que paga," *El Nuevo Día,* January 25, 1997, 83; and Luis Dávila Colón, "No disparen, que soy yo . . . ," *El Nuevo Día,* January 31, 1997, 69.

5. See Pabón's explanation of his article and of the provocative graphic in "Albizu y Madonna o la política de la representación," in *Bordes* 2 (1995): 129–30.

6. "La estadidad desde una perspectiva democrática radical," *Diálogo* (February 1997): 30–31. See also Ramón Grosfoguel, "Globalización y status," *El Nuevo Día,* October 35, 1997, 67.

7. See the articles by Juan Duchesne Winter, "Convalecencia del independentismo de izquierda" and "Nación, identidad y levedad," and by Carlos Gil, "Poder y fascinación: Respuesta amistosa al neo-independentismo," in *Postdata.*

8. See Luis Fernando Coss, *La nación en la orilla: respuesta a los posmodernos pesimistas* (San Juan: Punto de Encuentro, 1996). From a similar perspective, see Juan Manuel Carrión, *Voluntad de nación: ensayos sobre el nacionalismo en Puerto Rico* (San Juan: Nueva Aurora, 1996). For a discussion of contemporary thinking on the Puerto

Rican nation, see Jorge Duany, "Para reimaginarse la nación puertorriqueña," *Revista de Ciencias Sociales* 2 (January 1997): 10–24.

9. For a description and sampling of these new positions, see "Dossier Puerto Rico," in *Social Text* 38 (1994): 93–147, a Special Issue ed. Juan Flores and María Milagros López. See also Frances Negrón-Muntaner and Ramón Grosfoguel, eds., *Puerto Rican Jam: Essays on Culture and Politics* (Minneapolis: University of Minnesota Press, 1997); and Jorge Duany, "Después de la modernidad: debates contemporaneos sobre cultura y política en Puerto Rico," *Revista de Ciencias Sociales* 5 (June 1998): 218–41.

10. See Ella Shohat, "Notes on the'Post-Colonial'," *Social Text* 31–32 (1992): 99–113; and Anne McClintock, "The Angel of Progress: Pitfalls in the Term 'Post-Colonialism,'" ibid., 84–98. See also Anne McClintock, Aamir Mufti, and Ella Shohat, eds., *Dangerous Liaisons: Gender, Nation, and Postcolonial Perspectives* (Minneapolis: University of Minnesota Press, 1997).

11. Many of these alternative formulations are suggested in the collection *Puerto Rican Jam*, ed. Negrón-Muntaner and Grosfoguel. The editors' introduction proposes adoption of the term "ethnonation," while the essay by Agustín Laó, and the author and critic Mayra Santos Febres in another context, utilize the concept of the "translocal nation." The idea of "transnation" is explained in Arjun Appadurai, *Modernity at Large: Cultural Dimensions of Globalization* (Minneapolis: University of Minnesota Press, 1996): see especially, "Patriotism and Its Futures," 158–77.

12. Pabón, "De Albizu a Madonna," 32: "El surgimiento de un 'capitalismo lite.' Me refiero a un capitalismo que se ha hecho puertorriqueñista explotando para su beneficio los símbolos nacionales, que como la bandera, representan 'nuestras costumbres, tradiciones y modo de vida.' Es éste un capitalismo posfordista que como producto de los procesos de globalización e internacionalización de la economía y de la cultura busca incorporar al 'otro.' "

13. See Barry Buzan and Gerald Segal, "The Rise of 'Lite' Powers: A Strategy for the Postmodern State," *World Policy Journal* 13.3 (Fall 1996): 1–10. On the use of the concept of "flexibility" in cultural analysis, see Aihwa Ong, *Flexible Citizenship: The Cultural Logics of Transnationality* (Durham, N.C.: Duke University Press, 1998). The term "globaloney" is used by Robert Fitch in *The Assassination of New York* (London: Verso, 1993). See also Janet Abu-Lughod, "Going Beyond Global Babble," in Anthony D. King, ed., *Culture, Globalization, and the World-System: Contemporary Conditions for the Representation of Identity*, 131–38 (Minneapolis: University of Minnesota Press, 1997); Dani Rodrik, *Has Globalization Gone Too Far?* (Washington, D.C.: Institute of International Economics, 1997; and Luis Vidal Rucabado, "Tan lite que ni siquiera es de hoy," *Visión* (Mexico) (October 1–11, 1996): 5.

14. Walter LaFeber, *Michael Jordan and the New Global Capitalism* (New York: Norton, 1999).

15. Stuart Hall, "The Local and the Global," in King, ed., *Culture, Globalization, and the World-System* 30–31.

16. For an extended discussion of the role of commercial interests in the fashioning of contemporary Puerto Rican cultural identity, see Arlene M. Dávila, *Sponsored Identities: Cultural Politics in Puerto Rico* (Philadelphia: Temple University Press, 1997).

17. See Edouard Glissant, *Caribbean Discourse* (Charlottesville: University Press of Virginia, 1989), esp. 14–26. For an excellent discussion of Glissant's work in a Caribbean context and in relation to postcolonial theory, see Román de la Campa, "Mimicry and the Uncanny in Caribbean Discourse," in de la Campa, *Latin Americanism* (Minneapolis: University of Minnesota Press, 1999), 85–120.

18. The concept of the "modern colony" is applied effectively to some countries in the contemporary Caribbean by Gerard Pierre Charles in *El caribe contemporaneo* (Mexico City: Siglo XXI, 1985).

19. Glissant, *Caribbean Discourse*, 18.

20. See Mbmembe, "The Banality of Power and the Aesthetics of Vulgarity in the Postcolony," *Public Culture* 4.2 (Spring 1992): 1–30.

21. Glissant, *Caribbean Discourse*, 19.

22. Ibid., 20.

23. Ibid., 26.

24. See for example Álvaro Fernández Bravo and Florencia Garramuño, "La diseminación de lo nacional: Entrevista a Homi Bhabha," *Bordes* 1 (1995): 87–92.

25. On the omission of the U.S. Puerto Rican experience in Puerto Rican historical and theoretical work, see Arcadio Díaz-Quiñones, *La memoria rota: Ensayos sobre cultura y política* (Río Piedras, P.R.: Ediciones Huracán, 1993); see also "Broken English Memories," ch. 3 (present volume).

26. Glissant, *Caribbean Discourse*, 14.

27. Ibid.

28. Stuart Hall, "Cultural Identity and Diaspora," in Patrick Williams and Laura Chrisman, eds., *Colonial Discourse and Post-Colonial Theory* (New York: Columbia University Press, 1994), 392–403 (quote from 395).

29. Hall, "Cultural Identity and Diaspora," 394.

30. Ibid.

31. Abraham Rodriguez, *The Boy Without a Flag* (Minneapolis: Milkwood, 1992), 20–21. Subsequent page numbers are cited in the text.

32. Interview with Abraham Rodriguez in Carmen Dolores Hernández, ed., *Puerto Rican Voices in English* (Westport, Conn.: Praeger, 1997), 137–56 (quote from 142).

33. Ibid., 146.

34. See, for example, Manuel de J. González, "Aquí seguimos un siglo después," *Claridad* (January 9–15, 1998): 12; and Juan Manuel Carrión, "Sobre la nación sin bordes," *Diálogo* (March 1996): 41.

35. Dávila Colón, "En-madonnados," 69.

36. Ibid.

3. BROKEN ENGLISH MEMORIES: LANGUAGES IN THE TRANS-COLONY

1. Arcadio Díaz-Quiñones, *La memoria rota: Ensayos sobre cultura y política* (Río Piedras, P.R.: Ediciones Huracán, 1993).

2. Arcadio Díaz-Quiñones, "Puerto Rico: Cultura, memoria y diáspora," *Tercer Milenio* 1 (1994): 11–19.

3. The title of Luis Rafael Sánchez's story "La guagua aérea" [The air bus], trans. Diana Vélez, *Village Voice*, January 24, 1984, has become proverbial for the commuter status of Puerto Rican culture.

4. "Los emigrantes fortalecían—de una manera imprevista por el discurso excluyente de algunos sectores de las élites puertorriqueñas—la necesidad de conservar identidades, y, de hecho, la necesidad de fijar nuevas descripciones de la identidad." *And:* "Había en aquellas comunidades puertorriqueñas la posibilidad de un nuevo futuro que exigía conservar ciertos lugares reales y simbólicos, una nueva valoración de la geografía insular, de sus ríos y lomas, de sus barrios." Díaz-Quiñones, "La vida inclemente," in *La memoria rota*, 50–51.

5. "La *pertenencia*, el sentido de 'hogar' y comunidad, se afirma sobre todo en la distancia, con la incertidumbre del lugar. Ello explica, quizás, por qué se puede dar la paradójica situación de que algunos en Guaynabo desprecian su cultura, mientras que otros, en Filadelfia, la defienden con pasión" (ibid.).

6. Tato Laviera, *AmeRícan* (Houston: Arte Público, 1985), 53.

7. Homi Bhabha, "Between Identities: Homi Bhabha Interviewed by Paul Thompson," in Rina Benmayor and Andor Skotnes, eds., *Migration and Identity* (Oxford: Oxford University Press, 1994), 190.

8. Michel Foucault, *Language, Counter-Memory, Practice: Selected Essays and Interviews*, ed. Donald F. Bouchard (Ithaca: Cornell University Press, 1977), 33–34.

9. Sandra María Esteves, *Tropical Rains: A Bilingual Downpour* (New York: African Caribbean Poetry Theater, 1984), 26.

10. Esmeralda Santiago, "The Puerto Rican Stew," *New York Times Magazine*, December 18, 1994, 34, 36.

11. Martorell's performance-installation was first presented at the International Colloquium on the Contemporary Social Imaginary, held at the University of Puerto Rico in February 1991. The text, "Imalabra II," appears in Nydza Correa de Jesús, Heidi Figueroa Sarriera, and María Milagros López, eds., *Coloquio internacional sobre el imaginario social contemporáneo* (Río Piedras, P.R.: University of Puerto Rico Press, n.d.), 161–64. What Martorell means by "la lengua mechada" (as in "carne mechada," meat that has been larded and stuffed) becomes clear in the following sentence: "Like it or not, our tongue [language] has been stuffed and stuffed to the gills with other languages and with images which were dreamed up, remembered, forgotten, combated, surrendered, victorious and subversive, well versed or in verse, prosaic or precocious, silenced or no-lensed, incarnate or inchoate, tame or tempestuous, lending flavor and fullness to our appetite, length to our longing, endearment to our hunger" ["Nuestra lengua, querrámoslo o no, está mechada y requetemechada con

otras lenguas y con imágenes soñadas, recordadas, olvidadas, combatidas, rendidas, victoriosas y subversivas que versadas o en verso, prosáicas o procaces, silentes o sin lentes, encarnadas o bernejas, berrendas o virulentas dan sabor y grosor a nuestro apetito, estensión a nuestras ansias, caricia a nuestra hambre"].

12. "Qué alcance tiene la definición del idioma *único*, ante la hibridez y mezcla del español, del inglés y del spanglish que se oye en Bayamón, Puerto Nuevo o en Union City? Las élites puertorriqueñas defienden, con razón, su bilingüismo, que les permite leer a Toni Morrison o a Faulkner, y acceder a la alta cultura del Metropolitan Museum o el New York City Ballet, y, claro, a Wall Street. La diáspora de emigrantes puertorriqueños ha ido mezclando su lengua, una vez más, en sus continuos viajes de ida y vuelta." Díaz-Quiñones, "La política del olvido" (1991), in *La memoria rota*.

13. "¿Tendremos nosotros la capacidad para descolonizar nuestro imaginario, salir de la niebla colonial de que habló Hostos, sin renunciar a este revolú que nos identifica?" (ibid.).

14. Pedro Pietri, *Puerto Rican Obituary* (New York: Monthly Review Press, 1973), 12–16.

15. Coco Fusco, *English Is Broken Here: Notes on Cultural Fusion in the Americas* (New York: New Press, 1995).

16. "Porque se trata, precisamente, de un modo de concebir la identidad que escabulle las redes topográficas y las categorías duras de la territorialidad y su metaforización telúrica. En Laviera la raiz es si acaso el fundamento citado, reinscrito, por el silbido de una canción. Raices portátiles, dispuestos al uso de una ética corriente, basada en las prácticas de la identidad, en la identidad como práctica del juicio en el viaje." Julio Ramos, "Migratorias," in Josefina Ludmer, ed., *Las culturas de fin de siglo en América Latina* (Buenos Aires: Beatriz Viterbo, 1994), 60.

17. Tato Laviera, *Mainstream Ethics (ética corriente)* (Houston: Arte Público, 1988), 27.

4. "SALVACIÓN CASITA": SPACE, PERFORMANCE, AND COMMUNITY

1. Brochure for exhibit "Las Casitas: An Urban Cultural Alternative," Smithsonian Institution, Washington, D.C., February 2, 1991.

2. For other analyses of the casita phenomenon from various perspectives, see Luis Aponte-Parés, "What's Yellow and White and Has Land All Around It? Appropriating Place in Puerto Rican Barrios," in Antonia Darder and Rodolfo D. Torres, eds., *The Latino Studies Reader: Culture, Economy, and Society* (Malden, Mass.: Blackwell, 1998), 271–80; and Joseph Sciorra, " 'We're not here just to plant. We have culture.': An Ethnography of the South Bronx Casita Rincón Criollo," *New York Folklore* 20.3–4 (1994): 19–41.

3. For an introductory discussion of the history of plena music, see my essay "Bumbún and the Beginnings of *Plena* Music," in *Divided Borders: Essays on Puerto Rican Identity* (Houston: Arte Público, 1993), 85–91. On plena and other Puerto Rican musical forms in New York, see Ruth Glasser, *My Music Is My Flag: Puerto Rican Musicians and Their New York Communities, 1917–1940* (Berkeley: University of California Press, 1995).

4. On Cortijo, see Edgardo Rodríguez Juliá, *El entierro de Cortijo* (Río Piedras, P.R.: Ediciones Huracán, 1983). See also my essay "Cortijo's Revenge: New Mappings of Puerto Rican Culture," in *Divided Borders*, 92–107.

5. This point and other useful information about the early plena may be found in Félix Echevarría Alvarado, *La plena: Origen, sentido y desarrollo en el folklore puertorriqueño* (Santurce: Express, 1984).

6. For informative reports on recent developments at Rincón Criollo, see David González, "Atop a Mule to Serenade Woes Away," *New York Times*, January 1, 1996, 33, and "The Serpent in the Garden of Renewal," *New York Times*, August 29, 1998, B1. See also R.K., "Puerto Rican Institution Moving; Some Say Its Flavor May Not," *New York Times*, February 20, 1994, C11.

5. "CHA-CHA WITH A BACKBEAT": SONGS AND STORIES OF LATIN BOOGALOO

1. Unless referenced in the endnotes, all citations are from personal interviews and conversations conducted in June and July 1998 with the following musicians: Joe Bataan, Benny Bonilla, Johnny Colón, Joe Cuba, Andy González, Pucho Brown, Bobby Marín, Richard Marín, Eddie Palmieri, Tito Ramos, Richie Ray, Fernando Rivera (King Nando), Hector Rivera, Tony Rojas, Jimmy Sabater, Pete Terrace, and Willie Torres. I thank all of them for their time and generosity.

I also thank the following music historians and others knowledgeable about aspects of the boogaloo experience: David Carp, René López, Bob Moll, John Storm Roberts, Max Salazar, Harry Sepúlveda, Henry Medina, Richie Bonilla, Sonia Marín, Miriam Jiménez Román, John Sánchez, and David Maysonet.

Max Salazar in particular provided many key insights and opened many doors for me as I got started on the project, and his richly informative article, "Latinized Afro-American Rhythms," served as the basis of the present essay. That article appears in Vernon W. Boggs, ed., *Salsiology: Afro-Cuban Music and the Evolution of Salsa in New York City* (New York: Excelsior, 1992), 237–48.

Finally, I wish to thank my friend and colleague, the late Vernon W. Boggs, who first got me into the Latin R&B groove ten years ago, before his tragic and untimely death in 1994.

2. See especially the work of Vernon Boggs, "Rhythm 'n' Blues, American Pop, and Salsa: Musical Transculturation," *Latin Beat* 2.1 (February 1992): 16–19, and "Behind the Harptones and Mambo Boogie" (1954), *Latin Beat* 2.10 (December–January 1993): 32–35. See also the 1995 LP release disk *Vaya!!! R&B Groups Go Latin* on Verve, especially the liner notes by Donn Fileti.

3. King Nando, quoted in Salazar, "Latinized Afro-American Rhythms," 244.

4. Sanabria, quoted in Vernon W. Boggs, "Visions and Views of a Salsa Promoter—Izzy 'Mr. Salsa' Sanabria: Popularizing Music," in Boggs, ed., *Salsiology*, 187–93 (quote from 191).

5. The quote is from Salazar, "Latinized Afro-American Rhythms," 241.

6. Ibid., 240.

7. See Robert Pruter, *Chicago Soul* (Urbana: University of Illinois Press, 1991), 204.

8. Ibid.

9. Bobo, quoted in Salazar, "Latinized Afro-American Rhythms," 241.

10. Ibid., 242.

11. See David Carp, "Pucho and His Latin Soul Brothers," *Descarga Newsletter* 27 (1996): 14–15.

12. Pabón, quoted in Salazar, "Latinized Afro-American Rhythms," 243.

13. Ibid., 243.

14. See Langdon Winner, "The Sound of New Orleans," in Jim Miller, ed., *The Rolling Stone Illustrated History of Rock and Roll* (New York: Random House, 1980), 43. See also Jason Berry, Jonathan Foose, and Tad Jones, *Up from the Cradle of Jazz: New Orleans Music Since World War II* (Athens: University of Georgia Press, 1986), 126–28; and Grace Lichtenstein and Laura Dankner, *Musical Gumbo: The Music of New Orleans* (New York: Norton, 1993), 117 passim.

15. Salazar, "Latinized Afro-American Rhythms," 244.

16. Ibid., 245–46.

17. See Felipe Luciano, "The Song of Joe Bataan," *New York*, October 25, 1971, 50–53 (quote on 53).

18. Salazar, "Latinized Afro-American Rhythms," 244.

19. Ibid.

20. Ibid.

21. Ibid., 245.

22. Sanabria, quoted in Boggs, "Visions and Views of a Salsa Promoter," 191.

23. On the stereotyping in "Che Che Colé," see Juan Otero Garabis, "Naciones rítmicas: La construcción nacionales en la música popular y la literatura del Caribe hispano" (Ph.D. diss., Department of Romance Languages, Harvard University, 1998), 111–14.

24. See Vernon W. Boggs, "Willie 'El Trombonista' Colón" (interview), *Latin Beat* 2.10 (December–January 1993): 11. ("I feel that until things really change for Latinos in this country, they should really hold on to Spanish and not assimilate. . . . This is the only thing that they've got left. They don't have much, so I think they should hold on to the language rather than always use English lyrics.")

25. Salazar, "Latinized Afro-American Rhythms," 247

26. John Storm Roberts, *The Latin Tinge* (London: Oxford University Press, 1979; rev. ed., 1998), 169.

27. George Lipsitz, *Dangerous Crossroads: Popular Music, Postmodernism, and the Poetics of Place* (London: Verso, 1994), 80.

28. On the Puerto Rican role in early hip-hop, see "Puerto Rocks: Rap, Roots, and Amnesia," chapter 6 in the present volume.

6. PUERTO ROCKS: RAP, ROOTS, AND AMNESIA

1. Quotes of Charlie Chase are from my interview with him, "It's a Street Thing!" published in *Calalloo* 15.4 (Fall 1992): 999–1021.

2. See my article, written in 1984, "Rappin', Writin' and Breakin': Black and Puerto Rican Street Culture in New York City," *Dissent* (Fall 1987): 580–84 (also published in *Centro Journal* 2.3 [Spring 1988]: 34–41). A shortened version of the present chapter appeared as " 'Puerto Rican and Proud, Boy-ee!': Rap, Roots, and Amnesia," in Tricia Rose and Andrew Ross, eds., *Microphone Fiends: Youth Music and Youth Culture*, 89–98 (New York: Routledge, 1994). Other references are Craig Castleman, *Getting Up: Subway Graffiti in New York* (Cambridge: MIT Press, 1982); Herbert Kohl, *Golden Boy as Anthony Cool: A Photo Essay on Naming and Graffiti* (New York: Dial, 1972); Steven Hager, *Hip-Hop: The Illustrated History of Break Dancing, Tap Music, and Graffiti* (New York: St. Martin's, 1984). See also David Toop, *The Rap Attack: African Jive to New York Hip-Hop* (Boston: South End, 1984).

3. Quotes from Latin Empire are from my interview with them, "Puerto Raps," published in *Centro Journal* 3.2 (Spring 1991): 77–85.

4. Ed Morales, "How Ya Like Nosotros Now?" *Village Voice*, November 26, 1991, 91.

5. For an overview of Latino rap, see Mandolit del Barco, "Rap's Latino Sabor," in William Eric Perkins, ed., *Droppin' Science: Critical Essays on Rap Music and Hip-Hop Culture* (Philadelphia: Temple University Press, 1996), 63–84.

6. Elizabeth Hanley, "Latin Raps: Nuevo ritmo, A New Nation of Rap Emerges," *Elle*, March 1991, 196–98; C.A., "El rap latino tiene tumbao," *Más* 2.2 (Winter 1990): 81.

7. Joseph Roland Reynolds, "The Packaging of a Recording Artist," *Hispanic Business* 14.7 (July 1992): 28–30.

8. Ibid.

9. Cited in Flores, "Rappin', Writin', and Breakin.'"

7. PAN-LATINO/TRANS-LATINO: PUERTO RICANS IN THE "NEW NUEVA YORK"

1. Nancy Foner, ed. *New Immigrants in New York* (New York: Columbia University Press, 1987), 1, 3. See also *The Newest New Yorkers: An Analysis of Immigration into New York City During the 1980s* (New York: Department of City Planning, 1992).

2. As cited by Gabriel Haslip-Viera, "The Evolution of the Latino Community in the New York Metropolitan Area, 1810 to the Present," in Haslip-Viera and Sherrie Baver, eds. *Latinos in New York: Communities in Transition* (Notre Dame: Notre Dame University Press, 1996), 3–29.

3. See, for example, Saskia Sassen, *The Global City: New York, London, Tokyo* (Princeton: Princeton University Press, 1991). The idea of New York as "global city" was also an integral part of the mayoral campaign and administration of Ed Koch; see also Robert Fitch, *The Assassination of New York* (London: Verso, 1993).

4. Andrés Torres and Frank Bonilla, "Decline Within Decline: The New York Perspective," in Rebecca Morales and Frank Bonilla, eds., *Latinos in a Changing U.S. Economy* (Newbury Park, Calif.: Sage, 1993), 98–99.

5. Oscar Handlin, *The Newcomers: Negroes and Puerto Ricans in a Changing Metropolis* (Cambridge: Harvard University Press, 1959).

6. Torres and Bonilla, "Decline Within Decline," 99.

7. *Puerto Ricans in the Continental United States: An Uncertain Future* (Washington, D.C.: U.S. Commission on Civil Rights, 1976). That report states: "The Commission's overall conclusion is that mainland Puerto Ricans generally continue mired in the poverty facing first generations of all immigrant or migrant groups. Expectations were that succeeding generations of mainland Puerto Ricans would have achieved upward mobility. One generation later, the essential fact of poverty remains little changed. Indeed, the economic situation of the mainland Puerto Ricans has worsened over the last decade.

   "The United States has never before had a large migration of citizens from offshore, distinct in culture and language and also facing the problem of color prejudice. After 30 years of significant migration, contrary to conventional wisdom that once Puerto Ricans learned the language the second generation would move into the mainstream of American society, the future of this distinct community in the United States is still to be determined (145)."

8. Torres and Bonilla, "Decline Within Decline," 102–103.

9. For a discussion of pan-ethnic Latino organizations and activities in New York during the early decades, see Ruth Glasser, *My Music Is My Flag: Puerto Rican Musicians and Their New York Communities, 1917–1940* (Berkeley: University of California Press, 1995), esp. 94–97. See also Bernardo Vega, *Memoirs of Bernardo Vega: A Contribution to the History of the Puerto Rican Community in New York* (New York: Monthly Review, 1984).

10. See Jack D. Forbes, "The Hispanic Spin: Party Politics and Governmental Manipulation of Ethnic Identity," *Latin American Perspectives* 19.4 (1992): 59–78.

11. For this wider historical perspective, see Forbes, ibid.; Martha Giménez, "U.S. Ethnic Politics: Implications for Latin Americans," *Latin American Perspectives* 19.4 (1992): 7–17; William I. Robinson, "The Global Economy and the Latino Populations in the United States: A World Systems Approach," *Critical Sociology* 19.2 (1992): 29–59; Félix Padilla, "Latin America: The Historical Base of Latino Unity," *Latino Studies Journal* 1.1 (1990): 7–27.

12. On the question of terminology ("Hispanic" vs. "Latino"), see David E. Hayes-Bautista and Jorge Chapa, "Latino Terminology: Conceptual Basis for Standardized Terminology," *American Journal of Public Health* 77.1 (January 1987): 61–68; Fernando M. Treviño, "Standardized Terminology for Standardized Populations," *American Journal of Public Health* 77 (1987), 69–72; Earl Shorris, *Latinos: A Biography of the People* (New York: Norton, 1992), xv–xvii; Ilan Stavans, *The Hispanic Condition: Reflections on Culture and Identity in America* (New York: HarperCollins, 1995), esp. 24–27.

13. See David López and Yen Espiritu, "Panethnicity in the United States: A Theoretical Framework," *Ethnic and Racial Studies* 13 (1990): 198–224: Yen Le Espiritu, *Asian American Panethnicity: Building Institutions and Identities* (Philadelphia: Temple University Press, 1992); Howard Winant, *Racial Conditions: Politics, Theory, Comparisons* (Minneapolis: University of Minnesota, 1994), 60–62.

14. Félix Padilla, *Latino Ethnic Consciousness: The Case of Mexican Americans and Puerto Ricans in Chicago* (Notre Dame: Notre Dame University Press, 1985), vii.

15. See, for example, Félix Padilla, "Latin America: The Historical Base of Latino Unity," *Latino Studies Journal* 1.1 (1990): 7–27; and Padilla, "On the Nature of Latino Ethnicity," in Rodolfo de la Garza, ed., *The Mexican American Experience* (Austin: University of Texas Press, 1985), 332–45.

16. Misguided pomposity and downright errors abound in Stavans's book (*The Hispanic Condition*), as in his unreflected use of terms and phrases like "Latino metabolism" (14), "a five-hundred-year-old fiesta of miscegenation" (13), "our aim is to assimilate Anglos slowly to ourselves" (9), "society is beginning to embrace Latinos, from rejects to fashion setters, from outcasts to insider traders" (8), "yesterday's victim and tomorrow's conquistadors, we Hispanics" (10), etc.

17. See especially José Calderón, " 'Hispanic' or 'Latino': The Viability of Categories for Panethnic Unity," 37–44, and Forbes, "The Hispanic Spin," 59–78, in *Latin American Perspectives* 19.4 (1992).

18. See Suzanne Oboler, *Ethnic Labels, Latino Lives: Identity and the Politics of (Re)Presentation in the United States* (Minneapolis: University of Minnesota, 1995), 3–6. Subsequent page numbers are cited in the text.

19. Giménez, "U.S. Ethnic Politics," 8.

20. Linda Chavez, *Out of the Barrio: Toward a New Politics of Hispanic Assimilation* (New York: Basic Books, 1992), 156. See also the interview with Chavez, "How Welfare Has Hurt Puerto Ricans," *New York Newsday*, October 22, 1991, 97, 100.

21. Chavez, *Out of the Barrio*, 156.

22. Ibid., 158.

23. Colón, quoted in "Taking Exception with Chavez," *New York Newsday*, October 23, 1991, 86.

24. Serrano, quoted in ibid., 83.

25. Enrique Fernández, "Estilo Latino: Buscando Nueva York [*sic*]," *Village Voice*, August 9, 1988, 19.

26. Stavans, *The Hispanic Condition*, 42 passim.

27. Orlando Rodriguez et al., *Nuestra America en Nueva York: The New Immigrant Hispanic Populations in New York City, 1980–1990* (New York: Hispanic Research Center, Fordham University, 1995).

28. Evelyn S. Mann and Joseph J. Salvo, "Characteristics of New Hispanic Immigrants to New York City: A Comparison of Puerto Rican and Non-Puerto Rican Hispanics," Paper presented at the Annual Meeting of the the Population Association of America, Minneapolis, Minn., May 3, 1984.

29. "Understanding Socioeconomic Differences: A Comparative Analysis of Puerto Ricans and Recent Latino Immigrants in New York City," unpublished manuscript, dated June 1995 (in author's possession).

30. Ibid., MS pages 35–36.

31. Ramona Hernández, Francisco Rivera-Batiz, and Roberto Agodini, *Dominican*

New Yorkers: A Socioeconomic Profile (New York: CUNY Dominican Studies Institute, 1995), 5.

32. See Ramona Hernández and Silvio Torres-Saillant, "Dominicans in New York: Men, Women, and Prospects," in Haslip-Viera and Baver, eds., *Latinos in New York*, 30–56.

33. Jorge Duany, *Quisqueya on the Hudson: The Transnational Identity of Dominicans in Washington Heights* (New York: CUNY Dominican Studies Institute, 1994), 2.

34. See for example Torres and Bonilla, "Decline Within Decline," 102.

35. See Robert Smith, "Mexicans in New York: Memberships and Incorporation in a New Immigrant Community" in Haslip-Viera and Baver, eds., *Latinos in New York*, 57–103. See also Joel Millman, "New Mex City," *New York*, September 7, 1992, 37–43.

36. The phrase "transnational sociocultural system" was used in a study of Caribbeans in New York; see Constance R. Sutton, "The Caribbeanization of New York and the Emergence of a Transnational Sociocultural System," in Sutton and Elsa M. Chaney, eds., *Caribbean Life in New York City: Sociocultural Dimensions* (New York: Center for Migration Studies, 1987), 15–30.

37. Geoffrey Godsell, "The Puerto Ricans," *Christian Science Monitor*, May 1, 1980, 13.

38. The specification of Puerto Ricans as "colonial (im)migrants" and their parallel position to colonial or postcolonial immigrants in metropolitan contexts is noted but scarcely elaborated by Clara Rodríguez, *Puerto Ricans: Born in the U.S.A.* (Boston: Unwin Hyman, 1989), 18–19. For a fuller discussion see Ramón Grosfoguel, "Caribbean Colonial Immigrants in the Metropoles: A Research Agenda," in Antonia Darder and Rodolfo D. Torres, eds., *The Latino Studies Reader: Culture, Economy, and Society* (Malden, Mass.: Blackwell, 1998), 281–93.

39. See, for example, Andrés Torres, *Between Melting Pot and Mosaic: African Americans and Puerto Ricans in the New York Political Economy* (Philadelphia: Temple University Press, 1995).

40. Elena Padilla, *Up from Puerto Rico* (New York: Columbia University Press, 1958), 32.

41. See Jorge Oclander, "Latinos Split Over Keeping Their House District," *Chicago Sun Times*, December 13, 1995, 22–23.

42. "Hispanics Must Forget Politics, Focus on Unity," *Chicago Sun Times*, December 27, 1995, 30.

43. For a discussion of the relation of Puerto Ricans to the issue of immigration, see Franklin Velázquez, "Puerto Ricans and Immigrants: La Misma Lucha," *Crítica* 9 (February 1995): 1, 5–6. A valuable assessment of Latino politics in New York City may be found in Annette Fuentes, "New York: Elusive Unity in La Gran Manzana," *NACLA Report on the Americas* 26.2 (September 1992): 27–33.

8. LIFE OFF THE HYPHEN: LATINO LITERATURE AND NUYORICAN TRADITIONS

1. Nicolás Kanellos, "*The Mambo Kings Play Songs of Love*" (review), *Americas Review* 18.1 (1990): 113.

2. Cited in W. J. Stuckey, *The Pulitzer Prize Novels: A Critical Backward Look* (Norman: University of Oklahoma Press, 1966), 7. See also John Hohenberg, *The Pulitzer*

Prizes: A History of Awards in Books . . . (New York: Columbia University Press, 1974), and J. Douglas Bates, *The Pulitzer Prize: The Inside Story of America's Most Prestigious Award* (Secaucus, N.J.: Carol, 1991).

3. Stuckey, *The Pulitzer Prize Novels*, 262.

4. Cited in ibid., 250.

5. Kanellos, "*The Mambo Kings*" (review), 113.

6. Enrique Fernández, "Exilados on Main Street," *Village Voice*, May 1, 1990, 85.

7. Quoted in Alexandra Kuczynski, "Spider Man: Novelist Abraham Rodriguez Clocks the Bronx," *Paper* (May 1993): 20.1

8. Examples of this assertion as to the historical importance of *The Mambo Kings* and its Pulitzer may be found in Harold Augenbraum, ed., *Latinos in English: A Selected Bibliography of Latino Fiction Writers of the United States* (New York: Mercantile Library, 1992), 12, and from a very different perspective, Marc Zimmerman, *U.S. Latino Literature: An Essay and Annotated Bibliography* (Chicago: March/Abrazo Press, 1992), 38.

9. See, for example, Lori M. Carlson, ed., *Cool Salsa: Bilingual Poems on Growing Up Latino in the United States* (New York: Fawcett Juniper, 1994), and Delia Poey and Virgil Suarez, eds., *Iguana Dreams: New Latino Fiction* (New York: HarperCollins, 1992).

10. Historical overviews of the "Hispanic literary heritage" may be found in Ramón Gutiérrez and Genaro Padilla, eds., *Recovering the U.S. Hispanic Literary Heritage* (Houston: Arte Público, 19930, as well as in Harold Augenbraum and Ilan Stavans, eds., *Growing Up Latino: Memoirs and Stories—Reflections on Life in the United States* (Boston: Houghton-Mifflin, 1993), and Zimmerman, *U.S. Latino Literature*. See also William Luis, *Dance Between Two Cultures: Latino Caribbean Literature Written in the United States* (Nashville: Vanderbilt University Press, 1997).

11. See Gustavo Pérez Firmat, *Life on the Hyphen: The Cuban-American Way* (Austin: University of Texas Press, 1994), and Ilan Stavans, *The Hispanic Condition: Reflections on Culture and Identity in America* (New York: HarperCollins, 1995), whose first chapter is entitled "Life in the Hyphen," 7–30.

12. Pérez Firmat, *Life on the Hyphen*, 1.

13. Ibid., 136–53. Another lengthy discussion of *The Mambo Kings* may be found in Luis, *Dance Between Two Cultures*, 188–214.

14. Pérez Firmat, *Life on the Hyphen*, 1. Subsequent page numbers are cited in the text.

15. Stavans, *The Hispanic Condition*, 19. Subsequent page numbers are cited in the text.

16. See, for example, Augenbraum and Stavans, eds., *Growing Up Latino*, xi–xxix.

17. Stavans, *The Hispanic Condition*, 19. Subsequent page numbers are cited in the text.

18. For a discussion of the mambo-bolero contrast in *The Mambo Kings*, see Pérez Firmat, *Life on the Hyphen*, 149–53.

19. See Oscar Hijuelos, *The Mambo Kings Play Songs of Love* (New York: Farrar, Straus, Giroux, 1989), 165–66.

20. *Gráfico*, March 27, 1928, 2; as quoted (in part) in Virginia E. Sánchez Korrol, *From*

Colonia to Community: The History of Puerto Ricans in New York City (Berkeley: University of California Press, 1994), 73.

21. For an extended discussion of the concept of "cultural capital" and its bearing on literary canon-formation, see John Guillory, *Cultural Capital: The Problem of Literary Canon Formation* (Chicago: University of Chicago Press, 1993). See also, for the theoretical foundations of this analysis, Pierre Bourdieu, *The Field of Cultural Production* (New York: Columbia University Press, 1993), especially the essay "The Market of Symbolic Goods," 112–41.

22. See, for example, Eduardo Márceles Daconte, ed., *Narradores Colombianos en U.S.A.* (Bogotá: Instituto Colombiano de Cultura, 1993), and Daisy Cocco de Filippis and Franklin Gutiérrez, eds., *Stories from Washington Heights and Other Corners of the World: Short Stories Written by Dominicans in the United States* (New York: Latino Press, 1994).

23. On this point I am grateful for insights from Daisy Cocco de Filippis, Pedro López Adorno, and David Unger among others involved in the current "Latino literature" scene in New York. For a related discussion, see Arlene Dávila, "Art and the Politics of Multicultural Encompassment: 'Latinizing' Culture in El Barrio," *Cultural Anthropology* 14.2 (1999): 180–202.

24. For a more critical approach to Cuban American cultural experience and differentiation from that of resident Latino minorities, see the essays by Cuban American critic Román de la Campa, "The Latino Diaspora in the United States: Sojourns from a Cuban Past," *Public Culture* 6.2 (Winter 1994): 294–317, and "Miami, Los Angeles, and Other Latino Capitals," *Postdata* (Puerto Rico) 9 (1994): 65–74.

25. See Nicholasa Mohr, "Puerto Rican Writers in the United States, Puerto Rican Writers in Puerto Rico: A Separation Beyond Language," in Denis Lynn Daly Heyck, ed., *Barrios and Borderlands* (New York: Routledge, 1994), 264–69.

26. See Michael Lapp, "Managing Migration: The Migration Division of Puerto Rico and Puerto Ricans in New York City, 1948–68" (Ph.D. diss., Johns Hopkins University, 1990), 303ff.

27. See Lourdes Vázquez, "Nuestra identidad y sus espejos," *El Nuevo Día* (San Juan), February 9, 1997, 8.

28. Ibid., 9.

29. See Poey and Suarez, eds., *Iguana Dreams*, xviii.

30. Abraham Rodriguez, *Spidertown* (New York: Penguin, 1993), 267. Subsequent page numbers are cited in the text.

31. See Rodriguez interview in Carmen Dolores Hernández, ed., *Puerto Rican Voices in English* (Westport, Conn.: Praeger, 1997), 137–55 (quote from 152).

32. See Jonathan Mandell, "A Posse of One: The Balzac of the Bronx," *New York Newsday*, July 19, 1993, 39, 42–43.

33. See Steve Garbarino, "Urgent Fury: Abraham Rodriguez Jr.," *New York Newsday*, August 9, 1992.

34. Rodriguez, in Hernández, ed., *Puerto Rican Voices in English*, 140. Subsequent page numbers are cited in the text.

35. For further details and analysis, see "Pan-Latino/Trans-Latino: Puerto Ricans in the 'New Nueva York,' " ch. 7 of the present volume.

36. See Tato Laviera, *AmeRícan* (Houston: Arte Público, 1985).

37. María Fernández, "Ode to the DiaspoRican," in *AHA! Hispanic Arts News* (February–March 1998): 14.

38. Rodriguez, in Hernández, ed., *Puerto Rican Voices in English*, 140.

9. THE LATINO IMAGINARY: MEANINGS OF COMMUNITY AND IDENTITY

1. David González, "What's the Problem with 'Hispanic'? Just Ask a 'Latino,' " *New York Times*, November 15, 1992, sec. 4, p. 6.

2. Ilan Stavans, *The Hispanic Condition: Reflections on Culture and Identity in America* (New York: HarperCollins, 1995), 27. Another such unusual, and in my view confusing, usage of the terms may be found in William Luis, *Dance Between Two Cultures: Latino Caribbean Literature Written in the United States* (Nashville: Vanderbilt University Press, 1997), x–xi; here "Latino" refers to those of Latin American background born and raised in the United States, while "Hispanic" is taken to refer to those "born and raised in their parents' home country." Though the terminological distinction is questionable and remote from common parlance, Luis is accurate in calling for distinctions in group denomination when he states that "it would be incongruous to group Hispanics from privileged families who have superior educational backgrounds, traveling to the United States to pursue a post-secondary education, with Latinos living in the ghettos of East Harlem or East Los Angeles, attending inferior schools and lacking the economic support necessary to overcome the limitations of their existence" (xi). For an example of the overemphasis on language and an excessively expansive sense of "Latino" and "Hispanic," see Geoffrey Fox, *Hispanic Nation: Culture, Politics, and the Constructing of Identity* (Secaucus, N.J.: Carol, 1996).

3. The opening citations are renderings of statements I have encountered during the course of conversations and interviews, or in newspaper accounts. Examples of the abundant published discussion of the terms *Hispanic* and *Latino* may be found in Suzanne Oboler, *Ethnic Labels, Latino Lives: Identity and the Politics of (Re)Presentation in the United States* (Minneapolis: University of Minnesota, 1995); Earl Shorris, *Latinos: A Biography of the People* (New York: Norton, 1992); and *Latin American Perspectives* 19.4 (Fall 1992). See also my essay, "Pan-Latino/Trans-Latino: Puerto Ricans in the 'New Nueva York'," ch. 7 of the present volume.

4. Documentation of this widespread preference for national designations may be found in Rodolfo O. de la Garza et al., "Latino National Political Survey," as published in de la Garza, ed., *Latino Voices: Mexican, Puerto Rican, and Cuban Perspectives on American Politics* (Boulder, Colo.: Westview, 1992). For a response, see Luis Fraga et al., *Still Looking for America: Beyond the Latino National Political Survey* (Stanford, Calif.: Stanford Center for Chicano Research, 1994).

5. Benedict Anderson, *Imagined Communities: Reflections on the Origin and Spread of Nationalism* (London: Verso, 1983). As useful as Anderson's coinage may be for characterizing the cultural convergences among Latinos, to posit the idea of a "Hispanic nation," as in Geoffrey Fox's book of that title, would seem premature at best, and misleading in taking Anderson's analysis too literally (see Fox, *Hispanic Nation*, esp. 1–18).

6. The range of theoretical approaches from strictly quantitative to comparative to ideological is evident in the growing published literature on "Hispanics" or "Latinos," as cited in note 2 above (this chapter). See in addition, for example, Marta Tienda and Vilma Ortíz, " 'Hispanicity' and the 1980 Census," *Social Science Quarterly* 67 (1986): 3–20; Félix Padilla, *Latino Ethnic Consciousness: The Case of Mexican Americans and Puerto Ricans in Chicago* (Notre Dame: Notre Dame University Press, 1985); Rebecca Morales and Frank Bonilla, eds., *Latinos in a Changing U.S. Economy* (Newbury Park, Calif.: Sage, 1993). The concept of "ethnoscape" is set forth by Arjun Appadurai, *Modernity at Large: Cultural Dimensions of Globalization* (Minneapolis: University of Minnesota Press, 1996), esp. 27–65.

7. The present essay was originally intended as a general theoretical introduction to the projected catalogue of "Latino Voices," the first international festival of Latino photography, which opened in Houston in November 1994. The idea of conceptualizing and circumscribing a "Latino imaginary" arose while pre-viewing slides of images by Chicano, Puerto Rican, and Cuban photographers included in that historic exhibition, and deciding how best to present their theoretical and cultural significance to a broad United States audience of the 1990s. Although the catalogue did not materialize, I have presented the paper in a variety of settings across the country, incorporating insights as I went along. I especially thank Wendy Watriss, Frances Aparicio, and Marvette Pérez for their critical responses, though they are in no way to be held responsible for the arguments of the essay as it stands.

8. The most extended discussion of these instrumental uses of the "Hispanic" label may be found in Oboler's *Ethnic Labels, Latino Lives*, though I also find of some interest the exchange between Fernando Treviño and David Hayes-Bautista in the *American Journal of Public Health* 77.1 (January 1987): 61–71.

9. For examples of "Hispanics" in advertisements and other commercial uses, see Flores and George Yúdice, "Living Borders/Buscando América: Languages of Latino Self-Formation," *Social Text* 24 (1990): 57–84. That essay also appeared in my book *Divided Borders: Essays on Puerto Rican Identity* (Houston: Arte Público, 1993), 199–224. See also Arlene Dávila, "The *Othered* Nation: The Marketing and Making of U.S. Latinidad" (unpublished manuscript, 1999).

10. On the vast research on "modes of incorporation," see especially Alejandro Portes and Robert L. Bach, *Latin Journey: Cuban and Mexican Immigrants in the United States* (Berkeley: University of California Press, 1985), and Alejandro Portes and Rubén G. Rumbaut, *Immigrant America: A Portrait* (Berkeley: University of California Press, 2d ed., 1996).

11. See Candace Nelson and Marta Tienda, "The Structuring of Hispanic Ethnicity: Historical and Contemporary Perspectives," in Mary Romero, Pierrette Hondagneu-Sotelo, and Vilma Ortiz, eds., *Challenging Fronteras* (New York: Routledge, 1997), 7–29 (quotations from 26).

12. Roberto Suro, *Strangers Among Us: How Latino Immigration Is Transforming America* (New York: Knopf, 1998), 146–47. For Rumbaut, see the valuable essay, "The Americans: Latin American and Caribbean Peoples in the United States," in Alfred Stepan, ed., *Americas: New Interpretive Essays* (New York: Oxford University Press, 1992), 275–307; it is worth noting that while the author seems to have little difficulty speaking of "Latinos" as a group when contrasting them with African Americans, he otherwise voices skepticism as to the value of pan-ethnic, or what he terms "supranational," identities.

13. See, for example, Silvia Pedraza, "The Contribution of Latino Studies to Social Science Research on Immigration," JSRI Occasional Paper no. 36 (East Lansing: Julian Samora Research Institute, Michigan State University, 1998). Even broad historical overviews of Latino immigration may tend to abbreviate the duration of Latino presence in the United States; see, for example, Rubén G. Rumbaut, "The Americans," where preponderant attention goes to the post-1960s period.

14. See Arjun Appardurai,"Patriotism and Its Futures," *Modernity at Large*, 158–77.

15. See Fox, *Hispanic Nation*, esp. 237ff.

16. On Latino rap, see "Puerto Rocks: Rap, Roots, and Amnesia," ch. 6 of the present volume. For an interpretation of the casita phenomenon, see "Salvación Casita: Space, Performance, and Community," ch. 4 of the present volume.

17. See, for example, Peter Winn, "North of the Border," in *Americas: The Changing Face of Latin America and the Caribbean* (New York: Pantheon, 1992), 550–600. This chapter, like the book as a whole, is intended as the accompaniment to the ten-part public television series on contemporary Latin America. "North of the Border," the final chapter and segment, is about U.S. Latinos and is based on the research of Alejandro Portes and Rubén G. Rumbaut; their social science findings are significantly amplified by extensive references to rap music, casitas, and other cultural phenomena. See also Fox, *Hispanic Nation*, esp. 223ff.

10. LATINO STUDIES: NEW CONTEXTS, NEW CONCEPTS

1. The events at City College are reported in the *New York Times*, March 19, 1996, B4, and in the *Chronicle of Higher Education*, March 29, 1996, 18. Reporting on the strike at Columbia University appears in the *New York Times*, April 15, 1996, B1, B3.

2. The use of the term "globaloney" to refer to obfuscation of local, national, and regional realities and contradictions by imposing a "global" or "transnational" framework occurs in Robert Fitch, *The Assassination of New York* (London: Verso, 1993). See also "The Lite Colonial," ch. 2 of the present volume.

3. See Antonia Darder and Rodolfo D. Torres, eds., *The Latino Studies Reader: Culture, Economy, and Society* (Malden, Mass.: Blackwell, 1998).

4. Oscar Montero, "Coalitions/Collisions: Notes from a Latino Queer," in Robert Ji-Song Ku, ed., *Common Grounds: Charting Asian American Studies East of California,* East of California Network of the Association for Asian American Studies, Proceedings of the Fourth Annual Conference (New York: Hunter College/Columbia University, 1996), 45.

5. Angie Chabram, " 'Chicana! Rican? No, Chicana-Riqueña!' Refashioning the Transnational Connection," in David Theo Goldberg, ed., *Multiculturalism: A Critical Reader* (Oxford: Blackwell, 1994), 284.

6. Ibid., 290, 292.

7. It is interesting that Darder and Torres, the editors of *The Latino Studies Reader,* assume a strong stand against postmodernist orientations, while at the same time adopting much of the vocabulary and many of the theoretical concerns of postmodernist discourse (see esp. 5ff).

8. See, for example, Kelvin Santiago, *"Subject People" and Colonial Discourses: Economic Transformation and Social Disorder in Puerto Rico, 1898–1947* (Albany: SUNY Press, 1994).

9. See, for example, Partha Chatterjee, *The Nation and Its Fragments: Colonial and Postcolonial Histories* (Princeton: Princeton University Press, 1993), esp. 1–13. See also Patrick Williams and Laura Chrisman, eds., *Colonial and Post-Colonial Theory* (New York: Columbia University Press, 1994).

10. See Bertell Ollman and Edward Vernoff, eds., *The Left Academy: Marxist Scholarship on American Campuses,* 3 vols. (New York: Praeger, 1986); Noam Chomsky, ed. *The Cold War and the University: Toward an Intellectual History of the Cold War* (New York: New Press, 1997); and Mark T. Berger, *Under Northern Eyes: Latin American Studies and U.S. Hegemony in the Americas, 1898–1990* (Bloomington: Indiana University Press, 1995).

11. An account of the struggle for Chicano Studies, including the original "Plan de Santa Barbara," may be found in Carlos Muñoz, *Youth, Identity, Power: The Chicano Movement* (London: Verso, 1989). On Puerto Rican Studies, see María Sánchez and Antonio Stevens-Arroyo, eds., *Towards a Renascence of Puerto Rican Studies: Ethnic and Area Studies in the University* (Highlands Lakes, N.J.: Social Science Monographs, 1987). See also Frank Bonilla, Ricardo Campos, and Juan Flores, "Puerto Rican Studies: Promptings for the Academy and the Left," in Ollman and Vernoff, eds., *The Left Academy* 3:67–102; and Pedro Cabán, "The New Synthesis of Latin American and Latin Studies," in Frank Bonilla, Edwin Meléndez, Rebecca Morales, and María de los Angeles Torres, eds., *Borderless Borders: U.S. Latinos, Latin Americans, and the Paradox of Independence* (Philadelphia: Temple University Press, 1998), 195–215.

12. Geoffrey Fox, *Hispanic Nation: Culture, Politics, and the Construction of Identity* (Secaucus, N.J.: Carol, 1996).

13. On the term "ethnoscape" and other pertinent concepts of transnational cultural studies, see Arjun Appadurai, *Modernity at Large: Cultural Dimensions of Globalization* (Minneapolis: University of Minnesota Press, 1996).

14. Montero, "Coalitions/Collisions," 46.

POSTSCRIPT: "NONE OF THE ABOVE"

1. On the events and political situation in Puerto Rico in 1998, see Andrés Torres, "Cien Anos de Lucha: The Fight Over the Status of Puerto Rico," *Colorlines* (Winter 1999): 23–26, and Mireya Navarro, "Marking a Puerto Rican Anniversary," *New York Times*, July 26, 1998, 24.

2. See Mireya Navarro, "Plan to Sell Puerto Rico Phone Company Leads to Strike," *New York Times*, June 19, 1998, A18.

3. See Mireya Navarro, "With a Vote for 'None of the Above,' Puerto Ricans Endorse Island's Status Quo," *New York Times*, December 14, 1998, A18.

4. J. M. Garcia Passalacqua, "Puerto Rican Nationalism Hits Broadway," *San Juan Star*, December 14, 1997.

5. See Patricia Gonzalez and Roberto Rodriguez, "Puerto Ricans Complain About 'Yada Yada,' " *Column of the Americas*, May 15, 1998.

6. Don Feder, "No Statehood for Caribbean Dogpatch," *Boston Herald*, November 30, 1998.

7. See David Gonzàlez, "The Serpent in the Garden of Renewal," *New York Times*, August 26, 1998, B1. On current changes in the South Bronx, see Rachelle Garbarine, "Neighborhood Rises in the South Bronx," *New York Times*, December 25, 1998, B7, and Trish Hall, "A South Bronx Very Different from the Cliché," *New York Times*, February 14, 1999, sec. 11, pp. 1, 7.

8. See Chang Weisberg, "Hip-Hop's Minority? Latino Artists Unite and Speak Out," *Industry Insider Magazine* 15 (1998): 51–57, 96–97, and Rigs Morales and James "Chase" Lynch, "Latino Rap Lyricist," *Urban: The Latino Magazine* 3.2 (1998): 30–37. I thank Raquel Rivera for insights into the contemporary Latino rap scene and for new lines of cultural analysis. See Raquel Rivera, "Puerto Ricans in the Hip-Hop Zone" (Ph.D. diss., CUNY, 2000).

9. See Lucien Taylor, "Créolité Bites: A Conversation with Patrick Chamoiseau, Raphäel Confiant, and Jean Bernabé," *Transition* 74 (1998): 124–61. Subsequent page numbers are cited in the text. See also Lucien Taylor, "Mediating Martinique: The 'Paradoxical Trajectory' of Raphäel Confiant," in George Marcus, ed., *Late Editions 4 Cultural Producers in Perilous States: Editing Events, Documenting Change* (Chicago: University of Chicago Press, 1997), 259–329.

Selected Bibliography

Acosta, Leonardo. *Del tambor al sintetizador* (From drum to synthesizer). Havana: Editorial Letras Cubanas, 1983.

Anderson, Benedict. *Imagined Communities: Reflections on the Origin and Spread of Nationalism.* London: Verso, 1983.

Aparicio, Frances R. and Susana Chávez-Silverman, eds. *Tropicalizations: Transcultural Representations of "Latinidad."* Hanover, N.H.: University Press of New England.

Appadurai, Arjun. *Modernity at Large: Cultural Dimensions of Globalization.* Minneapolis: University of Minnesota Press, 1996.

Boggs, Vernon W., ed. *Salsiology: Afro-Cuban Music and the Evolution of Salsa in New York City.* New York: Excelsior, 1992.

Bonilla, Frank, Edwin Meléndez, Rebecca Morales, and Maria de los Angeles Torres, eds. *Borderless Borders: U.S. Latinos, Latin Americans, and the Paradox of Interdependence.* Philadelphia: Temple University Press, 1998.

Cohen, Robin. *Global Diasporas: An Introduction.* Seattle: University of Washington Press, 1997.

Darder, Antonia and Rodolfo D. Torres, eds. *The Latino Studies Reader: Culture, Economy, and Society.* Malden, Mass.: Blackwell, 1998.

Dávila, Arlene M. *Sponsored Identities: Cultural Politics in Puerto Rico.* Philadelphia: Temple University Press, 1997.

Dávila, Arlene and Agustín Laó, eds. *Mambo Montage: The Latinization of Nueva Yol.* New York: Columbia University Press, forthcoming.

De la Campa, Román. *Latin Americanism.* Minneapolis: University of Minnesota Press, 1999.

Dent, Gina, ed. *Black Popular Culture.* Seattle: Bay Press, 1992.

Díaz-Quiñones, Arcadio. *La memoria rota: Ensayos sobre cultura y política.* Río Piedras, P.R.: Ediciones Huracán, 1993.

Dolores Hernández, Carmen, ed. *Puerto Rican Voices in English.* Westport, Conn.: Praeger, 1997.

Fabian, Johannes. *Moments of Freedom: Anthropology and Popular Culture*. Charlottesville: University Press of Virginia, 1998.

Flores, Juan. *Divided Borders: Essays on Puerto Rican Identity*. Houston: Arte Público, 1993.

Fox, Geoffrey. *Hispanic Nation: Culture, Politics, and the Constructing of Identity*. Secaucus, N.J.: Carol, 1996.

Fusco, Coco. *English Is Broken Here: Notes on Cultural Fusion in the Americas*. New York: New Press, 1995.

García Canclini, Nestor. *Culturas híbridas: estrategias para entrar y salir de la modernidad* (Hybrid cultures: Strategies for entering and leaving modernity). Mexico City: Grijalbo, 1989.

Glasser, Ruth. *My Music Is My Flag: Puerto Rican Musicians and Their New York Communities, 1917–1940*. Berkeley: University of California Press, 1995.

Glissant, Edouard. *Caribbean Discourse (Discours antillais, 1981)*. Charlottesville: University Press of Virginia, 1989.

González, José Luis. *Puerto Rico: The Four-Storeyed Country*. Princeton and New York: Markus Wiener, 1993.

Guerra, Lillian. *Popular Expression and National Identity in Puerto Rico: The Struggle for Self, Community, and Nation*. Gainesville: University Press of Florida, 1998.

Hall, Stuart. "Cultural Identity and Diaspora." In Williams and Chrisman, eds., *Colonial Discourse and Post-Colonial Theory*, 392–403.

——. "Notes on Deconstructing 'the Popular.'" In Raphael Samuel, ed., *People's History and Socialist Theory*, 227–40. London: Routledge, 1981.

Haslip-Viera, Gabriel and Sherrie Baver, eds. *Latinos in New York: Communities in Transition*. Notre Dame: Notre Dame University Press, 1996.

Hijuelos, Oscar. *The Mambo Kings Play Songs of Love*. New York: Farrar, Straus, Giroux, 1989.

King, Anthony D., ed. *Culture, Globalization, and the World-System: Contemporary Conditions for the Representation of Identity*. Minneapolis: University of Minnesota Press, 1997.

Lipsitz, George. *Dangerous Crossroads: Popular Music, Postmodernism, and the Poetics of Place*. London: Verso, 1994.

Luis, William. *Dance Between Two Cultures: Latino Caribbean Literature Written in the United States*. Nashville: Vanderbilt University Press, 1997.

Martín Barbero, Jesús. *De los medios a las mediaciones* (From media to mediations). Barcelona: Grijalbo, 1987.

Negrón-Muntaner, Frances and Ramón Grosfoguel, eds. *Puerto Rican Jam: Essays on Culture and Politics*. Minneapolis: University of Minnesota Press, 1997.

Oboler, Suzanne. *Ethnic Labels, Latino Lives: Identity and the Politics of (Re)Presentation in the United States*. Minneapolis: University of Minnesota, 1995.

Pabón, Carlos. "De Albizu a Madonna: para armar y desarmar la nacionalidad." *Bordes* 1 (1995): 22–40.

Pérez Firmat, Gustavo. *Life on the Hyphen: The Cuban-American Way.* Austin: University of Texas Press, 1994.

Perkins, William Eric, ed. *Droppin' Science: Critical Essays on Rap Music and Hip-Hop Culture.* Philadelphia: Temple University Press, 1996.

Rivera, Angel G. Quintero. *!Salsa, sabor y control!: Sociología de la música tropical* (Salsa, flavor, and control: Sociology of tropical music). Mexico City: Siglo XXI, 1998.

Rivera Nieves, Irma and Carlos Gil, eds. *Polifonía salvaje: Ensayos de cultura y política en la postmodernidad* (Wild polyphony: Essays on culture and the politics of postmodernity). San Juan, P.R.: Editorial Postdata, 1995.

Roberts, John Storm. *Latin Jazz: The First of the Fusions, 1880s to Today.* New York: Schirmer Books, 1999.

——. *The Latin Tinge.* London: Oxford University Press, 1979; rev. ed., 1998.

Rodriguez, Abraham. *The Boy Without a Flag.* Minneapolis: Milkwood, 1992.

——. *Spidertown.* New York: Penguin, 1993.

Rodríguez Juliá, Edgardo. *El entierro de Cortijo* (Cortijo's funeral). Río Piedras, P.R.: Ediciones Huracán, 1983.

Rose, Tricia. *Black Noise: Rap Music and Black Culture in Contemporary America.* Middletown, Conn.: Wesleyan University Press, 1994.

Ross, Andrew and Tricia Rose, eds. *Microphone Fiends: Youth Music and Youth Culture.* New York: Routledge, 1994.

Sánchez, Luis Rafael. "La guagua aérea" (The air bus). Translated by Diana Vélez. *Village Voice,* January 24, 1984.

Santiago, Kelvin. *"Subject People" and Colonial Discourses: Economic Transformation and Social Disorder in Puerto Rico, 1898–1947.* Albany: State University of New York Press, 1994.

Shorris, Earl. *Latinos: A Biography of the People.* New York: Norton, 1992.

Stavans, Ilan. *The Hispanic Condition: Reflections on Culture and Identity in America.* New York: HarperCollins, 1995.

Sutton, Constance R. and Elsa M. Chaney, eds. *Caribbean Life in New York City: Sociocultural Dimensions.* New York: Center for Migration Studies, 1987.

Taylor, Diana and Juan Villegas, eds. *Negotiating Performance: Gender, Sexuality, and Theatricality in Latin/o America.* Durham, N.C.: Duke University Press, 1994.

Thomas, Piri. *Down These Mean Streets.* New York: Knopf, 1967.

Torres, Andrés and José E. Velázquez, eds. *The Puerto Rican Movement: Voices from the Diaspora.* Philadelphia: Temple University Press, 1998.

Vega, Bernardo. *Memoirs of Bernardo Vega: A Contribution to the History of the Puerto Rican Community in New York.* New York: Monthly Review, 1984.

Williams, Patrick and Laura Chrisman, eds. *Colonial Discourse and Post-Colonial Theory.* New York: Columbia University Press, 1994.

Zimmerman, Marc. *U.S. Latino Literature: An Essay and Annotated Bibliography.* Chicago: March/Abrazo Press, 1992.

ACKNOWLEDGMENTS AND PERMISSIONS

Many friends and associates offered invaluable help in studying and thinking through the issues treated in this book. In fact, *From Bomba to Hip-Hop* is the result of an ongoing dialogue and debate with a whole range of generous and intense people. In addition to those acknowledged in specific chapters, I am grateful to the following friends, among many others, who have been my intellectual companions over the past years: Edna Acosta-Belén, Luis Aponte-Parés, Antonio Arantes, Tony Boston, Arnaldo Cruz-Malavé, Arlene Dávila, Arcadio Díaz-Quiñones, Ricardo Dobles, Jorge Duany, James Early, Maria Fernández, Nestor García Canclini, Juan Gelpí, Gabriel Haslip-Viera, Agustin Laó, George Lipsitz, René López, Nicholasa Mohr, Gerardo Mosquera, Juan Otero Garabis, Deborah Pacini Hernández, Jorge Pérez, George Priestley, Julio Ramos, José Rivera, Raquel Rivera, Abraham Rodriguez, Rick Rodriguez, Edgardo Rodriguez Juliá, Mayra Santos, José Segarra, Diana Taylor, and Wilson Valentín.

I am especially thankful to Doris Sommer and George Yúdice, who read the complete manuscript at various stages and made a range of insightful criticisms and suggestions, as did Jean Franco and Robin Kelley. I have attempted to address their comments as I revised the text.

I also wish to thank all the photographers and visual artists for their guidance, and Roy Thomas, Ann Miller, and Brady McNamara of Columbia University Press for making the completion of this book an enjoyable and rewarding experience.

My compañera Miriam Jiménez Román was her usual intelligent and giving self, and saw me through all aspects of the book, from early inklings to repeated drafts and rewrites. To her I owe a very special gratitude and love.

Grateful acknowledgment is made to reprint material from the following copyrighted works:

Excerpts from "Kinda Hungry" and "Just Not Listed" (song lyrics) by the Latin Empire. Reprinted by permission of Anthony Boston and Richard Rodriguez of Latin Empire.

Excerpt from "melao" (poem) by Tato Laviera. From *Mainstream Ethics* (Houston: Arte Público Press—University of Houston, 1988). Reprinted by permission of the publisher.

Excerpt from "nuyorican" (poem) by Tato Laviera. From *AmeRícan* (Houston: Arte Público Press—University of Houston, 1985). Reprinted by permission of the publisher.

Excerpts from "La Vida Te Da Sorpresas," "Ven Acá (Tiguerito Tiguerito)," and "Puerto Rico No Te Vendas" (song lyrics) by Tomás Robles (TNT). Reprinted by permission of Tomás Robles.

Earlier versions of some of the essays included in this book were published in journals or essay collections. I thank the editors of these publications for permission to reprint revised versions of the original essays:

The Prelude is adapted from material originally published in *Diálogo* (Puerto Rico) (February 1995): 53.

Chapter 3 is adapted from material originally published in the *Modern Language Quarterly* 57.2 (June 1996): 381–95. Reprinted by permission.

Chapter 4 is adapted from material originally published in Diana Taylor, ed., *Negotiating Performance: Gender, Sexuality, and Theatricality in Latino/o America* (Durham, N.C.: Duke University Press, 1994). Reprinted by permission.

Chapter 6 is adapted from material originally published in William Eric Perkins, ed., *Droppin' Science: Critical Essays on Rap Music and Hip-Hop Culture* (Philadelphia: Temple University Press, 1996). Copyright (c) 1996 by Temple University. All rights reserved. Reprinted by permission of Temple University Press.

Chapter 7 is adapted from material originally published in *Centro Journal* 8.12 (Spring 1996): 170–86. Reprinted by permission.

Chapter 9 is adapted from material originally published in Frances Aparicio and Susana Silverman-Chávez, eds., *Tropicalizations: Transcultural Representations of "Latinidad"* (Hanover, N.H.: University Press of New England, 1997). Reprinted by permission.

Chapter 10 is adapted from material originally published in the *Harvard Educational Review* 67.2 (Summer 1997): 208–21. Copyright (c) 1997 by the President and Fellows of Harvard College. All rights reserved. Reprinted by permission.

INDEX

Sunsets (group), 88
symbolic inversion concept, 229n1
Symphony Sid, 101

Teenagers (group), 88
telephone company strike (Puerto Rico),
    221–23
tertulia: described, 4; Latino studies and,
    13
Third Base (group), 128–29
Thomas, Piri, 82, 180, 182, 183, 186, 225
timbales, 93–94, 99
"To Be with You" (song), 89–90, 93
Tom and Jerrio (group), 92
Tony Touch, 222
Toro, Yomo, 225
Torres, Willie, 81, 84, 89–91, 108
Tough Bronx Action, 135
Toussaint, Allen, 99
translocality, Latino studies and, 211, 214
transnational: 36, 38, 47, 158, 186, 209,
    211, 214, 232n11, 241n36; communi-
    ties, 161–62; consumer culture, 32;
    movements, 10, 26, 201

underground music, in Puerto Rico, 3

Valdéz, Vicentico, 96
Valentín, Bobby, 123
Vargas, Wilfredo, 127

Vázquez, Lourdes, 179
Vega, Bernardo, 51, 141, 239n9
Vega, Ed, 186
Vibrations (group), 92
Vico C, 3, 116
Victor Montañez y Sus Pleneros de la
    110 (group), 68
Viento de Agua (group), 226

"Watermelon Man" (song), 89, 93
"We're Puerto Rican and Proud" (song),
    131
West Side Story, 141
Whodini (group), 117
Wild Style (film), 117, 122
Williams, William Carlos, 174
women: in Latino literature, 181–82; in
    plena music, 69–70
women's studies, 216
Wright, Richard, 184
writers: from Martinique, 227–28;
    Nuyorican, 182, 186; on pan-Latin
    identity, 149–54; presence of, 20–21;
    Pulitzer Prize winner, 167; women,
    182, 187

Yúdice, George, 230n23

Zulu Nation, Puerto Rican chapter of,
    135